2004
Film Still / Filmnews Anandan Information Centre
Rickshawkaran (M. Krishnan: 1971)
Chennai

1993
Decorated Kite
Magazine image of actress Ayesha Zulka
Location unknown

2004
Abid Hussain Vora
Farida Traders, Cine Poster Supplies & Commission Agent
Mumbai

2003
Roadside Poster Display
Kaval Karan (Neelakanta: 1967)
Main poster shows MGR holding the A.I.A.D.M.K. party flag
Chennai

2003
'One In a Thousand' MGR Fans Association Souvenir Shop
A.I.A.D.M.K. Party Flag, images of MGR and J Jayalalithaa
Chennai

2003
Discarded Hoarding
Seven Stars Film Distribution Industrial Estate
Thiruvananthapuram, Kerala

2003
Roadside Poster Display
Kakha Kakha (Gautham Menon: 2002)
Chennai

2003
Madras Safire Lithographers / Design Studio
Image on screen: Kushi (S J Surya: 2000)
Chennai

2003
Film and Film Poster Distributor
Elegant Publicities
Chennai

2002
Roadside Poster Display
Left: Agaaz (Yogesh Ishwar: 2001). Right: Naseeb (Manmohan Desai: 1981)
Juhu, Mumbai

2003
Cinema Hall
New Theatres
Thiruvananthapuram, Kerala

1992
Rickshaw Decoration
Central figure: Bruce Lee. Flanked by: Rajinikant
Madurai, Tamil Nadu

1992
Rickshaw Decoration
Top: Lord Krishna. Bottom left: Lord Venkareshwara & Padmavathi. Bottom right: MGR
Madurai, Tamil Nadu

2004
Roadside Vinyl Film Hoarding Display
Relax (S.S. Raja Mouli: 2000)
Chennai

2004
National Film Archive of India
Kalyan Khajina (Baburao Painter: 1924)
Pune, Maharashtra

1993
Roadside Poster Display
Pallandu Valzhai (K Shankar: 1975)
Chennai

LIVING
PICTURES

The title of this publication is appropriated from a copy line that was used to publicise the Lumière Brothers' cinematography when it was first presented to public audiences in India on 7 July 1896. The programme of entertainment was advertised as a spectacle of 'living photographic pictures'.

EDITED BY DAVID BLAMEY & ROBERT D'SOUZA

LIVING PICTURES

PERSPECTIVES ON THE FILM POSTER IN INDIA

First published in London 2005

Open Editions
45 Handforth Road
London
SW9 0LL

www.openeditions.com

ISBN 0-949004-15-4

British Library Cataloguing in Publication Data
A catalogue record for this book is available in the British Library

Printed and bound in Europe
DL B-41074-05

TRANSLITERATION

The names of films, places and people have been used in the transliteration style of the Indian film industry and our authors. For example, where Homi Wadia has used, in written correspondence with the editors, the spelling 'Tufaani Teerandaaz' as the transliterated title of his 1947 film and the *Encyclopaedia of Indian Cinema* has favored the spelling 'Toofani Teerandaz', we have opted for our author's preference of 'Toofani Tirandaaz'. All are equally correct.

Likewise, although Bombay is now called Mumbai we acknowledge that the colonial name is still widely in use in India and worldwide and have thus followed the authors' lead and sought not to impose a regime of linguistic protocol on the names of places.

We have not translated any of the film titles into English. Where films appear with English titles, as in the case of *Mother India* or *Love And God,* it is because they were made or released with English names.

DAVID BLAMEY
PREFACE

The filmmaker John Cassavetes once observed that he saw no reason to make a film about something he already knew. The inference here is that knowledge – particularly perhaps in the form of conventional wisdom – can be seen as a pre-condition of the desensitized artwork. Since it was essentially a need to understand more that caused both of us, as editors, to embark upon this project we took nourishment and passport from Cassavetes' assertion throughout our field studies and subsequent presentation here. Moreover, given that the commercial film poster in India seemed to exist as both an object and a visual space for dialogue between different media and users, we had no desire to fortify intellectual or artistic perimeters and instead pursued our curiosity in preference to being shown the way. Our objective was – and still is – to keep moving, questioning and reporting.

It was a chance encounter that first inspired us to look beyond the visual appearance of film posters in India and consider how their value might be located not solely in their effectiveness as advertisements but also in their importance as signifiers within a broader cultural context. We recall the pivotal moment when we first observed movie publicity material being circulated and exchanged as artifact instead of being consumed subliminally within the hubbub of visual persuasion that is the experience of walking or driving in Indian streets. Having entered a shop that was located in a Muslim rag 'n' bone market in Bombay, an innocuous roll of paper was presented to us by the proprietor and ceremoniously unfurled for our examination. The bland tubes of thin grey paper were turned inside out to reveal their brilliant contents. We bargained for a while and eventually left with a selection of Bollywood posters under our arms, carefully rolled-up into pages of *The Times of India* for protection.

Subsequent to this initial episode, we have visited film producers, production houses, design studios, film distributors, poster printers, auction houses and poster traders across India in order to collect a representative body of work for further scrutiny and reflection. Central to our inquiry has been the hypothesis that there is an inherent and interconnecting relationship between these posters and both the perception and construction of national and regional cultural identities in modern India.

The rationale for detecting and selecting our data has been shaped by a combination of artistic discernment and pragmatism. As a consequence, we have only included material that both held creative graphic interest to us, and that could for practical reasons, be acquired to take away to be digitally scanned. In addition to this – and by way of pre-empting any accusation of omissions, oversights or eccentricity in the final selection of material – we claim to have accurately reflected the uneven experience of encountering posters on India's streets. We have purposely juxtaposed publicity notices from a number of important film-producing regions with films made in different genres and during different periods of time. Arranged as a chronology, C-grade sex and horror films and Hindi language classics are obliged to occupy the same physical space as 'foreign' films – such as the Indian release poster for the Bruce Lee film *The Return of the Dragon** – and 'bogus' films like *Kachchi Umar Mein** that have dodged the certification process to be distributed throughout networks of private 'adult' clubs. Under this particular set of visual, sequential and spatial circumstances we have therefore been able to contest the primacy of existing Bollywood visual ideology and reveal an intrinsic contradiction in attempting to view this multifarious visual culture as a generic whole.

The collection of posters reproduced here is restricted to a post-colonial period of production from 1950 to the present day. One of the oldest films, Homi Wadia's *Toofani Tirandaaz*, was actually released in the year of Indian Independence, 1947. The oldest film that was available to us in poster form is for Merian C. Cooper & Ernest B. Schoedsack's *King Kong**, which was made in 1933; it has been dubbed into Hindi and re-released for an Indian audience. One of the most recent films is the 2002 action blockbuster *Kaante**, a Bollywood take on the Hollywood film *Reservoir Dogs*, which stars Amitabh Bachchan and includes mandatory singing and dancing interludes. With a few exceptions, we have posters for films made every year between 1949-2004. When reviewed as a timeline, the posters that we have selected reveal many narratives – the most notable being that of the decline and demise of the traditional commercial artist working for the promotion of movies. The impact of photographic technology on the viability of illustration and painting and later of computer design programmes on the artwork production technique of cut-and-paste montage have thus been major contributory factors in shaping the development of Indian film poster styles.

* *The Return of the Dragon,* see illustration on page 161.

* *Kachchi Umar Mein,* see illustration on page 223.

* *Toofani Tirandaaz,* see illustration on page 92.

* *King Kong,* see illustration on page 91.

* *Kaante,* see illustration on page 244.

While many of the posters are produced in the year that the films were released in, it should be noted that others represent the commonplace practice of cannibalising original artwork in the cause of supplying a demand for re-runs or updating the visual appeal of failing designs. To demonstrate the ease with which Indian poster artists have absorbed and appropriated influences from their own cultural heritage as well as the rest of the world, at times we have included multiple images for the same film, made over a period of time. This opportunity to visually compare variations on a primary pictorial theme allows us to see how original designs have evolved to meet the demand of changing circumstances and how any concept of fixity is inappropriate to the porous characteristic of Indian mass communication in this context.

A consequence of this commonplace practice of redeploying and reconfiguring principal design elements has been the unusual amount of detective work required to establish definitively the creative source of every poster. Where an artist's signature or a credit for a design studio has appeared on the printed work we have recognized that person or studio as the poster artist in our captions. Where it has not been possible to detect an artist's credit from the poster information alone we have contacted the film producer or production company and obtained the necessary information directly from this source. In instances where studios have closed down, or the custodians of a film producer's estate could not clearly recall an artist's name, we have excluded the information from the caption.

Finally, in acknowledgment of the occasionally oblique correlation between the texts that follow this preface and the images of posters that we are presenting as a symbolic corpus for the purpose of assessment, we should perhaps state that we encouraged a degree of open-ended rapport from our writers. Since we regarded the film poster's existence as an ongoing process of redefinition and change, it seemed logical to canvass opinion from a number of perspectives: art and design criticism, film history, filmmaking, sociology and visual anthropology. The assignment was simply to reflect on the meaning of this unique and forceful visual medium, back from the surface of its physicality, through its everyday use and out into the world.

ROSIE THOMAS
ZIMBO AND SON MEET THE GIRL WITH THE GUN

1966

London swings under Wilson's Labour, Christine Keeler's only just faded out of view and the Beatles claim they are more famous than Jesus. Indira Gandhi becomes India's third Prime Minister, the rupee is devalued, and Homi Wadia releases Zimbo Finds a Son.

The Beatles make their first visit to India, get mobbed by fans in Delhi, visit outlying villages in 1950s Cadillacs and George buys a sitar. Did they see those Zimbo *posters?*

1968

Student protest sweeps Europe and America, workers man the barricades in Paris, and Mrs Gandhi prints a postage stamp to launch the Wheat Revolution. Whip-cracking Emma Peel bows out of The Avengers *as actress Diana Rigg becomes a Bond girl, and Bombay movie legend Fearless Nadia makes her feisty come back in the James Bond spoof,* Khilari, *at the age of sixty.*

The Beatles and their wives return to India, meditate in Rishikesh, find peace and love, and discover that the Maharishi is a sham. George and Patti extend their stay and study ragas with Ravi Shankar in Bombay. George does yoga and practices his sitar every day. We know a lot about that six-week trip but none of them has ever mentioned those Khilari *posters.*

When the Beatles famously went to India in the 1960s posters of *Zimbo Finds a Son* and *Khilari* would have been on the hoardings – and their films in the cinemas – in all the poorer areas of India's cities and larger towns. From everything we know, this is an India that George and the boys never really even noticed.

LEFT – Poster for Homi Wadia's 1966 film, *Zimbo Finds A Son*. Also see illustration on page 130.

RIGHT – Poster for Homi Wadia's 1968 film, *Khilari*. Also see illustration on page 137.

While *Zimbo Finds a Son* (John Cavas, 1966) promised its audiences alluring fantasies of a pristine, lush, green jungle where, just like Tarzan, a handsome couple swings from trees and tastes forbidden fruits of sexual plenitude, *Khilari* (*The Player*, Homi Wadia, 1968) gave tantalising glimpses of a different kind of paradise. Here, audiences could dream of the planes, helicopters, skyscrapers and guns of an exciting modern world where, just like James Bond, secret agents run dangerous global missions. Two exotic utopias, two complementary fictions of modernity. Evil lurks in both: the jungle is a space of wild and primitive nature, the city one of villainous corruption. Our heroes and heroines posture triumphantly across these seductive scenes, promising their audiences full-colour thrills of gutsy innuendo and larger-than-life, playful violence, all within a recognisably Indian format.

Both films were produced by Homi Wadia at Basant Studios, neither was a critical success nor major hit, both were in black and white, and both were aimed at the 'C grade circuit', the term by which the film industry and cosmopolitan elite dismiss the barely literate urban and rural poor who make up the largest share of India's vast movie audiences. While Homi Wadia had been known as 'king of the stunt film' since the 1930s, and Basant was unquestionably the leader in its field, by 1968 audience tastes were changing, especially with the massive influx of the rural dispossessed into the cities in the 1960s. Many rivals had sprung up and Basant's films had begun to look tired and old-fashioned, now working their magic primarily with the poorest of these audiences. The secret of Basant's success had always been to keep their films alive to global popular culture, notably Hollywood; to push whatever technical or cultural boundaries they could; and to integrate and fuse all this with Indian entertainment conventions, traditional storytelling and populist fantasies.

While the Beatles returned to Europe in the late 1960s to feed Western fantasies with a vision of a pure, timeless, spiritual India – and launch a million 'gap years' – Basant Pictures quietly fed the Indian popular imagination over a period of almost forty years with a series of visions of East and West, jungle and city, tradition and modernity. It drew on Hollywood and popular entertainment forms, plundered with abandon and 'Indianised'. The Beatles drew on Indian classical and traditional cultures, plundered with abandon and 'Westernised'. While the Beatles fed an eccentric version of India back to Western popular culture, Basant fed an eccentric version of a *different* Western popular culture back to a *different* India. The Beatles Westernised their India, Basant Indianised its West.

But what did these two posters mean to Indian audiences in the 1960s? What might the Beatles have learned from chatting with the drivers of those shiny Cadillacs? What might the north Indian villagers have told the most famous English lads in the world about their favourite movies, the film stars that excited them, and their passion for cinema?

REMAKES AND HOLLYWOOD

It would be hard for Indian audiences in the sixties to see either *Zimbo* or *Khilari* posters without thinking back to earlier movies. Both films explicitly revisit the 1930s heyday of Homi Wadia and his brother Jamshed, known as JBH.

Zimbo was clearly Tarzan, and in *Toofani Tarzan* (*Tempestuous Tarzan*, Homi Wadia, 1937) the Wadia brothers' studio, Wadia Movietone, had brought India its *deshi* [1] Tarzan. Proudly advertised as India's first jungle adventure film, this had been such an extraordinary success that it continued to rake in profits for more than twenty years.[2] Moreover John Cavas, *Zimbo Finds a Son's* director, had become a household name playing the original Indian Tarzan. Known for his astonishing world records that had included carrying a Chevrolet containing four passengers on his bare back, he had been lovingly admired for his brawny frame, superhuman strength and simple charm. The *Zimbo* series of three films, which began in 1959, were openly advertised as *Toofani Tarzan* remakes.

1 – Indian, home-grown, local.

2 – Material on the Wadias draws on interviews by the author with Homi and Mary Wadia in 1986; the documentary *Fearless: the Hunterwali Story* (Riyad Wadia, 1993); the published writings of JBH Wadia, together with JBH's unpublished essays, courtesy of Wadia Movietone archive.

Khilari, on the other hand, built its appeal around an even bigger household name –
and former co-star of John Cavas – Fearless Nadia. Nadia had been queen of the
Bombay box-office of the 1930s and1940s. Known as *hunterwali* or 'woman with the
whip' after her 1935 debut film of the same name, she had played a swashbuckling,
horse-riding, masked avenger who championed India's independence and women's
rights. A white-skinned, blue-eyed blonde sporting hot pants, leather boots, plunging
necklines and a voluptuous body, she had tossed burly villains over her golden curls,
beaten hapless men to pulp, swung across ravines and rescued her heroes before taking
the reins in a no-nonsense romance. Her success had made Wadia Movietone its
reputation and considerable fortune. *Khilari's* promise to its audiences was another
chance to enjoy Nadia, now aged sixty, nine years older than her last screen role
but just as feisty.

But while both films make much mileage of their Indian pedigree, they also both
bathe in Hollywood's reflection. Like many Indian studios of the early years, Wadia
Movietone had built Hollywood associations for its stars. Nadia had been popularly
known as "India's Pearl White" – referring to the star of *The Perils of Pauline*, who had
been a favourite of Indian audiences in the silent era, and *Toofani Tarzan's* opening
credits had introduced John Cavas as "Indian Eddie Polo." Whilst this suggests a form
of mimicry familiar in colonial discourse, it was also clever marketing: JBH Wadia and
others clearly recognised the commercial value of the brand name (1980:94).

However *Khilari* and *Zimbo* also cite Hollywood more openly, directly milking two
of the biggest global phenomena of the 1960s: James Bond and Tarzan. Although both
imperialist adventure stories, they were as popular in the former colonies as in the
West. *Khilari* promoted itself as a James Bond spoof. By 1968 the Bond series, based
on English author, Ian Fleming's, racy novels, had become a worldwide success, with
a string of five spectacular hits between *Dr No* (1962) and *You Only Live Twice* (1967).
In fact in India, with swingeing censorship cuts and import controls that limited
distribution, the films were rarely seen in full and only infrequently outside the larger
cities. Despite this, James Bond made his mark on the Indian market and spawned
a host of local imitators. The name signalled global sophistication: Bond was a cool
superhero and to know about Bond was to be up-to-date, Westernised, modern, with
the additional frisson that the films were known to be more sexually explicit than
anything the Indian censors allowed.

Zimbo Finds a Son, and its 1930s predecessor *Toofani Tarzan* were, on the other hand,
Indian versions of the Hollywood Tarzan movies – *Zimbo Finds a Son's* English title
itself a brazen rip-off of a famous MGM title. Of course, all the movies were versions
of Edgar Rice Burroughs' popular American novels. Whilst the novels' first craze was
from 1912 until the 1930s, there was a global Tarzan revival in the 1960s. By 1963 one
in 30 paperbacks sold worldwide was a Tarzan novel and Hollywood's *Tarzan Goes to
India* (1962) – with music by Ravi Shankar – became the most profitable yet of the
world's most lucrative film series, making more than 50% of its profits outside America.[3]

3 - Torgovnick, 1991:42; Essoe,
1968:187.

However it was the 1930s MGM films starring Johnny Weissmuller that directly inspired the Wadia brothers and remain worldwide the classics of popular memory. While Elmo Lincoln's 1918 silent version had first popularised Tarzan throughout India, JBH Wadia tells us: "Johnny Weissmuller, with this fantastic jungle cry and swimming abilities, made Tarzan a household name even in remote small towns in India." As JBH himself puts it, (somewhat quirkily writing of himself in the third person): "Borrowing heavily from the original, JBH placed his screenplay in an Indian setting."[4]

Toofani Tarzan is far from being a simple copy of *Tarzan, The Ape Man*, just as the Nadia films were crucially different from anything Hollywood produced, and *Khilari's* similarities with a Bond movie lie primarily in its exuberant pace, fantasy modernity, irreverent humour, and knowing jokey references. The accusation that Bombay filmmakers simply copy Hollywood has often been made but does not stand scrutiny. As I have argued elsewhere (Thomas, 1985:121), no close copy of a foreign film has ever been successful and, whilst borrowing elements from wherever they need, Indian filmmakers know that the key to success lies in knowing how to adapt and 'Indianise' their material, although association with a successful foreign brand does no commercial harm. JBH was always the first to acknowledge his sources – and ultimately part of the Wadia brothers' credibility with audiences lay in their being seen as 'modern' and glamorously 'westernised' whilst still proudly local, in many ways the most cosmopolitan of filmmakers, in others the most *deshi*.

THE WADIAS AND THEIR STUDIOS

The Wadia brothers had been a phenomenal force in the early sound era. Sons of a wealthy respectable Bombay Parsee family, they had been passionate filmgoers in their youth, world cinema enthusiasts who openly enjoyed the early Hollywood comedy and action films that many others of their class dismissed as 'trash'. While JBH was an intellectual, writer and political visionary, Homi was a technical genius and astute businessman. The combination was dynamic and, after a run of successful stunt films in the silent era, they quickly adapted to sound and raised finance to set up Wadia Movietone in 1933. Whilst there was always some tension between JBH's aspirations to produce 'quality' cinema and Homi's box-office flair, these differences were productively harnessed throughout the 1930s to produce some of the era's most radical – and popular – films. The Nadia films, scripted by JBH, championed education and independence for women, Hindu-Muslim unity and the Freedom movement, and also attacked caste and class – all within a highly entertaining format that was massively popular at the box-office. Other stunt films, including *Toofani Tarzan*, demonstrated a pioneering technical approach. Unlike some other studios which relied on foreign technicians, Wadia Movietone encouraged enterprising, gifted, local young men to find their own solutions to special effects and camera technique: they built their own camera crane and dolly, set up the best back projection and matte effects systems in Bombay, and regularly shot with multi-camera set-ups. JBH and Homi scoured Hollywood technical journals and kept in touch with all new developments.

4 – JBH Wadia, *The Making of Toofani Tarzan* (unpublished essay quoted courtesy of the Wadia Movietone archive).

Wadia Movietone also used its technical expertise to produce spectacular Arabian Nights magic and fantasy films as well as swashbuckling costume pictures. Such films drew, on the one hand, on Hollywood's Douglas Fairbanks tradition, on the other on Urdu Parsee theatre, which itself was influenced by Shakespearean conventions. At its height in the mid-1930s Wadia Movietone was a massive business enterprise with 600 people, including its stars, on its payroll and clocking in daily. It was the most profitable studio of its day.

Despite – and undoubtedly also because of – their success, the brothers suffered critical disapproval. Gallingly for JBH, as his political and intellectual credentials were unmatched,[5] rival studios such as Bombay Talkies were lauded for the 'realism' of their melodramatic 'socials'.[6] JBH's response was to push his own studio output towards more serious social films and high culture experiments, such as *Raj Natarki* (*Court Dancer*, 1941) which boasted top classical dancers and an English language version for its American release. Meanwhile Homi's stunt, comedy and action films became increasingly elaborate and expensive as he aspired to compete with Hollywood technical accomplishments. He built spectacular sets and set new challenges for his burgeoning special effects team, including complicated storm sequences in a mock-up jungle and high-speed car chases. Their business partners were not happy as, by the early 1940s, none of their films were making much money.

Ostensibly to circumvent wartime raw stock restrictions, the brothers set up Basant Pictures in 1942, with Homi as producer/owner and JBH a silent partner. The combination of the flop of their first film, a social melodrama starring Nadia as a vamp, and escalating personal differences provoked a crisis. The brothers fell out and parted company.

At this point Homi, his back against the wall, followed a hunch that the key to Basant's survival lay in his only remaining assets, Fearless Nadia and John Cavas. If produced cheaply enough, films starring the original whip-cracking Nadia and her partner John Cavas might just succeed. Whilst Nadia was already taking lessons in hairdressing to prepare for a new career, Homi persuaded her to give him one last chance. On borrowed time and hired studio floors he produced a shameless sequel to her original 1935 hit. *Hunterwali ki Beti* (*Daughter of Woman with the Whip*, 1943) revived the old magic and was an immediate success. Homi had found his formula: cheap, quickly made stunt, action and jungle films followed with exciting titles such as *Flying Prince, Tigress, 11 O'clock, Baghdad ka Jadu* (*Magic of Baghdad*), *Toofani Tirandaaz* (*Whirlwind Archer*) and *Circus Queen*. Nadia was once again queen of the box-office and Basant's fortunes rose. Gradually its repertoire expanded and, when Homi and JBH teamed up once again to produce the successful *Ram Bhakt Hanuman* (1947), Basant also became renowned for its quality 'A-grade' mythologicals, a tradition that raised its status considerably. Homi was now able to build his own studio facilities at Chembur on the outskirts of Bombay. Between 1942 and 1981 Homi's well-run production company continued to produce a stream of unpretentious but quietly successful films aimed at the mass audience. Much of the success of the early

5 – He had an MA in English literature and an LLB and was actively involved in nationalist politics, at first a Congress supporter, later a founder member of former Marxist M.N. Roy's Radical Democratic Party.

6 – 'Social' strictly refers to any film in a contemporary setting but many also had (loose) pretensions to social concern and themes addressing social inequalities.

years lay in being always just slightly ahead of the game. Continuing Wadia Movietone's tradition, Basant's innovative special effects department found low cost, creative and *deshi* solutions to the technical problems crucial to its two key specialisms: stunts and mythologicals. A talented team grew up, many of whom stayed for years, for example *Maya Bazaar's* director, Babhubhai Mistry, who began as a hot SFX technician at Wadia Movietone. Despite the huge difference in status between Basant's two core genres, the same technicians and directors worked on both and workers used to quip: "mythologicals are just stunt films that happen to be about gods".

Basant's legacy is remarkable not least for the stream of stars and directors whose early careers it moulded. Meena Kumari began her adult career playing Hindu goddesses for Basant. Others include Feroz Khan, who starred in the Wadia Brothers' detective thriller *Reporter Raju,* and director Manmohan Desai, king of the 1970s/80s spectacular multi-starrer films such as *Coolie* and *Naseeb.* Even independent producers using Basant as no more than a hired studio facility cashed in on the kudos of its name to promote their film, as the poster for the swashbuckling costume drama *Talwaar ka Dhani**(*Gift of the Sword*) indicates.

With a rewriting of Indian cinema history which began in the post-Independence era, the Wadias' pioneering work became marginalised and began to disappear from historical accounts. With po-faced government censorship in the 1950s "which did not look favourably on magic and fighting scenes,"[7] stunt films, as such, became less viable although mythologicals were still favoured. 'Realist' socials ruled the day. These tuned with the European-educated Congress intellectuals' vision of an Indian modernity which combined humanist social reform and scientific rationalism with proud display of an essentialised 'pure' Indian traditional culture. The Wadias themselves were torn between this and a radically different vision. Understanding market forces, they knew that popular passions would be the seeds for new modern Indian identities and that these could not be neatly imposed from above. Representing much that was, in practice, peripheral within the nationalist project (Parsees, Muslims, Christians), Wadia Movietone, and later Basant, well understood the hybridity and fluidity of identities within the porous borders of a modern India in a transnational context. Drawing eclectically on global popular culture, including 'trash' and popular entertainment forms from India and elsewhere, their films celebrated diversity, revelled in playful mimicry and impersonation, and provided a space within which the gamut of modern Indian identities could be explored. It is hardly surprising that their films were simultaneously immensely popular with subaltern audiences and rubbished by the mainstream nationalists. Zimbo's 1937 prototype, *Toofani Tarzan,* written and produced by JBH Wadia and directed by Homi, provides a useful example of these processes.

INDIA'S TARZAN

Toofani Tarzan Storyline
Unlike the Weissmuller movies but in the tradition of the first Rice Burroughs' books and all good Hindi films, *Toofani Tarzan* begins in Tarzan's childhood. Tarzan's father,

* *Talwar ka Dhani,*
see illustration on page 104.

7 – K.A. Abbas quoted in Chakravarty 1993: 51.

Ramu, is a scientist boffin who lives with his wife and young son in a comfortable but ramshackle jungle bungalow. While Uma cooks in her kitchen, he does chemistry experiments in his makeshift laboratory next door. One day he discovers "the truth", a potion that will confer immortality. He decides the family will visit his millionaire father in the city, with whom relations seem strained on account of Ramu's love-marriage with the humble Uma. On the eve of the visit, where Ramu will announce his scientific discovery to the world, tragedy strikes. Ramu is killed by a pride of lions and Uma becomes separated from her son. With the help of Dada, an ape-man family retainer, and accompanied by Moti, the family's pet terrier, the son escapes in a hot air balloon, survives a dramatic thunderstorm and lands by a lake. Round the boy's neck is an amulet containing Ramu's miraculous scientific formula.

Fifteen years later Ramu's father leads an expedition to the jungle to search for his long lost grandson who, according to local rumours, survived and, now known as Tarzan, lives happily in communion with nature. With the party, in white solar *topis* [8] and hunting gear, are an adopted daughter, Leela, who obsessively makes-up her face; a lecherous villain, Biharilal; a qawwali-singing philosophiser guide, together with a buffoonish servant and an army of muscular porters and bodyguards. When local cannibals attack with poisoned arrows, Tarzan, with pals Dada and Moti, comes to the rescue, fights off the tribals and dispatches them with an elephant stampede. Out of the foliage appears a ranting mad woman wearing a necklace of stones and armbands of skulls. She rails at the party as "liars and sinners", decries the wicked ways of city folk and urges Tarzan to follow her back into the jungle and ignore Leela's approaches. Despite this Tarzan and Leela meet again when, having rescued her from Biharilal's lecherous advances, Tarzan abducts her himself. Gradually he proves his innocent and gentle nature and they fall in love. Leela joins Tarzan in his tree-top home, exchanges her blouse and slacks for a leopard skin minidress, and spends her days riding elephants, swinging through trees and swimming in crocodile infested lakes.

After a series of adventures in which all members of the grandfather's expedition are kidnapped by cannibals, Leela is lowered into a pit to be fed to the cannibals' giant gorilla chief. Moti, the brave little dog, escapes and raises the alarm and Tarzan swings to the rescue, overpowers the gorilla by brute strength and finally frees the whole party. He leads them to safety by making his own taut body into a bridge over a ravine. Now fuelled by his greed for the secret in Tarzan's precious amulet, the ruthless Biharilal attacks Tarzan and, in the ensuing tussle, shoots and mortally wounds the mad harridan. Uma's memory returns and the party discovers that she is Tarzan's long-lost mother, who went insane when she believed both husband and son had perished. She dies reunited with her beloved son, Tarzan. Nudged on by Moti, Biharilal falls to his death from a precipice. Leela refuses to return to the city with her adopted father and insists on living with lover Tarzan in their jungle paradise. Only when the qawwali poet reminds the old man that "whatever God does is good", does her father finally agree to bless the union between his grandson and adopted daughter. As the sun sets, the qawwal sings: "What you could not find in the city, you have found in the jungle, Celebrate the happiness found by love, May God fill your life with happiness, Stay Happy".

8 - *Topis* – a white cloth hat worn as protection against the sun.

'Indianisation'

Although JBH writes of "borrowing heavily from the original" and there are undoubtedly many echoes of, and quotes from, the Johnny Weissmuller movies, particularly in the characterisation of Tarzan and in the love scenes, the process of "placing the screenplay in an Indian setting" has provoked substantial and significant changes.

Formally the film follows Indian structural conventions. The first reel, set in the hero's childhood, sets up the first narrative disruption. The rest of the film traces its consequences fifteen years later. A comedy sub-plot with its own burlesque characters weaves through the main action and romance plot, and poetic songs interrupt the narrative flow and comment on what unfolds. Heroes and villains are sharply differentiated and Biharilal, the unremittingly lecherous, callous and greedy city scoundrel, has to be killed before the narrative can be resolved. The backbone of the narrative is the drive to reunite the hero's dispersed family, finally resolved when grandfather finds his lost heir and effectively provides him with a mate.

JBH also made thematic changes. Some of these key in to Indian cultural concerns, for example the introduction of Tarzan's mad mother. Others result from a more subtle shift in the film's underlying dynamic. The explorers are not white colonialists but westernised Indians from the city. The jungle is peopled not by black African 'pygmies' but quasi-Indian tribal peoples. The film's underlying opposition is thus between westernised, educated, wealthy, city-dwelling 'modern' India and non-westernised, uneducated, impoverished, rural or 'primitive' India. Evil lies in both: the former is the domain of 'false ways', immorality and greed for material gain; the latter is tainted with cruelty and savagery.[9] In the course of the film, Tarzan, Leela and other characters take a variety of positions in the space between these poles, including Tarzan's pals Moti, a curiously domesticated pet terrier, who is neither wild jungle beast nor pampered city pooch, and the mute, arm-swinging ape-man Dada, an overt cross-breed.[10] Only Leela can move freely between the two domains.

By substituting the 'nectar of immortality' for the material wealth – elephant tusks, lost jewels and suchlike – that motivates most American versions of the tale, Wadia significantly changes its thrust. Tarzan's father is a 'modern' Indian who attempts a rapprochement between city and jungle and fails. He is simultaneously a rational scientist – the epitome of the acceptable face of westernised modernity according to the nationalist intellectuals – and a traditional ur-Indian sage, finding a magical elixir of life akin to the alleged discoveries of an ancient Indian wisdom that operated centuries before western science. Ramu is from a wealthy city background but chooses to live in poverty in the jungle pursuing his altruistic quest. Significantly, at the very moment when he has apparently conquered nature, his idyll is disrupted. The forces of nature – wild lions and fierce thunderstorms – punish his arrogance. Later, when the villainous Biharilal covets the wealth to be made from Ramu's discovery, he is also killed. Only when Tarzan and Leela submit to God's will and live in harmony with the forces of nature, within the plenitude of true love – discovering that it is quality not length of life that matters – can the narrative be resolved, thereby situating the film's moral

9 – Interestingly, the epitome of both evils is ultimately 'westernised' as the evil cannibals are dressed in the generic face paint and feather headdress of the wild-west Indians of American movie mythology.

10 – Wadia explains that he was forced to create this strange, and by today's standards offensively racist, character as Professor Deval's Circus had no trained apes. He is played by Boman Shroff who himself had a reputation as one of the Wadia's stunt heroes.

universe firmly within the emotional and metaphoric sensibilities of 'tradition', here the Indian art form of Urdu qawwali poetry.

Probably Wadia's boldest innovation was Uma, the mad mother. For Indian audiences, she would be coded as a Kali figure, the goddess of creation and destruction, who conventionally represents the terrifying force within femininity. At each appearance Uma's insane cackle dominates the soundtrack as she harangues and challenges the city-dwellers. Ultimately the raw, dysfunctional feminine energy thought to belong to a woman without a man – unleashed by the death of her husband and son and her retreat from 'civilisation' – has to be controlled. Biharilal's bullet wound 'brings her to her senses' so she can die as a loving, nurturing mother in her son, Tarzan's, arms.

Tarzan's mother scarcely figures in any American versions of the story, although Rice Burroughs' early books made something of his aristocratic father. But in Hindi cinema mother and son is invariably a key dynamic. As Ashis Nandy puts it: "the mother-son relationship is the basic nexus and the ultimate paradigm of human social relationships in India" (1980:37). Whilst the MGM film hints evasively at an incestuous bond between Jane and her father,[11] and her father has to die before Tarzan and Jane can live happily ever after, in *Toofani Tarzan* it is Tarzan's *mother* that has to go, releasing the Indian Tarzan from his (in all practical senses invisible) Oedipal bond.

Tarzan and Leela
If Tarzan's father and mother offer models of modernity – ways of bridging the opposition between city and jungle – which are both ultimately flawed and fail, Tarzan and Leela themselves offer more hope. Both figures provide spaces within which 'modern' identities are fluid and open to exploration and negotiation.

Leela is an intriguing mix of 'modern' independence, coquettish helplessness and unconstrained sexuality. She encompasses two facets of decadent city femininity: the vanity and 'falseness' signalled by her obsessional attachment to her make-up bag, and the assertive toughness of a woman in slacks who stands up to men, wields a gun and defies her father to choose her own sexual partner. The movie transforms her into a free spirit in a miniskirt whose hedonistic sexuality becomes, through a series of moves and denials, acceptably identified with the innocence of the jungle. Thus, for example, an erotic bathing scene, in which she (purportedly) bathes nude while singing a sensual song about "a burning rising in my body," is immediately followed by a comedy gag in which Moti the dog steals her clothes, and then her kidnap by the cannibals. Whilst on one level clearly presenting her as both sexually desiring and desirable, the film simultaneously disavows this. Not only does she, in a 'conversation' with Moti, coyly deny sexual relations: "You think I let Tarzan have his way? You think I'm wild (*junglee*) like Tarzan?" but the overt sexual energy of the scene is sharply displaced onto the lust of villainous cannibals and their voracious gorilla chief.[12] It is also not insignificant that the figure of Fearless Nadia would inevitably have coloured any audience viewing of Leela in 1937.[13]

11 - Creed has pointed this out (1987:4).

12 - Creed describes a similar series of moves in *Tarzan The Ape Man, Ibid: 3-5.*

13 - Even the camera angles of the bathing scene echo a famous *Hunterwali* scene. Leela, however, is neither a fighter nor stunt woman.

As Barbara Creed has argued of their American alter egos, Tarzan and Leela's relationship is fundamentally – and quite radically – one of mutual interdependence (1987:6). Both Leela and Tarzan move between being active figures that push the narrative on and erotic spectacle for the camera. While Tarzan demonstrates brute strength and the ability to protect Leela from danger, Leela not only feminises him, by for example powdering his face and treating him as a naughty but charming child, but she also controls and teaches language. Their love scenes include many direct quotes from the Weissmuller movie, including the famous naming scene. But interestingly, what in the American film is simply "Jane, Tarzan, Jane, Tarzan",[14] here becomes "Main Leela, Tum Tarzan," (Me Leela, You Tarzan) emphatically placing control with Leela's voice.

Ultimately, however, it is Tarzan who is central to the film's power and success with its audiences. Wadia found the casting of Tarzan his greatest challenge – no suitable actors could be found in Bombay. John Cavas, the 1930 Body Beautiful Champion of India had to be lured away from a quiet life in Poona, where he lived with his mother and taught physical culture and weight-lifting classes. Before winning the Tarzan role he first had to prove his screen charisma as second hero in *Hunterwali*. Much of *Toofani Tarzan*'s pleasure centres around admiring shots of the strength and beauty of Cavas's body and awe at his acrobatic feats and fighting skills. These include dangerous animal stunts, learned through an arduous early morning training schedule with the animal tamers at Professor Deval's circus which JBH insisted he attend before clocking in at the studio each day. As with other stars of the era who came out of popular vaudeville and showmanship traditions, the fact that he did all his own stunts was an integral part of the appeal. Cavas's Tarzan is modelled closely on Weissmuller,[15] with a similar mix of animal beauty, gruff brute strength, childish helplessness and a strong moral sensibility.

Tarzan's Appeal

What seems, at first sight, most surprising about the Tarzan crazes of the early decades of the twentieth century and again in the 1960s, is the popularity of such overtly colonialist books and films with vast audiences in former colonies. The films of the 1930s made more than 75% of their profits abroad, and even Haile Selassie, Emperor of Ethiopia, used to demand his own African premieres of the Weissmuller films (Essoe, 1968:87).

Why did Tarzan resonate so widely? Why did Indian audiences enjoy the Hollywood Tarzans so much and what was the appeal of the Indian versions? On the one hand the films' pleasures are obvious: beautiful bodies, both male and female, thrilling shots of jungle animals, exciting stunts and fight scenes, and in the Indian version, songs and poetry. But perhaps another key lies in the points of identification the Tarzan figure itself offers.

Contrary to common misrepresentations of Tarzan, the character as originally conceived was not one-dimensionally chest pounding and macho. As Torgovnick points

14 – And not, as invariably misquoted in accounts of the MGM movie, "Me Tarzan You Jane." Creed suggests it is so conveniently misremembered because "Me Tarzan, You Jane" returns control to the male voice *Ibid: 6.*

15 – Interestingly, given JBH's explicit acknowledgement of his inspiration whilst writing and casting the film, Cavas was billed as "Indian Eddie Polo" *not as* "Indian Johnny Weissmuller". Perhaps this would have been seen as too much like copying, placing Cavas as second-rate – the MGM films were in distribution there at the time. More intriguingly it suggests the magic of the silent era stars was still unsurpassed: the capital accrued from the brand-name Eddie Polo – who never himself played Tarzan – places *Toofani Tarzan* beyond a simple copying of the US Tarzan films and into the realm of great cinema nostalgia.

out, Burroughs's early Tarzan story "begins with scenes which dramatise confusion and contradictions about black-white relations, about maleness, and about man's treatment of women" – themes gradually suppressed as the books went on (1990:42). Perhaps more than most other heroes – Indian or Hollywood – the movie Tarzan is a fluid character. He is neither of the city nor properly of the jungle; neither civilised nor primitive; neither western nor traditional; ultimately neither conventionally masculine nor feminine. As such he allows for points of fluctuating identification within the liminal zone between such oppositions, an arena within which contemporary power and gender relations can be explored. Although not in any simple sense a role model for 'modern' Indian masculinity,[16] the Tarzan figure allows space for negotiation of where modern Indian masculine identity might lie.

Three points are pertinent in relation to India.

Firstly, in the context of the nationalist movement, the fluidity of Tarzan's masculinity would have been particularly radical, for it moves beyond the limited oppositions nationalist ideologies had proposed. Cavas's Tarzan offers neither the hard, callous, emotionally impoverished masculinity of the coloniser nor the more effeminate masculinity of Gandhian ideology. Instead it keys in to traditions of subaltern popular culture, from the wrestling and body-building sub-cultures associated with the monkey god, Hanuman, to the martial male cultures of Sikh and Muslim men, as well as to role models from popular Indian performance traditions and Hollywood. By the 1960s there was also another level at play as masculinity was being redefined worldwide. John Cavas had opened up an Indian screen space which produced not just Azad, the star of the three Zimbo films and more than a dozen other Tarzan-style movies, but a number of rival 1960s Indian Tarzans, notably the bodybuilder Dara Singh, a major cult figure of the era who took the display of rippling brawn to increasingly hysterical levels, as comparison between the posters of *Zimbo* and *Faulad** indicates.

Secondly, there is the question of mimicry. Whilst on the one hand John Cavas was known to be a Parsee actor playing an implicitly Hindu character (Wadia's Tarzan), he was also an Indian man playing an American actor (Weissmuller), who plays a lost English aristocrat (Burroughs' Tarzan). Homi Bhabha and others have alerted us to the radical potential of mimicry within colonialist sites. The Wadias' appropriation of Hollywood to their own ends was not simply good commercial sense. By incorporating and reworking MGM and Weissmuller's Tarzan within Indian conventions, the scope for playful identification and appropriation was considerably extended. Cavas's muscular frame bears a load even more formidable than the famed Chevrolet: it simultaneously stands in for and displaces Weissmuller, accruing to itself all the power of his global marketing appeal. It becomes the white superhero of the coloniser, at one level a fictional British aristocrat, at another the global success story of American media imperialism. But at the same time it converts an overtly colonialist film to its own needs. Tarzan could be owned and played with and – interestingly – the Wadias felt no compulsion to clear copyright, at least the first time round.[17]

16 – Except, one might argue, in fantasy.

* *Faulad,* see illustrations on pages 117 & 119.

17 – JBH seems genuinely astonished that a legal representative from the Burroughs' estate had the temerity to visit him a couple of months after *Toofani Tarzan*'s release demanding all references to the copyright name be wiped. He congratulates himself on charming the agent into dropping the legal case but with the remakes from 1959 onwards the Wadias played safe and changed the name to *Zimbo*. Other 1960s Indian Tarzan producers had no such scruples and, when challenged about 10 films using the Tarzan name between 1963 and 1965, Sargaam Chitra Ltd claimed the films were only for the Nigerian market (Essoe, 1968: 204-7).

Thirdly, in claiming Tarzan for Indian audiences, the Wadias were also reclaiming the whole concept of 'jungle' from several centuries of colonialist appropriation. The word itself is of Sanskrit origin and is found in thirteenth century literature meaning uncultivated ground. By 1804 we find *junglo* used in the vernacular to mean a wild or uncivilised person – here a group of Gujarati women's scathing reference to a white colonial man who didn't understand their language.[18] Like thousands of other words it came into the English (and French) language – and global culture – through Anglo-Indian parlance.

Much is made of the word *'junglee'* in *Toofani Tarzan*. Leela constantly but fondly berates her lover: *"Tarzan tum bilkul junglee ho"* [19] and, as they banter the term around between themselves, it is clearly ambivalently valued, being mostly used to mean not only uncivilised but – in the loosest sense – uncontrolled sexuality. By the mid 1960s the word *'junglee'* had acquired a new and more specific meaning following the sensational success of the film *Junglee* (Subodh Mukherjee, 1961). In this Shammi Kapoor kick-started the 1960s for Indian youth and achieved instant stardom as an Indian rock and roller, a 'wild thing' with his hair slicked back in an Elvis quiff. As the persona developed this romantic hero frolicked in the snows of fashionable mountain resorts and raced sports cars around glamorous European capitals with a new breed of 'mod' heroine, superficially Westernised but indubitably virtuous and traditional at heart. Although in his debut film the term *junglee* in fact refers to (a caricature of) unfeeling, cold, westernised masculinity, *junglee* gradually became associated with Shammi himself and became an ambiguously desirable quality, with suggestions of a different sort of uncivilisedness – an excitingly dangerous sexual energy and ultra-modernity. It thus signified both the exotically primitive and the exotically westernised, and inadvertently became one of several terms at play in the negotiation of modernity and a concept which, unconsciously and perhaps unexpectedly, underpins the *Khilari* poster as much as the *Zimbo* poster. It is time to return to the posters.

GIRLS AND GUNS

The Wadias didn't need Jean Luc Godard to tell them that, "all you need for a film is a gun and a girl". *Khilari*'s poster takes no chances: three guns, four 'girls'. Its promise is clear: spectacle, action, 'thrills', sexual titillation and exciting – if jokey – violence within a glamorous modern world. Images of *Khilari*'s stars have been cut out from photographic stills of the film, overpainted in vivid colours and mounted over swirling brushstrokes which roughly sketch in backgrounds and loosely unify the picture. While Hollywood posters often organise their imagery around an unresolved narrative dilemma, this poster offers a montage of figures in a range of settings and moods, condensing through its spatial relationships the key themes of the film.

18 - Hobson Jobson, 1985: 470-1.

19 - Transl. "Tarzan, you're such a wild thing/uncultivated person"

The poster for *Zimbo Finds a Son* uses the same production technique but is, at first glance, thematically less complex. Spatial relationships set up a basic opposition around which the image is structured. Virile masculinity dominates the left-hand side of the poster, accentuated by an hysterical excess of phallic attributes: a lethal knife, rippling muscles of a bare torso, and an erect elephant trunk that dutifully echoes the bulge in the flame-red loincloth of our priapic hero. His sexy mate in skimpy golden bra-top and miniskirt averts her gaze and submits her body full-on to the camera. Bridging this exaggerated opposition between active masculinity and passive femininity (and literally placed to join the two figures) is the son, echoing his father's stance but dressed in his mother's golden loincloth. Confidently disregarding the conventions of Western perspective his placement within the frame visually mediates the key opposition, suggesting both the nurturing qualities of his father (under – and in front of – whose arm he appears) and the potency of his mother (above whom he stands erect).

However, 1960s Indian audiences would have brought well-developed knowledges about Tarzan movies – Indian and Hollywood – to this poster: the amulets Zimbo and his son wear around their necks, as well as the heroine's dress code and the wispy jungle background, would have provided condensed references to *Toofani Tarzan's* storyline and city/jungle theme. Although the posters of *Zimbo* and *Khilari* might appear to the casual observer dramatically different in theme, there are remarkable continuities. Similar oppositions underlie and structure both, broadly a development of themes already revealed in *Toofani Tarzan*: urban vs. rural, civilised vs. primitive, westernised vs. traditional, masculine vs. feminine, and both, in their different ways, make considerable play with the fluidity of gender roles.

The poster for *Khilari* offers more of a puzzle, coding its themes within a more complex layout, as well as assuming a broader range of cultural knowledge and references that audiences would draw on. The top right-hand corner is a dystopic urban nightmare: vivid red and yellow brushstrokes suggest the turmoil of a fiery hell. It is a site of frenzied action: an aeroplane shoots out at a dramatic angle, a helicopter hovers over toppling tower blocks, a posse of survivors hangs precariously from a net beneath. This is equally the Indian metropolitan dream turned sour, a just punishment for a wicked Western world and, for many rural audiences, a vision of Kaliyug itself.[20] Guarding against this inferno is an exotic, gun-toting, sexy siren from the 'westernised' world, in black catsuit and high heels, a flaming mane of auburn hair and large red belt emphasising her curvaceous body and her fiery, dangerous but powerful, sexuality.

Directly opposite, in the bottom left, against the wet dream idyll of a steamy waterfall, another dangerously enticing sexuality beckons. This is nature's rural temptress, the exotic, 'primitive' tribal belle whose sexuality is 'untamed', a vamp whose skimpy ethnic clothes reveal her sensuous and alluring body as she dances seductively for the camera.

Mediating between these two extremes are three figures. The hero and his sexy sixties babe lie across the poster's central ground, offering a promise that order will ultimately be restored and hinting that, within a glamorously westernised world, the paradise of traditional rural life is still nearby. Hovering over this couple, like an avenging guardian angel, is the reassuringly triumphant and heroic Nadia.

20 – For more on this concept (lit. the era of Kali) expressing the degradation of the modern world see Pinney's analysis of a calendar poster (1995: 84).

Four female figures dominate the poster: two, with guns, take active control, two present themselves as erotic display. Despite this, the hero comfortably controls the centre ground, his hands firmly clasped around the biggest gun of all, his eyes masterfully focussed on a distant target. As he snakes along a grassy bank, hints of the trees of the jungle behind him implicitly identify him with the virile muscular action and ur-Indian romance of Tarzan's world. But Dileep Raj's boyish, smiling features and exaggerated rock and roll quiff (complete with dramatic blue highlight) simultaneously evoke that other *junglee*, Shammi Kapoor, whose 1961 film had unleashed on India, to the tirades of scandalised traditionalists, its own energetic youth pop culture, and Dileep is excitingly 'westernised' by these associations. Where the *junglee* of both Tarzan and Zimbo swings from trees in a forest, *Khilari*'s modern '*junglee*' will swing from cranes and helicopters over a city skyline, leading a fast life as a debonair, handsome, young man-about-town.

His sex kitten partner displays herself in classic pin-up pose, engaging our gaze and teasingly presenting herself, through contradictory signals, as both demure and sexually available. This figure combines and unifies visual motifs from the rest of the image. The towel around her head suggests she has just bathed, evoking the sexiness of the waterfall but simultaneously modestly covering her hair. The sizzling orange flame-like pattern of her mini-dress echoes the inferno of the cityscape and the fiery sexuality and hot passion of the cat-suited femme fatale. The white brushstrokes behind her head, and arms opened to display her breasts and voluptuous but vulnerable body, echo – and subvert – the masterful figure of Nadia, commanding the skies of the top left. To fire, water and air is added earth: her snake-like, plump, bare legs, tantalisingly displayed but modestly half-crossed, lie alongside the hero, firmly grounded on the brown earth. However excitingly modern she may seem, she is still safely traditional, still a daughter of mother earth and Mother India.

Khilari's major selling point was Fearless Nadia and the two gun-toting female figures were undoubtedly key to the poster's appeal. Commanding the top left-hand corner of the frame, and echoing the placement of the Tarzan figure and his knife in the *Zimbo* poster, is Nadia's victorious and heroic spy-mistress, Madam XI. Left hand firmly on her hip in a gesture of control and authority, a masculine jacket zippered almost to the top, she brandishes her powerful gun high above her head, the only feminising touch her blood red fingernails and lips. Eyes raised heavenwards, she is the picture of the 'courage, strength, idealism' of her early years. Her cat-suited double, the fetishistic sexualised side of Nadia's feisty persona, stands guard behind. She is simultaneously a protective cover for alter ego, Madam XI, and also our protection against the terrifying cityscape. How could such apparently transgressive images of female power and authority have been popularly accepted as a heroine figure by Indian audiences over more than thirty years?

Since the groundbreaking success of her first film in 1935 Nadia carved out a unique place for herself in Indian cinema. She had debuted in *Hunterwali* as a swashbuckling princess with a double life, who traded her sari for mask, whip, cloak, hot pants and boots whenever the need arose. As her films went on Nadia became increasingly identified as 'Bombaiwali' – the woman from Bombay – connoting cosmopolitan sophistication and modernity, and the settings of the films ranged from Ruritanian palaces to fashionably contemporary art deco sitting rooms, or, in the case of *Diamond Queen* a quasi-wild-west frontier town. Her weapons ranged from swords and whips to guns and bows and arrows, but her fists and feet could be equally devastating. She regularly punched burly villains to pulp or carried them triumphantly over her head before tossing them to an undignified and gory end. She was an impressive acrobat, could swing from chandeliers and somersault from great heights, and shots of her training in her gym started something of a keep-fit craze at that time. She was also an accomplished horsewoman. As one fan fondly remembers:

"The single most memorable sound of my childhood is the clarion call of Hey-y-y as Fearless Nadia, regal upon her horse, her hand raised defiantly in the air, rode down upon the bad guys. To us schoolkids of the mid-forties Fearless Nadia meant courage, strength, idealism" (Karnad, 1980:86).

She was frequently identified with the accoutrements of modern technology where she was emphatically in control: she ran, fighting, along the tops of moving trains, she drove fast cars, and she hung from aeroplanes. She signified much that was considered dangerously exciting about westernised modernity and her films were a reverie of potency within this world. Not only did many of them boast English titles, but the fact that she was a blue-eyed, blonde-haired white woman added a frisson to this, especially as many of her 1930s films were recognisably championing the Freedom Struggle.[21] However, modernity could be signalled in various ways. Even with a Hindi title and the ahistorical setting of a Ruritanian kingdom, an art deco inflection to the poster design, as in *Toofani Tirandaaz**, might be enough to suggest the film's modernist credentials. As Nadia's career continued in the 1940s and 1950s her range widened to include jungle and circus pictures as well as films with an Arabian ambiance, which won her fans throughout the diasporic distribution networks of the Arab world. Her appeal failed only when she was given emotional scenes in social melodramas or played the 'vamp' role.

However radical Nadia might seem, the Wadias did not invent the masked fighting woman. This was a well-established convention of the silent cinema. There has, in fact always been a space within the Indian imagination for the strong female figure, as the ubiquity of powerful female deities such as Kali, indicate. However, another tradition also grew up, that of the *virangana*, or warrior woman. Kathryn Hansen, in her study of Nautanki Theatre, describes how historical and legendary figures from various eras and different parts of India (from Razia Sultana to Lakshmibai, Queen of Jhansi) fed the imagery and stories of much popular theatre and early cinema, as well as folk songs, comic books and calendar art (1992:188-98). The prototypical *virangana* is a good queen, who takes over a throne when a male kinsman dies, leads her people into battle dressed as a man, displays astonishing military skills and dies defending her kingdom against invaders. Four features characterise what Hansen refers to as "this startling

21 – I have written elsewhere about this apparent paradox (Thomas, 1991 and 2005).

* *Toofani Tirandaaz,* see illustration on page 92.

counter-paradigm of Indian womanhood": emphasis on the physical strength of an active body, on moral strength, masculinised dress, and sexual freedom. The *virangana* is one of the only models of Indian womanhood in which notions of 'purity' are irrelevant and active sexual desire is not punished.

If the Wadias' Cavas, as Tarzan, had opened up a fluid space for exploration of modern Indian masculinity, their Nadia persona opened a similar – and arguably even more important – space for femininity. Where Cavas offered a 'counter-hero' to the soft romantic male leads of the mainstream social melodramas, Nadia offered a 'counter-heroine'. Where Tarzan's masculinity could be simultaneously virile, potent, muscular, compassionate, childish and feminised, Nadia's femininity was charming, compassionate, moral, independent, tough, aggressive and sexy. Fashioned out of the 'counter-paradigm' of the *virangana* warrior woman, the 'Bombaiwali' legitimated Nadia's rebelliousness and westernised cosmopolitanism within a traditional framework: she became a *virangana* for the modern Indian world.

Whilst the motif of the masked fighting woman runs throughout Indian cinema history, Nadia's contribution was key. Her success undoubtedly helped audiences to accept, for example, the tougher aspects of the Leela character in *Toofani Tarzan* in 1937. The 'girl with a gun' motif has retained its currency in Indian cinema, not only with the real life *virangana*, Phoolan Devi, played by Seema Biswas in *Bandit Queen** in 1994, but also the blatantly fetishised Kiran Kajal in *Main Khilona Nahiin** or Rekha's *Madam X.* Here the mask of Nadia's early years, (as seen in *Toofani Tirandaaz's* poster), is combined with Nadia's guns, attitude and even fictional name (Madam XI) from *Khilari*. But Nadia herself remained a legendary force until her very last film, *Khilari*. Even at sixty she continued to punch her weight: larger than life, sexy and irreverent, she was still subverting stereotypes as she confidently redefined the boundaries of what older women could do.

CODA

While Mrs Gandhi was launching her Wheat Revolution, and the Beatles unleashed peace and love on the world, what were Indian audiences making of the *Zimbo* and *Khilari* posters? All but the poorest ignored them completely, these were not 'A-grade' films, the world had moved on and Nadia was well past her prime. But for subaltern audiences who still responded to the Wadia magic, here was an entry into exotic other worlds, packaged with comic book violence, sex, and a self-parodic, wacky humour, incorporated within conventions and stories they knew. Most importantly the films were fun, playfully opening up myriad new ways of being both modern and Indian, whilst gently spoofing the popular culture of a transnational world.

Too bad the Beatles never made it out to Basant Studios. *'Zimbo and Son Meet the Girl with a Gun'*… it could almost have been on the White Album.

* *Bandit Queen,* see illustration on page 238.

* *Main Khilona Nahiin,* see illustration on page 213.

* *Madam X,* see illustration on page 238.

In 1965 Christine Keeler was credited with a bit part in Tarzan And The Circus, *a cheap Bombay film aimed at the Nigerian market. Azad, who'd made his name as Zimbo, starred as Tarzan.*

Emma Peel's Diana Rigg spent her childhood in India (1938-46) where she learnt Hindi, went to the movies and… well… just must *have seen those whip-cracking Fearless Nadia films.*

In May 1968, just weeks after returning from India (and while Paris burned), the Beatles recorded the first version of Happiness Is A Warm Gun *at George's house in Surrey. Had they, perhaps, caught a glimpse of that* Khilari *poster after all…?*

CHRISTOPHER PINNEY
NOTES ON THE EPIDEMIOLOGY OF ALLURE

When I arrived at Balkrishna Vaidya's film-hoarding atelier in Dadar, Bombay, he was already engaged with another visiting researcher. A Canadian filmmaker of South Asian heritage, understandably annoyed at my arrival, was making a movie about Bombay's visual culture. Balkrishna's workshop was an ideal setting. An assistant worked on a huge billboard advertising *Lagaan*, Amir Khan's international hit about a plucky village cricket team and their victory over a bunch of grotesque colonial oppressors. Working from a small, cross-hatched, reference print the assistant deftly worked swathes of vibrant colour across stretched white canvas. The intensity and movement bewitched the filmmaker whose cameraman mimicked the painter's movements, digitally capturing every flick and every splash. On the other wall of the workshop lay an equally vast billboard for the remake of *Devdas* on which former Miss World Aishwarya Rai's peacock eyes flared dramatically.

I skulked by the side sensing that my presence was disturbing the filmic scenario of the solitary artisan heroically producing this distinctive visual wonder. The workshop with its pulsating slabs of colour surreally stacked in a small lane, seemed ontologically necessary, like the trolleys in the bazaar stacked with luminous aubergines, or the red chillies spread out on sheets. What would Bombay be without these?

Balkrishna started work as a hoarding artist in 1952, and the relationship he had with the makers of the films he publicised was uni-directional: distributing companies would preview the film and distribute stills and Balkrishna would "get an idea of what the story is about, who the hero is, what the mood is like". Occasionally in the early days, stars would come to Balkrishna's studio to be painted directly. The artist would then produce two or three layouts and the distributor and producer would decide which one(s) should receive the full hoarding treatment. In those days Balkrishna's art was a crucial mediator between commodity and consumer: his paintings aimed to "attract the lower classes, the people working in factories, to provide people with small incomes with a reason to go to the movie theatre and see a film". His images reflected what filmmakers had already decided although some had surprising incidental benefits. His hoardings were so prolific, so large, that some served simultaneously as ideological superstructure and material infrastructure, a source of dreams and a means of keeping the rain out: "If a film [was] successful... the paintings [were] taken down and put up somewhere else... And during the monsoon season we g[a]ve some of them to poor people to cover their homes with."

But all that was a long time ago, before the computer rendered his skills marginal and European art museums recoded his work as a sign of golden age Bollywood. Balkrishna and his son Rajesh are no longer commissioned to produce works that publicize specific films, but rather are asked to create signs of a particular, past, moment of Indian visual culture. The *Lagaan* and *Devdas* hoardings were destined for art galleries. I should have talked with his son about this, Balkrishna suggested, but unfortunately he was in London working on commissions from high-class restaurants. Interviewed in Austria in 1999, where he was performing in an art gallery, Balkrishna commented that in Europe "the kind of recognition we get is rather extraordinary..."

That Balkrishna's hoardings are now part of a commodification of nostalgia reflects an elaborate ecology of changing image production in India. As artisanal curiosities they appeal (chiefly to a European intelligentsia) precisely as the antithesis of the industrial capitalism of film production that they celebrate. Within India they have been displaced by a digital technology that is better able to capture the gloss of commodities and which itself embodies in its own materiality a more perfect form of the kind of capitalism it serves.

In the icy air-conditioned chill of Glamour Studios in Santa Cruz, "handpainted" has become a potential "treatment". Computer aided design encompasses all previous technologies as *effects* and the mouse can become the paintbrush, timidly constructing on a 17 inch screen what the painter's body previously mapped across 20 feet of stretched canvas. The wayward brush of the billboard artist reflecting the contingency of a body in front of a canvas becomes a planned event. But it is one likely only to be understood by an elite that can recognize the knowingness of such a gesture. For the masses, "handpainted" or other nostalgic effects will backfire: "If it doesn't look glossy, if it doesn't look glamorous and if it isn't westernised enough they will take it as a low quality film".

At Glamour Studios I saw what had killed Balkrishna's art, rendering it fit only for nostalgia. Talk here was of design briefs, producers' expectations, dummy posters and client feedback. The seamlessness of digital technology was mirrored in an entrepreneurial ideology that dissolved form into the desire of the client and technological expertise of the designers. "We decide the look", two erudite young female designers tell me: they have been professionally authorised to control the overall style and it is they who direct the photo shoot, asking for a particular kind of lighting, specific regimes of clothing etc. The most important work occurs before a photo shoot however, specifying what kinds of expressions they want: first they decide what they want, then they go and get it. From initial concept to final execution is usually two or three months' sustained work.

But the designer can often play a constitutive role in the development of a film for producers will frequently arrive with only a vague idea, seeking the creation of a stylistically persuasive finance brochure. This outlines the plot, cast and conveys a "feel" of the film – what its "mood" and genre will be. In developing these extended advertisements for a concept, the designers frequently give shape to what has previously been formless. If finance is subsequently arranged and the film goes into production the brochure becomes a point of reference in the whole process of "picturisation".

Bombay cinema has always essentialised itself, choosing to see itself as completely different to Hollywood where everything is grey and plot driven. Designers at Glamour invoke similar, and increasingly untenable, oppositions between the constraints they labour under and the expectations that prevail in Hollywood: whereas in Hollywood they say, the theme might triumph (an action movie might content itself with a helicopter) in Bombay, the star always triumphs. The face and the star are irreducible: "If Shah Rukh [Khan] is in the film no matter how bad your poster, people will definitely go and see it".

By contrast, another film (*Koi Mere Dil Mein Hai*) "has to be really glossy because it doesn't have a big star cast". Bright colour and glossiness can hail viewers in the absence of any familiar star physiognomy. In a transparent circularity bright colours indicate a "fun film, romantic, bright". A transparent narrative also helps, in the absence of opaque star faces: *Koi Mere Dil Mein Hai* was a triangular love story and so the main poster featured a couple in the middle and three characters on either side. Narrative was spatialised, space itself became transparent and worked, so the designers believed, to hail its audience. Always there is a strong imperative to "make it for the masses" so as to ensure an adequate return on investment in film production.

Glamour Studio, while so centrally committed to the metropolitan glamour of Bollywood is also at heart a difference-producing machine; it sorts audiences, mediates their expectations and produces publicity for different spectators accordingly. If there are several different posters for a film then one might be an action poster aimed specifically at north India's young males and a more "glossy" one will be developed for the overseas diaspora market.

Digital technology's transcendental signified is "glossiness". It is a balm: "… a certain amount of gloss really works. Not everyone can visually understand everything and if we're talking about the masses, gloss really works". Gloss signifies not only a look but also a technical perfectibility immanent not only in the digital technology of Glamour Studios but the films that they publicise, and the entire system of industrial capitalism and the consumption patterns which film helps to fuel.

It has often been remarked that since the late 1980s, Hindi film has increasingly reflected and appealed to the consumption expectations of the emergent middle class in a post-liberalisation economy. Middle class gloss coats real transformations in class structure and an intensification of consumption. *Maine Pyar Kiya* (1989) is the film generally credited with inaugurating this new aesthetic of gloss and was in part defined by a look created by the photographer Gautam Rajadhyaksha. Rajdhyaksha is a well-informed lover of Italian Opera, and the leading photographer working in film publicity in contemporary Bombay. Relaxing in his informal Chowpatty apartment, he told me that, "I feel sorry that I was partly responsible for displacing this great art of hoarding painting. I still remember the hoardings for *Kagaz ke Phool* and *Sujata*... these posters were extraordinarily bright so you [could not] miss them. You may not like them but you [could not] miss them. These are the kind of images [that posters] embedded." At this point he points his fingers to his head, as though to indicate a heritage of public images sedimented in his memory.

His CD collection of Verdi and Puccini is the most well chosen and extensive I have ever seen. His photographic style perhaps owes something to the latter composer: it is theatrical and romantically lush. Puccini's seamless lyricism and polarised vocal colours find a parallel in Rajadhyaksha's technical sophistication and ability to create a shimmering and accessible surface. This Rajadhyaksha 'look' has contributed fundamentally to the definition of Bombay filmi aesthetics since *Maine Pyar Kiya*, Sooraj Barjatya's romantic smash hit.

Rajadhyaksha was brought into *Maine Pyar Kiya* at a late stage, as part of what he terms "a damage control shoot". Thereafter, he was involved in the publicity for all Rajashree Productions movies including their biggest blockbuster *Hum Aapke Hain Koun...!* featuring Salman Khan and Madhuri Dixit. He also became involved with the director Yash Chopra, working on *Dilwale Dulhania Le Jayenge*, *Dil to Pagal Hai*, *Ranglila*, and on films such as *Ishq*, *Kuch Kuch Hota Hai*, *Kabhi Khushi Khabhi Gham*, *Dil Se* and *Raja Hindustani*. He became something of a "good luck mascot" for "superstitious" people in the film industry.

For *Ishq* Rajadhyaksha was to have a significant impact on the look of the final film itself. Brought in while twenty per cent of the film shooting remained, Rajadhyaksha was able to define looks and styles for the publicity which were then incorporated into key episodes of the film itself. For other movies he is brought in only after the completion of the film: he has always tried to link the images to the content of the film and then gets the actors to re-enact key scenes during the shoot. "If there were tears there should be tears, if a certain kind of lighting then try and reproduce that kind of lighting".

Rajadhyaksha counterpoints his own intimate engagement with the specifics of each film with the tactics of other Bombay-based publicists. Certain people (who will remain nameless) "get anthologies of world cinema posters in London, or they take illustrations for the covers of Mills & Boon [but] they don't realise that they are blond or that you can use furs over there to add to the glamour but that you can't use furs in India". He, by contrast, engages with the precise narratives and locality of films.

His working practice varies according to the directors: with the Barjatyas he is involved from the very start; with Aditya Chopra he rarely sees the film before the shoot –

Chopra narrates the story and provides an interpretive frame. But Rajadhyaksha's aim is always the same: to get close to the affect of the film. "I always ask what is your character, what are you doing? I try and talk to the star... I ask, now this particular costume that you are wearing in the film at that particular juncture – what are you feeling and can we possibly recreate those feelings?"

He is always searching for the dramatically defining moment, a comic situation or an "extremely emotional clinch" that can be developed into the main motif. He refers to this as "the main signature mnemonic" and gives as an example Madhuri Dixit bending over a very sedate, quiet, Salman Khan in an image used to promote *Hum Aapke Hai Koun...!* "In most cases you more or less grasp the feeling" (he gesticulates abstractly). "Sometimes it may not be truly representational but, if it captures the magic of two people, the chemistry works..."

He perceives an increasing focus on the "main signature mnemonic". "Subsidiary characters are no longer important. In the 40s, 50s, 60s, even 70s you had small little heads [on the poster] but nowadays it's not important because what sells are the two people who are saleable and you concentrate on those. Or if you are lucky to have four, or if you are lucky to have six like in *Hum Aapke Hain Koun...!* then [concentrate] on those". Alongside this, Rajadhyaksha isolates an increasing focus on the face for which he claims some credit, having become renowned for his close ups. Full-length shots are required only for show cards ("landscape" format images printed on card which are usually displayed outside the cinema) and are very rarely used in the main publicity.

Reflecting on his immense success and profound impact on the aesthetic of film publicity he calmly concludes: "I don't think for a moment that any of the films that I have so proudly listed and have been associated with have done anything to push the parameters of Indian cinema. In fact I would call it regressive cinema – they've taken cinema back. It's now purely escapist farc".

I visited Gautam Rajadhyaksha with an old friend, Ravi Aggrawal, who runs the Bombay branch of S.S. Brijbasi. Rajadhyaksha drew a telling contrast between the images he produces for posters and those that Brijbasi publish as postcards, many of which are also photographs taken by Rajadhyaksha: "His market is very different – it is the true Indian market, unlike what we do..." Whereas Rajadhyaksha saw himself as part of an elite that produces images in order to gain the approbation of a few close industry contacts ("We want to create something that our contemporaries and colleagues will say, "Hey, that was *good*""), Brijbasi's market is "The true Indian filmgoer who actually buys a ticket and goes into the darkened halls [even if] it might be bug-infested, hot and sultry [these are] the people for whom these are the dream gods and goddesses".

Poster images of the kind produced by Glamour Studio are disseminated to major cities and other urban areas but only reach a minority of India's population. At small town level a set of posters and lobby cards may accompany a print of a film but then moves

Bollywood film star publicity
sheets manufactured by the
Bombay publishers S.S. Brijbasi.

on with the film when the period of screening ends: the publicity becoming progressively more tatty as the film travels. Films and *filmi* glamour leave their permanent trace in small towns and villages in the form of the kind of postcards that S.S. Brijbasi print in their multitude. Their Bombay office, at the heart of bustling Zaveri Bazaar, is crammed with stacks of religious and other posters, and many thousands of postcards.

In March 2004 the most popular set of postcards were 18 images of Salman Khan whose recent film *Tere Naam* had been a great hit with adolescent boys. More precisely, the hairstyle he sported in the film had been hugely popular and most of the postcards prominently featured his coiffure styled with a central parting in a manner that in an English context would be called "curtains". The popularity of *Tere Naam* was also the catalyst for Brijbasi's reprinting of a large number of earlier Salman Khan images. Salman Khan, who first shot to stardom in *Maine Pyar Kiya* in 1989 (this film, recall was also the first that Gautam Rajadhyaksha produced the publicity for) is what I often heard referred to as a "bare chest specialist". For the purpose of postcards he is usually clad only in jeans so that his muscular torso can be displayed to best effect. The consumers of these images are largely small town and village boys who aspire to a similar physique.

Postcards are printed on sheets which, when cut, produce eighteen postcards. In March 2004 only Salman Khan and Ajay Devgan were sufficiently popular to warrant such treatment. Aishwarya Rai, Preiti Zinta, Sunny Deol and Sanjay Dutt were also extremely popular but only warranted sharing mixed sets with each other (and hence finding themselves on nine postcards each).

Ravi Aggrawal explained that, generally speaking, boys buy pictures of male stars and girls buy pictures of females. Male stars evoke bodily and behavioural aspirations, and female stars serve as grooming and fashion role models. If only it were possible to get a photo of Salman Khan wearing a bikini, I was once told, he would also start to appeal to female consumers. This in part explains why the more female stars "expose", the less they sell: "a beautiful smiling pose of Madhuri Dixit fully clothed will give me a longer print run than a fully exposed pose of Mumta Kulkarni". But there are some significant regional variations: sultry images, especially of Mumta and Manisha Koirala sell especially well in the east of the country where there is a taste for 'exposure'.

Good sales depend on a continuing visibility through the regular release of new films: "too few releases and they slip out of the public mind. Out of sight, out of mind. You need to be constantly releasing to sell, you need at least one major hit and 5-10 releases to deserve your position in our postcard collection!" But there is an illuminating exception to this. Brijbasi's long-term best-selling postcard, photographed by Gautam Rajadhyaksha, depicts Amitabh standing by a horse. Slightly out of focus and not especially striking, its popularity puzzled Ravi until it transpired that it was being purchased in bulk by a Ludhiana garment manufacturer who was manufacturing white sweaters in the style that Amitabh wore in this photo. The cards were attached to the packaged garment, which had now become the "Amitabh sweater".

The long-term best-selling post-card of Bollywood film star Amitabh Bachchan produced by the Bombay film publicity publishers S.S. Brijbasi.

Filmi images also circulate through other routes. During the school holidays between April and June, Brijbasi sells large numbers of 8x14 sheets on which are printed 20 small images. Mostly these are scanned in from the covers of cassettes of film music and are hence atrophied remnants of the original posters for the film whose music appears on each cassette. These tend to be hastily created montages depicting the main characters in the films and lie closer to the kinds of posters that artists such as J.P. Singhal were producing in the 1970s, rather than the narrative motifs of Gautam Rajadhyaksha. Occasionally they are versions of the postcard images or montages specially created for this genre. The reverse of the sheet is printed with a light blue, designed to reduce the transparency of the sheet for these are sold to schoolchildren who collect them through playground blind swap procedures that depend on their anonymity. One child will hold out a fan of images, blue side up and the excited transactor will select one, turning it over to reveal its identity. By this route film posters make their way into the hands of schoolchildren and into the intimate spaces of the everyday.

Gautam Rajadhyaksha had earlier observed that he, "just works in [his] own ivory tower… but how [images] trickle down and [are] interpreted by the market that pushes this country forward is something that needs a lot of research". An inroad into this intriguing question had been provided by a marketing device created by Ravi Aggrawal. Several years ago he started to print the following on the back of all Brijbasi postcards: *panch alag alag 'brijbasi' postcard nimnalikhit pate par dak se bhejie aur zordar inaam paiye* (post five different Brijbasi postcards to the address below and you'll receive a fantastic gift). The gift was one large laminated poster of Aishwarya Rai and a telephone index illustrated with small images of film stars. Ravi hoped to elicit information about the location of consumers and to his surprise "found that 99% of the respondents were from villages of block level, *panchayat* level, below *taluka* level, i.e. villages of below 5,000 or 1,000. So that's where they're most starstruck I guess – more than people in urban areas". A telephone directory for a telephone that doesn't exist, decorated with stars they will never meet, is a powerful metaphor of this rural craving for the fusion of glamour and commodities.

This *mofussil* (provincial) engagement with the metropolitan allure of film was also confirmed by a large number of letters Ravi received following the release in 1993 of the film *Khalnayak* which featured a celebrated, indeed notorious song sequence *Choli ke peechhe?* (What's underneath my blouse?). In this erotically charged sequence, Madhuri Dixit taunted Sanjay Dutt with the prospect of a resolution to that question. For many mofussil consumers, Brijbasi was the gateway to this cinematic world and consequently about twenty marriage proposals were sent to their Bombay office from villagers addressed to Madhuri Dixit and including photographs, declarations of abiding love and pleas such as, "I'm very poor, but I'm very rich at heart".

It is quite likely that these matrimonial aspirants first saw Madhuri's beatific face on a village lottery *jhanki*. The dreamworld of mass consumption is often conveyed through this device, a sheet of card, about 30x40 inches, mounted on a pole so that it may be held aloft, and on which are glued and stapled watches, children's plastic toys and Brijbasi postcards of film stars. At the top is usually a wooden ruler, a prize but an object which also provides structure to the display. Beneath this, symmetrically arranged are a cornucopia of stickers, silver foil coins, tiny plastic shopping bags, plastic mice, cars, fans, guns and telephones, with a single postcard in each corner.

The filmi imagery of village lotteries expresses a symmetrical and complementary allure to that evident in the work of Balkrishna Vaidya. The contemporary consumers of Balkrishna's images find in his work the allure of a lost world. His images conjure not only the nostalgia of the work of the artisan but also make possible the imposition of fixity on the fluid world of Bollywood. Viewed through Balkrishna, popular Indian cinema is distilled from a living practice into an idealised history: the golden age of Raj Kapoor and Guru Dutt, the revolutionary threat of the angry young men of the 1970s and 80s defused by the passing of time, and more recent successes sieved of the tedious and unpredictable dross that constitutes much day to day film production. Balkrishna's work, dislocated from its original function provides a nostalgic canon, retrospectively providing an easy closure on a tempestuous world. Filmi images, of the kind that appear in village lottery *jhankis*, project forward to a world of the city, of movement and glamour, invoking a world not of nostalgia but of future potentiality.

The power, the plausibility of this gesture rests, however, on its reciprocation. The village reaches out to the allure of the cinematic city but periodically Bollywood bounces its fantasies back into the heart of the *mofussil*.

These observations draw on research conducted in Bombay in late March and early May 2004. This period was immediately prior to the national elections in which the BJP-led administration would be replaced by the current Congress coalition. Many film actors stood in key constituencies and mobilised the allure of their cinematic personalities in pursuit of their political ambitions.

Three of the most visible figures were Dharmendra, Govinda, and Sunil Dutt. In Mumbai North the Congress candidate Govinda, known for his dancing and vulgar comedic ability, projected his subaltern identity as a humble man of the people rather than Bollywood establishment. In the neighbouring Mumbai North West constituency the veteran actor Sunil Dutt, widower of *Mother India* star Nargis and father of leading actor Sanjay Dutt, stood a fifth time for Congress under the slogan, "We are polishing the exterior, but the interior is starving" (*India Today,* 19/4/04, p. 28). He is an embodiment of a seriousness that seems diametrically opposed to Bollywood and yet he too projects a gravitas that was sculpted through his own film career.

Dharmendra, now aged 69, came out of retirement to stand for the BJP in the desert constituency of Bikaner in Rajasthan. Known widely as "Garam Dharam" (Spicy Dharam), he made much of a celebrated line from his most famous movie, G.P. Sippy's *Sholay* (1975). Newspaper coverage documented his campaigning strategy: "he unleashes a barrage of emotion-packed dialogues, plays the drunken prankster, turns into a romantic poet and even flexes his muscles" (*Hindustan Times* [Delhi] 12/4/04). Jai and Veeru, two characters from *Sholay* were invoked continuously and describing what he would do if the Vajpayee Government refused his demand for more water for this drought stricken area of northwest India he declaimed, in reference to his drunken water tower suicide sequence in *Sholay*, "I will climb a water tank and shout… *"Vajpayeeji agar Bikaner walon ko unki cheez nahin mili toh – suicide"* (Vajpayee, if the people of Bikaner don't get what they need, then [I'll commit] suicide). The 10,000 crowd roared their delirious approval.

As Bollywood is exported to the west as a sign of India, it is increasingly forced to signify a totality. We are told that its posters line every city street and that its film music blares from every taxi. Bollywood certainly plays a key role in the cultural life of modern India but it does so in different ways, at different levels, and through different forms. We need detailed and nuanced accounts of this film world's strange compulsions. We need an "epidemiology" of this allure.

M.S.S. PANDIAN
PICTURE LIVES

Tamil film magazines of the 1930s and the 1940s were suffused with complaints about the condition of cinema halls. We repeatedly get to read about overcrowding, bedbugs in the seats, lack of ventilation or fans, cigarette and beedi smoke and being seated very close to the screen. A writer in *Aadal Padal*, a well-known Tamil film magazine, posed the question, "Where is hell?" and answered, "cinema halls". [1] He drew careful parallels between the alleged forms of torture practised in hell and the experience of the audience in cinema halls.

Over time the condition of this hell has improved. Part IV of the Madras Cinemas (Regulation) Act 1957 gave detailed instructions about the building of cinema halls. The Act dealt with booking windows, doors, staircases, entrances and exits, gangways, angle of vision etc. Instructions were indeed detailed. For instance, on the angle of vision, it mandated, "The angle of elevation subtended at the eye of any person seated in the row nearest to the screen by the length of vertical line dropped from the centre of the top edge of the picture to the horizontal plane passing through the observer's eye, shall not exceed 35 degrees, the height of the eye of the person so seated being 3 feet, 6 inches above the floor level. A strong barrier or other efficient partition shall be provided to enforce this provision". [2] It also directed the cinema hall owners to provide basic facilities to the filmgoers: "The licensee shall provide (i) a sufficient supply of wholesome drinking water for the use of persons employed in and frequenting such buildings; the quantity and the places and the method of storage and supply being prescribed by the licensing authority; and (ii) spittoons of such description, in such numbers and in such places as may be prescribed on the recommendation of the Health Officer concerned." [3]

Though the quality of life in cinema halls has improved over time, part of the hellishness remains in place. Uncomfortable seats, bedbugs, switched off fans and air-conditioners, accommodating beyond the prescribed capacity – all continue to be part of the present day cinema hall experience. But the irresistible seduction of the film medium makes people endure the hell. Protests against the condition of cinema halls do take quotidian forms; one of the most widely prevalent forms is to damage seats by tearing the cushions.

1 - *Aadal Paadal*, January 1938.

2 - *Madras Film Diary* 1958, Madras, 1958, p. 45.

3 - *Ibid*, p. 50.

Outside this hell however, films have their own enchanted lives. This is the world of posters, cutouts, fan magazines, handbills, newspaper advertisements, still photographs and hand-painted film hoardings. If cinema halls render one more or less helpless, in the world outside, the viewer exercises greater autonomy. If the flow of the film on the screen renders it relatively unavailable for personal appropriation, these artifacts can be individually appropriated and returned to in self-willed contexts. In critical ways, these fragments drawn from films but rendered in a state of stasis provide this autonomy. Writing about the technique of close-ups in film text, Laura Mulvey writes, "…the star close-up would hold the story in stasis, cutting her image out from the flow of the narrative, emphasizing her function as spectacle in its own right."[4] If close-ups are moments of stasis heightening eroticised visual pleasure, the film artifacts that circulate outside the film and cinema halls are in an accentuated state of stasis and hence could be appropriated and taken to varied sites and put to different uses. I will return to this point later. Now to the many lives of these artifacts.

In the enthusiasm to invest film artifacts with the status of art, what is forgotten often is the commercial intent that gives life to them. The meticulous planning by film producers and distributors to make their films a commercial success lay concealed behind them. Let me illustrate this by giving some details about the advertising department of the once famous but now defunct Gemini Studios. Located in Madras and owned by S.S. Vasan, the heydays of the Gemini Studios were from the 1940s to 1960s.

Ashokhamitran, a reputed Tamil writer who worked in the public relations department of the Gemini Studios, writes, "In the advertisement department, there was a cupboard with pigeonholes. The pigeonholes were allotted for important Indian periodicals, each containing a sample copy of the publication and their advertisement tariff. What sort of photographs and news should be sent to which periodical and how much advertisement should be released to different periodicals were all planned."[5] The studio also employed a lot of artistes to paint advertisements and posters on big canvasses as well as people with skill in different languages to do the lettering part of the canvasses.[6] This tightly-controlled and commercially motivated release of information and visuals was a corollary to the deliberately orchestrated sense of secrecy, and hence curiosity, produced around forthcoming releases. Describing his job in the public relations department of the Gemini Studios, Ashokamitran writes, "Gemini Studios did not admit visitors. Whenever there was a compulsion to admit visitors, it was my job to show them nothing but give them the feeling that they had seen everything."[7]

A massive film-producing machine like the Gemini Studios constantly innovated methods to commercially promote their films. To promote the Gemini production *Samsaram* (L.V. Prasad: 1950), the head of the advertisement department V.K.N. Chari got the addresses of housewives from the electoral register and sent them tens of thousands of letters written as though the heroine of the film herself asks them to watch the film.[8] The promotion of *Avvaiyar* (Kothamangalam Subbu: 1953), a Gemini mega hit, is again a tale of commercial innovation. As Ashokamitran recalled, "From the public we received a lot of letters appreciating the film *Avvaiyar*. I replied for months

4 – Laura Mulvey, *Fetishism and Curiosity*, Bloomington and Indianapolis, 1996, p. 41.

5 – Ashokamitran, *Iruttilirundu Velicham*, Chennai, 1997, p. 35.

6 – *Ibid.*

7 – *Ibid.*, p. 36.

8 – *Ibid.*, p. 41.

thanking one hundred of them everyday. There was a scene in the film where Avvaiyar worships Lord Muruga and his consorts Valli and Deivanai. We printed this picture in thousands and send them with the 'Thank You' letters. There were also thousands of letters requesting this picture."[9] The publicity blitz unleashed by the Gemini Studios for its hugely successful *Chandraleka* (S.S. Vasan: 1948), a Tamil film of 18,634 feet, made such an impact that the Bombay producers passed a resolution that there should be a limit imposed on advertisements for any film in periodicals.[10] All these activities produced an avalanche of visual artifacts outside the film text, but parasitical on it.

For those who did not have the resources to do what Gemini Studios could do, there were specialist service providers. In the 1950s *The Madras Film Diary*, an annual directory of the film trade, classified those who provided film publicity as "commercial artistes and publicity directors", "publicity consultants and advertising agents", and "printers and suppliers of publicities". The first of these groups seems to be the most important. While the Bharat Studio was described as "specialists in banners, stills, boards, slides etc.", Balu Brothers were portrayed as "publicity artistes, designers and consultants on all matters on publicity; specialists who serve film producers and film trade with their complete full-fledged publicity department." The list included names of individual artistes too – G.H. Rao, Nageswara Rao, U.S. Menon, K. Madhavan, J. Nath, O.T. Rajan, and M.R.S. Mani. Significantly, despite being producers of popular forms of art, in their self-description, they were not artists, but artistes.

The commercial intent which produced posters, banners, still photographs and other film artifacts was not confined to the world of cinema alone. Film stars became advertising vehicles to sell other commodities. Mobilising images of female stars to sell soaps is a common practice. The practice seems to have had a long past. In 1938 Baby Saroja, a well-known juvenile star of the period, figured as a complainant in an injunction suit filed before the Madras High Court by her father. The suit sought to restrain Khader Ismail & Co. from selling soaps imported from Japan bearing the name "Saroja Sandal Soap" with her portrait on the wrappers and covers of boxes.[11]
In today's vocabulary, film stars have become brand ambassadors. Of course, it is not only soaps that have been promoted in this way. A recent issue of the *Economic Times* reports, "The fizzy crown is passing on. Simran has been replaced with Trisha in the *Fanta* ad. The latter, who is currently on a high in Tamil and Telugu cinema, has been signed on by the fizzy drink brand as their brand ambassador. It may be recalled that the same lass had featured in a commercial for the rival *Pepsi* brand with the Tamil film star Madhavan some years ago. It remains to be seen whether *Pepsi* will counter the Trisha onslaught with some other heroine."[12] For the time being Trisha will be on billboards, newspaper advertisements and television spots along with a *Fanta*.

The visual artifacts, though brought to life by the commercial intent of the film industry and beyond, have lives of their own. They circulate in unintended domains and perform unintended tasks.

9 - *Ibid.*, p. 84.

10 - *Kundoosi*, January 1959.

11 - *Madras Film Diary 1942*, Madras, 1942, p. 65.

12 - *Ibid.*, p. 41.

Film posters and hand-painted banners, though often consumed in distraction in the fast-moving urban milieu, provide visual pleasure and a sense of curiosity. If Siegfried Kracauer claimed that flânerie is "a wonderful virtue made out of the necessity of limited space",[13] the condition of limited space abounds in the over-populated roads of Madras and other towns. Writing about Thiruvanmiyur, a neighbourhood on the outskirts of Chennai city, Ashokamitran reminisced, "Two cinema halls – Jayanthi and Thyagaraja – screen new films as well as old ones. More than the names of the films, the women on the posters would trouble one. It would astonish [me] that such films are made at all. Cinema halls in the outskirts mean films with uninhibited scenes."[14] Ashokamitran is a quintessential flâneur – a stroller, a detective and a journalist rolled into one.

The poster images of stars are regularly removed from the walls and re-sited – either in full or in fragments – in bicycle hire shops, tea-shops and barber shops as decorative material. Their popular images are hand-painted on to the signboards of shops and on auto rickshaws. Paradoxically, it is their condition of stasis and being in a state of freeze, that makes them mobile. In their mobility, they are used in unintended ways – though their life is meant to be transient on city walls.

Still photographs from films, which are sold outside cinema halls, city pavements and village fairs or published in film and fan magazines and in the Friday film pullout of dailies, are collected avidly, preserved and revisited in privacy. Thus one escapes the helplessness and the sense of confinement which cinema halls impose, even while offering visual pleasure. Even someone like S. Satyamurthy, a well-known nationalist politician of the pre-independence period who was a member of the Madras Legislative council, was no exception to this tendency of collecting pictures. As film historian Theadore Baskaran records, "Satyamurthy's fascination with film stars at times went beyond their utility for propaganda purposes. He requested Gohar of Bombay, a star of the silent era, to send an autographed photo; she did, along with a note which said, 'I will be greatly delighted to meet you whenever you come to Bombay'.[15] Pictures of stars are also imprinted on rings, lockets, key-chains, wall calendars and T-shirts and sold and bought extensively.

13 – Siegfried Kracauer quoted in David Frisby, *Cityscapes of Modernity*, Cambridge, 2001, p. 48.

14 – Ashokamitran, *Oru Paarvaiyil Chennai Nagaram*, Chennai, 2002, p. 54.

15 – S. Theadore Baskaran, *The Eye of the Serpent: An Introduction to Tamil Cinema*, Madras, 1996, p. 77.

16 – I am grateful to Venkatesh Chakravarthy for this insight.

But cutouts are of a different kind. They come in two shapes – horizontal and vertical.[16] The horizontal ones accommodate a range of narrative elements. Usually, they portray, apart from the hero and heroine of the films, fragments from song-and-dance and fight sequences as well as comedians and other actors in the film. They are thus inclusive in nature. Vertical ones are of the films of established and popular stars. They usually portray the star hero, and occasionally with the heroine. The star himself is the message. At times, the vertical cutouts super-emboss the star on the foreground of hoardings, producing a kind of three-dimensional effect. They could be gigantic. Recently, there were 100ft by 20ft hoarding-cum-cutouts for the films *Puratchikaran* (2000) and *Valarasu* (2000) on Anna Salai in Madras. Given their sheer size, they could be viewed only from a distance. They dwarf the viewer and exude the aura of films and film stars. Unlike posters or still photographs, they cannot be relocated in the private domain of the viewer and returned to at will. However there are other kinds of cut-outs which can be personally appropriated. These are the life-size cutouts of stars such as M.G. Ramachandran, Rajinikant and Kamal Hassen that are kept in small-town photo studios, or in travelling ones, which set-up their shops in village and urban fairs. In these studios, one can be photographed with the life-size cut-out of one's favourite hero. Being reduced back to life-size and shrunken further to regular-sized still photographs, the cutout heroes thus reach the personal domain of the filmgoers and film fans.

Film artifacts are not only appropriated by filmgoers for personal reasons. They have also become channels for making larger public statements. This is particularly so with film (and other) posters.

The rivalry between the fans of two Tamil mega-stars, M.G. Ramachandran and Shivaji Ganesan, was legendary during the 1960s. One of the ways in which the fans endorsed their loyalty was to deface the film posters of the other star. Cow dung was the preferred medium extensively used to deface them. In their defacement the posters which were normally consumed in distraction, acquired a certain aura. Poster wars continue. In 2002, the Pattali Makkal Katchi (PMK), a Tamil regional party, appealed to the youth not to watch films of Rajnikant claiming that they were not in conformity with Tamil cultural ethos. When his 150th film *Baba* (2002) was released, the PMK cadres went on a rampage tearing down *Baba* posters.

Fan loyalty is occasionally converted into enduring political capital. The well-known case again in this regard is the incredible political success of the Tamil film star MG Ramachandran. He forged a Robin Hood-like image on the screen and capitalized on it to form his own political party and ruled Tamil Nadu state as its Chief Minister for thirteen years.[17] This is a possibility generally not available to female stars. Given their scxualized image on the screen, it is difficult to mobilize them into the realm of politics. After entering a political career, J. Jayalalithaa, once a successful film star, discounted her association with films. In an interview she claimed, "Where films were concerned, I worked hard, though unwillingly as I never wanted to be in films in the first place. I was compelled to join films by my mother."[18] Her political opponents circulated an image of her as a cabaret dancer from the Tamil film *Vairam* (1974) to discredit her.

The urban cultural elite stage their public wars on posters mainly on two grounds – vulgarity and civic sensibility. Anxiety about films as a key source of vulgarity and obscenity is long-standing. For example, the Advisory Committee constituted by the Government of Madras in 1968 for drafting a code to avoid obscenity in film publicity, defined the following as obscene and authorised the Commissioner of Police to take suitable action: "(1) The low-cut neck-line of the blouse making the cavity visible in a prominent way to the eyes. (2) The tight fitting dress of the skin-colour, making it appear as if there was no dress at all. (3) Swimming costume or bathing dress. (4) Bharathanatyam dress should not be shown without a veil cloth on the human body. (5) Mere brassier alone, without a covering cloth. (6) Proximity of two artistes

17 - M.S.S. Pandian, *The Image Trap: MG Ramachandran in Film and Politics*, New Delhi, 1992.

18 - *Aside*, January 22-28, 1984.

(Male and Female) in such a way, either suggestive or open, such as one lying over the other, rolling, attempt to kiss or kissing, holding close woman artiste by men with their hand at improper place, men holding the women close with hands at suggestive and similar postures." [19]

It was merely a code without the force of law. The Cinematograph Act 1952 does not cover posters which are considered obscene, and these come under section 292 of the Indian Penal Code and the Indecent Representation of Women (Prohibition) Act, 1986. The posters therefore, for most part, escaped state censorship. However, the Tamil Nadu Government enacted the Tamil Nadu (Compulsory Censorship of Film Publicity Materials) Act 1987 to deal with "obscene and indecent posters".

Even in those times when there was no adequate legal provision to deal with posters, there was enough public noise made about vulgarity in film posters – often it was a cinephobic response of the elite to claim a higher aesthetic self for themselves. The Tamil film magazine *Bommai*, once widely-circulated but now defunct, wrote in 1966, "The vulgar posters and big advertisement banners displayed in streets, walls and important road crossings in Madras, are creating a rage in the minds of the respectable people... There was opposition. The President of the Film Chamber issued a warning... The police department issued new orders. As all this was happening, the storm and rain that hit the city had felled the banners and washed away the posters. We think that the blemish of Madras has been removed. If there is no vulgarity in the posters and banners, Madras will not only be a clean city but also a respectable one." [20]

The Gandhian-inspired Sarvodaya Movement in the past and women's wings of the Left parties in the present, are in the frontline of the war against obscene film posters. In March 1965 women belonging to the Sarvodya movement in Madras pasted their own posters on bi-lingual film posters advertising the foreign film *Women by Night*. With a semi-clad woman prominently in the foreground, the poster declared the film's "third glamorous week" in the Shanti deluxe air-conditioned theatre. At the bottom of the poster, it was printed, "Important note: We invite outstation viewers to come to Madras to watch *Women by Night*. Due to unavoidable reasons, this film will not be screened within 100 miles around Madras." While the film exhibitor bemoaned the loss of posters, the city corporation officials claimed that their job was only to collect taxes on each film poster pasted in the city walls. [21]

Though posters do earn the city money, they have been and are viewed by the urban cultural elite as disfiguring urban space and being generally aesthetically unacceptable. Civic sensibility is the ground on which periodic campaigns to clean the city walls of posters are launched. The list of participants in the campaign to clean the walls of Anna flyover in Madras's most important thoroughfare launched by a civic NGO, Exnora, in June 1992, could give a glimpse of who wants the posters off the walls. Apart from members of Exnora, the participants included the District Collector of Madras, the Commissioner of Madras City Corporation and the Commissioner of Police.

19 - *Madras Film Diary 1970*, Madras, 1970, p. 97.

20 - *Bommai*, December 1966.

21 - *Kumudam*, 1 April, 1965.

Their motive is to regulate and control the presence of posters on city walls: "A memorandum was given to the Chief Minister through the Collector suggesting the government should put up a wall or hoarding every 500 metres or so for posters. It also suggested that an unemployed youth may be assigned to manage the walls and nominal user fee may be charged to use the wall space for a designated time. Pre-designated areas for arches and cut-outs were also suggested."[22]

The old world of film artifacts is slowly changing. As much as close-ups on the screen, these artifacts, by exceeding the commercial intent which produced them, endeared and sustained film stars as stars for their fans. But the very same stars, in the fast globalising world, are trying to monopolise and control the circulation of film artifacts. Digital reproductions of images have made their circulation cheaper and faster. And hence spawned the new anxiety.

The first film star to entertain desires of such total control is Rajinikant, a Tamil film actor with a following of 12,000,000 fans. It began with his 150th film *Baba*. The day after the film was announced, Rajinikant inserted a legal notice in prominent Tamil and English dailies, which patented the film's posters, drawings, and costumes. It also prohibited persons and firms from imitating his screen persona or using the character of *Baba* for commercial gain. Further, it banned the use of his photographs, sketches, head-scarves and pendants for selling or branding products. Usually it is small-time manufacturers who use film images of stars without their permission, to promote their products in limited markets. The legal notice also meant that printers and distributors could not print Ranjinkant's *Baba* images and sell them in the market as in the past.

Despite the legal ban, *Baba* images circulated in unintended domains. Name hoardings of shops carried hand-painted images of Rajinikant in *Baba* along with the name of the shops. The backs of the ubiquitous auto rickshaws carried his images. The key poster for the film, released by the publicity company Lotus International, had Rajinikant in profile, clenching a beedi with his teeth and holding up his right hand. His fingers imitate in the poster the classical dance *mudra* of a deer. A hand-painted advertising hoarding for beedis copied the image and Rajnikant ensured that it was removed. Even though the film failed at the box office, the efforts of Rajinikant to monopolise the images of *Baba* perhaps indicates a different future for the erstwhile free consumption and appropriation of film artifacts.

The second major change is directly technology-induced. In the place of hand-painted hoardings, the advertisers increasingly prefer vinyl hoardings covered with thin polythene sheets. This combination of computer and plastic is jeopardising hand-painted hoardings and the livelihood of 20,000 hoarding artists in Madras. The decline of the old world is looming large. Young hoarding artists take about a decade to master their art. They begin by following the 'graft method' where they divide the entire space of the hoarding into squares and paint square by square. As they gain experience, they give up the squares but paint the images as they are.

This was a collective work, with the master artist drawing the outline and giving the final touches while apprentices filled in the broader subject matter. There are other kinds of division of labour among the hoarding artistes – letter painters and figure artists. Most often, the letter painters would not know the language they painted. They just copied the letters as though they were images. Interestingly, a large number of hoarding artists belong to the single caste of Acharis. [23]

Digitalised vinyl hoardings which are produced quickly and are glossy are fast rendering a large number of hoarding artists jobless. As a recent newspaper report notes, "If they had jobs to do for Rs. 1,000 a week four years ago, now it was only Rs. 250, the artist says, pointing out that several artists have now taken to driving auto rickshaws. Others are even painting buildings or working as construction labourers to earn a living." [24]

Gemini Studios is dead. Its former premises now occupied by an unedifying highrise building and one premium boutique hotel, the Park Hotel. The death of the Gemini Studios and the fact that its contemporary presence is only as a memory, haunts the Park Hotel's self-description. As the hotel is introduced, "This elegant and lavish 215-room hotel stands on the historic premises of the erstwhile Gemini Film Studios. The precincts that created larger than life heroes and heroines since the 1940s, mesmerised millions with Technicolor dreams have now been transformed to house the theatre of life in its private and public spaces." [25] Even its restaurant 'Six-O-One' does not let go of the Gemini Studios: "Six-O-One (601) pays tribute to our historic location in the heart of the city. It is this address, housing Gemini Film Studios, which redefined film and creativity. This all-hours restaurant promises to take the same creativity and experience forward on a platter." Finally, to the rooms themselves. The Park Hotel claims, "The show continues within the confines of the rooms of this urban haven. The colours are muted, the mood is calm, the feeling utterly peaceful. Contemporary décor and rich textures create the perfect backdrop for your dramas. Pale beech wood flooring and frosted glass weave translucent dreams… Original film posters adorn the walls."

23 – Acharis are an artisanal Tamil caste.

24 – Akila Dinakar, *Digital Technology Displacing Signboard Artists*, The Hindu, December 15, 2003.

25 – All details of the Park Hotel's self-description are taken from http://www.theparkhotels.com

If posters belonged to the republic of popular visual culture, now they are appropriated to the narrow privacy of the super-rich in the Park Hotel. The statement about the Park Hotel rooms that, "The colours are muted, the mood is calm, the feeling utterly peaceful", stands in sharp contrast to the raucous vibrancy of the world of popular Tamil films and film artifacts. If the quality of stasis renders film artifacts mobile beyond their commercial intent, their presence on the walls of the Park Hotel has a different quality. On the walls of the Park Hotel, the quality of stasis is one of immobility. It is something like a hunter's trophy. A sense of death pervades.

EMILY KING
THE POSTER ON THE BEDROOM WALL

In 2003 I made a brief appearance on Radio 4's film review programme *Back Row* promoting a coffee-table book on movie posters that I had just written. The first question thrown at me and the young male film critic who had been drafted in to keep me company was, "Which poster did you have on the wall of your student bedroom?" A simple enough enquiry, but I was dumbfounded. Throughout the writing of the book I had been considering the posters' relationships with the films they promoted, the industry that generated them and the individual designers who created them. What I had not thought about was their meaning to those who put them on their walls. As the two men in the studio sauntered off down a memory lane furnished with images of *Betty Blue* (1986) and *Jaws* (1975), I became increasingly agitated. Had I written a book that missed the point?

It was only when I left Broadcasting House that I began to feel on firmer ground. Movie posters must be given credit for more than their ability to inspire nostalgia, even in a publication destined for coffee tables. That said, the bedroom wall tack does have its virtues, and particularly so in relation to my writing on Indian film poster graphics. To be honest, it is the only approach available to me. I know little about Indian cinema and even less about the production and distribution of the images associated with it. I do, however, know several people who have hung these images in their houses, and on those grounds, I am prepared to speculate.

Of course the phenomenon of identifying yourself through the posters on your wall is nothing new. Susan Sontag described it more than 30 years ago in her essay, *Posters: Advertisement, Art, Artifact, Commodity*, first published in Duguld Stermer's book, *The Art of Revolution: 96 Posters from Cuba* (New York: McGraw-Hill, 1970). Characterising the behaviour negatively as "cultural boasting" and less so as a means by which "cultural subgroups announced themselves to each other", she pointed out that the image on the wall does not necessarily communicate uncomplicated approval. Instead it acts as an indication of awareness of the "worldly value, with some nuances" of the posters' subjects, and is often laden with "nostalgia and irony".

Poster for Steven Spielberg's 1975 film *Jaws*.

Broadly speaking, Sontag is right and, just as I doubt that those critics' favourite films were *Jaws* and *Betty Blue*, I am also extremely sceptical about the depth of the enthusiasm for commercial Indian film communicated by the Bollywood poster in the European or American domestic interior. Very few Westerners can take traditional Bollywood produce undiluted. A dance number here and there, great, but seen from start to finish these films tend to disorient the uninitiated viewer. They seem both too fast and too slow, making rapid assumptions about character and plot and then stopping for a protracted musical sequence. In a review of Amitabh Bachchan's recent remake of the blockbuster *Deewaar* (2004), the Guardian's film critic Peter Bradshaw complained that the movie was riddled with "the kind of unreflective wartime stuff popular in our industry decades ago" and its "song-and-dance numbers are under-par and relentless". I have not seen this film, but I would guess that Bradshaw's criticisms are founded more on his expectations of Bollywood (fuelled by the posters as much as anything) than any genre-specific shortcomings of the film. Us would-be Bollywood fans are a bunch of predominantly white urban sophisticates, with a gloss of everyday multiculturalism. We would love to think we love this stuff, but really most of us don't.

Possibly the most significant element in the European and American desire to love Bollywood is the wish to express enthusiasm for an alternative celebrity culture: a local culture that has been pitted against the ranks of global celebrity and emerged unequivocally triumphant. The idea (possibly a fantasy) that Brad Pitt could walk down the streets of Mumbai unmolested, but Bobby Deol would need a bodyguard soothes our anxieties about increasing homogeneity and globalisation. Like Pitt, Deol has a look and a mode of living that could be accused of inspiring impotent frenzies of consumerist envy, but hey, at least he's home-grown.

Of course, it would be wrong to imply that the Indian preference for Bollywood stars above their Hollywood counterparts is a straightforward affair of preferring like above like. The ethical content of commercial Indian movies lends Bollywood actors greater moral weight than their American equivalents. What's more, Bollywood's financial success is a matter of national concern; the 1950s advertising slogan 'Be Indian, Buy Indian' still has currency. But as far as the Bollywood-movie-star-as-broader-cultural-emblem goes, there is a tendency among soft anti-capitalists to regard non-Western consumerism as an entirely unrelated phenomenon. Where Hollywood is seen as a purveyor of false consciousness, Bollywood is regarded as a manufacturer of authentic desire.

A design-oriented take on the same set of issues pits standardised international movie advertising against the idiosyncratic, handcrafted type and imagery used to promote Bollywood produce. In a parallel to the enthusiasm for Indian film stars, the European and American appetite for Indian cinema graphics represents the longing to see the local triumph against the global. In the face of the increasing uniformity of Hollywood film advertising, with most local distributors choosing or being coerced into adopting consistent visual styles, our hunger for singular graphic idioms becomes ever keener. The lack of imagination or verve in the graphics used to promote mainstream film leaves us craving alternatives. In the face of the bland set of celebrity portraits that appear on most mainstream film posters, the crazy disjunctive collage images such as that on the poster for Chandra Barot's *Don** (1978) become very appealing. In this image, soulful black and white portraiture clashes with inexpertly cropped stills of action scenes. Rather than selling the movie as a seamless whole, it suggests a kit of parts, which could be taken as a reflection of the theme of the film, that of mistaken identity.

In the mid-1980s the graphic designer and educator Katherine McCoy encouraged her graduate design students at Cranbrook Academy of Art in Michigan to explore vernacular type and imagery as an option preferable to the prevalent graphic language of corporate modernism. They were set exercises that required replacing the ubiquitous typefaces Univers and Helvetica with fonts taken from food packaging or the more outré sections of the Letraset catalogue. The purpose of this procedure was to demonstrate the communicative potential of the unschooled everyday, the assumption being that vernacular graphic expression was more authentic than its sophisticated counterpart. In retrospect, McCoy's educational protocol seems to involve an absurd degree of fetishisation (type as the fall-guy of capitalism), yet the feeling that design is better for having not been through the corporate mill survives. Most of us have little understanding of the nature of the design and marketing industry behind Indian movies, yet we retain a belief that it is an arena where idiosyncrasy and personal expression are more likely to have persisted. Hand-drawn type and illustration, such as the perky letterforms on the poster for *Mehboob Ki Mehndi** (1971) or the comic-book aesthetic of *Pran Jaye Per Vachan Na Jaye** (1973), have come to represent a communicative ideal.

I have been to India twice, once in the late eighties and more recently in 2004. I visited different parts each time, travelling between Delhi and Ahmedabad the first and remaining in Calcutta the second. Of course my experience is limited, but it did strike me that in the nearly twenty-year gap between the two encounters, Western advertising and graphic styles had become much more prevalent in India's urban environments. In particular, I noticed the campaign for Hutchison's mobile phone network '3' with its extensive use of white space and stock photography. It could have been lifted straight from the streets of London, or Frankfurt, or Stockholm. In comparison with the slickness of this sort of Western advertising, with its nod to moneyed minimalism (think also of the advertising campaigns for Gap or Apple), Bollywood posters of the kind shown in this book seem to represent an alternative that is worth preserving. Maybe once it would have seemed vulgar, but now we cherish the campaign for Yash Chopra's family drama *Sawaal** (1982), with its inexplicable use of a rainbow background, or that for *Sholay** (1975) with its extravagant fireball. Overwrought graphics and evidence of hand-made production such as over-inking, misregistration and clumsy montage have become emblems of authenticity.

Of course it's not just Indian movie posters that are viewed this way. Illustrated movie posters from all over the world merit the same kind of treatment. In particular, the posters that emerged from Poland in the 1950s and 1960s are often held up as the most

* *Don*, see illustration on page 178.

* *Mehboob Ki Mehndi,* see illustration on page 147.

* *Pran Jaye Per Vachan Na Jaye,* see illustrations on pages 166–167.

* *Sawaal,* see illustration on page 202.

* *Sholay,* see illustration on page 173.

perfect examples of the graphic expression of cinematic themes. Designed to promote Polish films and international films within Poland, these posters were distributed by a centralised government agency and were collectible from the outset. Rather than simple advertisements – entertainment in 1950s Poland was scarce and an empty seat at a screening near unthinkable – they are expressions of a national cinematic philosophy, a belief that filmic narratives should be viewed as metaphors for the core themes of human existence.

The distinctive Polish film poster breathed its last just before the fall of the iron curtain in the late 1980s and now the Poles enjoy the same mundane cinematic graphics as the rest of us. It is probably not long before Indian movie graphics go the same way and, as with Polish posters, increasing rarity will almost certainly enhance our sense of their worth, both cultural and financial.

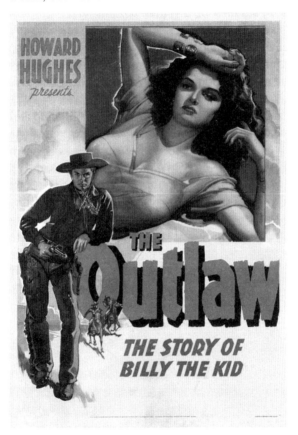

Jane Russell featured on the 1941 film poster for *The Outlaw*.

Moving on from graphic nostalgia, the posters in this book satisfy longing on many other levels. Particularly striking is their treatment of sexuality. Bellies, upper arms, thighs and backs are invested with an erotic charge that has long evaporated in our porn-hardened climes. They appear, to put it bluntly, like something from the 1960s. And the nature of those bodies too. Great handfuls of upper arm, soft folds of flesh on bellies and backs, hips that look like they might wobble. The internal corset of solid muscle nurtured by

Hollywood movie stars, male and female, since the 1980s has rendered the Bollywood body a thing of exotic rarity. Then there is the extra charge of having your titillation illustrated rather then photographed. It harks back to the extraordinary poster of Jane Russell for the 1941 film *The Outlaw**. Drawn by an Italian watercolourist, the lovingly painted strain on the fabric over Russell's chest brings to mind the hand of the artist, adding another layer of eroticism.

Most Europeans and Americans who have been to India first encounter the country in the course of gap-year travel. The contemporary equivalent of the grand tour, the 'year off' is intended to furnish young people with a burst of exoticism so concentrated that they are able to go about the real business of living with their sense of adventure sated. Westerners arriving in India tend to be stunned by the visual noise of the cities created by the interplay of graphic saturation and life conducted in the open. While Sontag argued that domestified collections of posters act as "substitutes for experience", in the case of Bollywood images they are often mementoes of genuine instances of culture shock. And along with memories of the noise, the heat and the smells, the posters bring back a sense of youth and lack of responsibility. For many of us, Indian graphics are inextricably tied with the transition to adulthood, the years between 18 and 22. Sontag argued that "modern tourism" turns "travelling into something more like buying", but she didn't acknowledge that the act of buying could be an experience in itself.

Of course it's not enough to view another culture's graphics as part of your own emotional history, but I have gone so far down this road that I will close with a specific instance of nostalgia. In the early 1980s, when I was a young teenager, I spent a few years living with my family in Egypt. I attended a British school and one of my best friends was the daughter of an Indian family who were living in Cairo in similar circumstances – although they lived in a carpeted modern flat, while we lived in a tile-floored traditional villa. My friend was a cousin, I don't know how close, of the actor Amitabh Bachchan and we spent several weekends at her place watching videos of Bollywood extravanganzas while consuming a steady stream of Indian food. It was the case of swapping what had become the everyday peculiarity of being an English thirteen-year-old in Cairo for a new, more luxurious strangeness. Now, when I see Indian posters, I remember the distinctive smell of over-efficient air-conditioning, the taste of carrot halva and the thrill of proximity to a family member of someone who was such a demonstrable celebrity.

* *The Outlaw*, see illustration on previous page.

SARA DICKEY
STILL 'ONE MAN IN A THOUSAND'

Late in 2004, I saw my neighbor Darshini standing at a bus stop on a Madurai street. When I stopped to say hello, Darshini excitedly pointed out a poster advertising her favorite movie, which was pasted on a wall across the street. Looking over, I saw a stream of brightly printed posters for the latest Tamil films. But Darshini was directing me to a smaller, less glossy print for the 1965 film *Ayirathil Oruvan (One Man In A Thousand)* starring MGR and Jayalalithaa. The film was playing at one of the local theatres specializing in old MGR films. MGR – easily the most enduringly popular hero of Tamil cinema – acted in films for 40 years before becoming Chief Minister of Tamil Nadu in 1977. Jayalalithaa, the last of his major co-stars, is the current Chief Minister. Before I went on my way that afternoon, Darshini explained that *Ayirathil Oruvan* was important to her because it had garnered MGR's party its first electoral success. Darshini's praise for this movie took me by surprise: all of the truly enthusiastic MGR fans I had known until then were poor or lower middle class, and most had minimal education. Darshini has a Ph.D. in History, teaches high school, and tutors private students in English at her home. Her son is in medical school and her daughter develops computer software. She was in fact the first solidly middle class, well educated person I had known to profess respect for MGR as both an actor and a political leader.

Darshini's use of the poster, however, was typical. Film posters are one of the several vivid signs of films, film stars, and actor-politicians found all over the city. The range of these signs, ordered roughly from small to large and from temporary to long-standing, includes small glossy decals, printed posters, painted fan club signboards, giant movie hoardings (billboards) clustered in central crossroads, and even the towering cut-outs and gilded statues of present and past Chief Ministers (such as MGR and Jayalalithaa) who used film stardom to launch political careers.

Posters are arguably the most proliferated and the most ephemeral of all these film visuals. They are more low-cost and widespread than the other publicly erected cinema advertisements, and they appear in the visual field of everyone who walks or rides in the streets. Posters rotate frequently, lasting only as long as the film's run, or until fans of rival stars deface them. They often spark comments and conversations. Passersby remark on favored actors and filmmakers, speculate about new films, and recall the plots of the old MGR and Shivaji films being advertised. And as I learned, even posters of 40-year-old films can also engender discourses on what is right and what is wrong with the contemporary social and political world.

In this case, seeing the *Ayirathil Oruvan* poster also sparked later conversations that wove together Darshini's and my mutual interests in film, politics, and social change. Over the next month, whenever we visited, Darshini talked about MGR, Jayalalithaa, the social and economic contributions of their political parties, and how such advances had combined with economic liberalization to change the class and gender landscape in Tamil Nadu.

I must note at the outset that these conversations were eye opening for me. I have studied class relations in urban Tamil Nadu for over 20 years, and the first years of this research were on film watching and fan clubs. As an anthropologist who studies class as a system, I try to examine evenly the perspectives of people in different class positions. My aim is to understand how individuals, as well as larger economic processes, work continually to reproduce and to alter class – in its local forms – as a socioeconomic system. But I am also highly critical of political and social systems that entrench poverty, and these aims often pose tensions in my work and daily life. Because (like many social critics and academics) I have always reacted to the claims of MGR's apologists with skepticism at best, such tensions quickly came to the fore as I spoke with Darshini. Yet Darshini made me realize something I later confirmed by talking with others – that there is a significant highly educated, middle-class contingent of people who continue to support MGR (and to a somewhat smaller extent, Jayalalithaa), who look back on MGR's rule with longing, and who have well articulated, strongly felt reasons for doing so – largely because of the social welfare programs enhanced by MGR's government, as well as a less clearly stated nostalgia for the social and cultural values that they feel are irretrievably slipping away.

Whenever she visited after showing me the poster of her favorite film, Darshini brought along some of her latest MGR fan magazines, and she soon persuaded me to buy a VCD of *Ayirathil Oruvan*. In this film, MGR plays Manimaran, a brilliant indigenous doctor who leads a rebel group against a series of tyrants, including an island king, a pirate chief, and a dictator. Each foe is felled by Manimaran's singular intelligence and fighting skills. When he and the rebels are enslaved and then bought by an island king, the beautiful princess Punkodi (Jayalalithaa)[1] is entranced by Manimaran's good looks, bravery, and selfless leadership. The slaves escape the island, only to be coerced by a pirate chief into joining his band. When Punkodi follows after Manimaran, she too is captured by the pirate chief, but Manimaran valiantly saves her honor when the chief

1 – Until late 2000, Jayalalithaa's name was written in English as 'Jayalalitha'. She added the final letter, on numerological advice, to enhance her party's chances in the 2001 Legislative Assembly elections.

auctions her off. Although she first spurns Manimaran for his apparent turn to piracy, Punkodi quickly recognizes his true character again, and soon they are wed. Manimaran defeats each of his opponents in quick succession, but despite great acclaim, he refuses to become either pirate chief or king. Instead he humbly declares his service to the people, and leaves with Punkodi to become an itinerant doctor once more.

MG Ramachandran left his impoverished family to join a drama troupe at the age of 7. He entered the Madras film studios in 1936, and in 1953 became a member of the Dravida Munnetra Kazhagam party (DMK, the Dravidian Progressive Federation). The DMK had grown out of the Non-Brahman Movement in southern India, and was initially founded on rationalist principles (anti-religion and anti-caste). MGR left the party in 1972 to form his own party, the Anna Dravida Munnetra Kazhagam (ADMK).[2] The ADMK quickly became highly successful, in large part due to MGR's fan club support, and MGR was elected Chief Minister of Tamil Nadu in 1977, a position he held until his death in 1987.[3] J. Jayalalithaa was MGR's third and final major co-star, and she joined his party leadership at MGR's invitation in 1982. After MGR died, Jayalalithaa consolidated the party under her leadership. She has since been Chief Minister three times, holding the position from 1991-1996, for a brief period in 2001 (when she was forced to leave office after the Indian Supreme Court ruled that a corruption conviction made her appointment unconstitutional), and then again from 2002 to the present (after the Madras High Court acquitted her of the corruption charges).

MGR's film and political personae were closely linked, as is clear in *Ayirathil Oruvan*. Specializing strategically in heroic figures, MGR played swashbuckling renegades and triumphant underdogs, portraying characters that elevated and glorified 'the people'. Fans used glowing terms to praise his virility, power, generosity, and selflessness. In this way, his film roles were taken as illustrations of his character, on the premise that he would not have chosen such roles had they not mirrored his own moral code.[4] These qualities are captured – stilled and distilled – in posters of MGR's films, where his power and virility are advertised in a muscled physique, his selfless innocence in the shining eyes of an open face, and his identification with working-class people in portrayals of (well attired) laborers.

The romantic lover, dancing rickshaw driver, and sword-wielding fighter were abandoned in favor of new visual representations after MGR became Chief Minister. Sometimes he smiled in those pictures of his last ten years, and sometimes not; often he was shown helping elderly women or sick children; but almost always he wore a trademark cap and dark glasses. These accessories hid the aging that would have belied the 'evergreen', immortal image that many fans fervently believed in. His death in 1987 came as a shock to these fans, and the breadth and depth of their adoration was revealed as the news spread. Riots and several suicides followed, dramatically enacting fans' grief and devotion, and three million people attended MGR's funeral.

In succeeding MGR, Jayalalithaa was unable to build on her film roles as MGR had; film heroines of the time rarely depicted publicly powerful figures. Instead, her early

2 – The party was named after C.N. Annadurai, founder of the DMK; in later years it was renamed the AIADMK, for the All India ADMK.

3 – See Sara Dickey, *The Politics of Adulation: Cinema and the Production of Politicians in South India*, The Journal of Asian Studies 52, 2: 340-372, May 1993.

4 – On the relationship between MGR's film roles and political career, see also M.S.S. Pandian, *The Image Trap: MG Ramachandran in Film and Politics*, New Delhi: Sage (1992).

political following was based on her relationship to MGR. Before his death, Jayalalithaa was widely referred to by fans as 'Anni', elder brother's wife, and was assumed to be his 'second wife'. Soon after she first became Chief Minister, Jayalalithaa began to encourage followers to call her 'Amma', mother, and worked to de-feminize and de-sexualize her image, both in person and in her cut-outs. She transformed her image from a lithe and attractive heroine, to a demure if anointed devotee of MGR, and finally to a staunchly bulky, heavily draped, and independent figure of power.[5]

MGR'S GIFTS TO THE PEOPLE

After Manimaran escapes from the island kingdom, the distraught Punkodi sings his praises. She lauds his 'golden [hued] body', his 'heart like a small child', and his generosity, calling him 'one among a thousand' and 'the leader of the poor'.

Economic liberalization was instituted formally in India in 1991. Its policies are touted as having substantially benefited India's middle classes. The quantity and quality of consumer goods have increased, and lower-interest loans have become far more accessible for major expenditures such as vehicles, homes, and business equipment. New kinds of employment range from prestigious managerial and IT positions with multinational firms to a large number of lower-level service positions. Theoretically, at least, the purchasing power of the middle class has grown simultaneously with the increase in quality, variety, availability, and accessibility of the consumer goods for which they constitute the major market.

But the effects of liberalization have in fact been mixed for middle and lower classes alike.[6] While Madurai residents who see themselves as middle class almost always state that people in Madurai are better off now than they were, say, 20 years ago, they express numerous concerns about the social changes that have accompanied economic improvement.[7] Darshini was even more directly critical of economic liberalization, which she felt had had a largely detrimental impact on culture and values. Although Darshini is happy to have easier access to computers and other technologies, her thoughtful commentaries reveal her sense that Tamilians have lost various kinds of freedom with liberalization – freedoms that she associates with MGR and his parties.

The first time we met after seeing the *Ayirathil Oruvan* poster, I was talking with Darshini about a common belief that the middle class was growing in Tamil Nadu, and poverty was decreasing. Darshini agreed with this view, and had an explanation for the (apparent) phenomenon. She began with an explication that went straight to my interests in consumption and class:

> "The poverty line has improved here. You don't find people in rags, people who are hungry. The standard has improved. Almost everyone has a TV, tape recorder, and synthetic saris now. The major difference from the past is that now, people's basic needs are satisfied. Nowadays, it's amenities and electronic goods that separate the poor from other people".

5 – On the changing visual imagery of Jayalalithaa, see Preminda Jacob, *From Co-star to Deity: Popular Representations of Jayalalitha Jayaram*. In Vidya Dehejia (Ed.), *Representing the Body: Gender Issues in Indian Art*, Delhi: Kali for Women, 1997.

6 – On these impacts of liberalization, see Leela Fernandes, *Nationalizing 'The Global': Media Images, Cultural Politics and the Middle Class in India*, Media, Culture & Society 22: 611-628 (2000), and *Restructuring the New Middle Class in Liberalizing India*, Comparative Studies of South Asia, Africa and the Middle East XX, 1 & 2: 88-104 (2000); Jayati Ghosh, *Gender Concerns in Macro-Economic Policy*, Economic and Political Weekly (April 30, 1994), p. WS-2-WS-4; Rajni Kothari, *Poverty: Human Consciousness and the Development of Amnesia*, Atlantic Highlands, NJ: Zed (1995).

7 – Most people who are poor, on the other hand, believe that the general populace is worse off than before, although they recognize that wealthier people have made significant gains.

In her view, the dividing line between the poor and others is no longer whether people possess adequate food and shelter, but how high the quality and quantity of their consumption is. Darshini is a keen social observer, and she was able to articulate a detailed vision of the process that she believes has created these improvements. Her explanation began with national changes but moved immediately to local programs:

> "Food has become cheap because of the agricultural revolution, and textile industries have made synthetic fabrics cheaper. Then health – [Tamil Nadu] government health schemes have given the people good health. Government free schools make children go to school now – plus there has been a free meals scheme since 1981 for children up to age 15. When the mother is four months pregnant, she can go to the Free Meals Scheme and get nutrition balls. When the child is two years old, she can leave the child at the Nutrition Scheme Center. MGR brought this – now children are cared for from 4-month-old fetuses to 15 years old. But the major scheme that eradicated poverty is the Family Planning Scheme. Child mortality is down, the life span is up, children are fed and educated, women can go to work. When the DMK came to power, they propagated the idea that children are not a gift from God – they are biologically produced. Women were very ready to have family planning. So the need for food was reduced, while the supply of food was increased".

Darshini felt that MGR had done 'all good for the people'. She said he was indeed 'one among a thousand', and she reminded me that one of his standard titles was Puratci Talaivar (Revolutionary Leader). The programs she credited him with were all initiated, however, by other Chief Ministers and previous parties. The Nutritious Noon Meal Scheme, for example, was begun as the Mid-day Meal Scheme in 1956 by K. Kamaraj, Congress Party leader and state Chief Minister, and targeted the poorest and most disadvantaged children. In 1982, MGR expanded the program to include pre-school children and pregnant women. Tamil Nadu is indeed seen as a leader in this arena; some analysts attribute Tamil Nadu's relatively high literacy rate to the Nutritious Noon Meals program,[8] since the program encourages parents to send their children to the schools.[9] Like many people, Darshini associates the benefits of this program with MGR's generosity and concern for all of the people of Tamil Nadu.

Similarly, government incentives for 'Family Planning' (which in most of India is now synonymous with female sterilization) were implemented in Tamil Nadu in the early 1960s, before the DMK came to power in 1967. Darshini, however, attributes changing attitudes toward family size with the DMK's rationalist ideology, rather than with specific programs. And because MGR still belonged to the DMK at this time, Darshini is able to associate this social development with him.

While Darshini recognizes a national economic context that contributes to economic changes in significant ways – including increasing industrialization and productivity in agriculture and manufacturing – she chooses to highlight the contributions that MGR made to improved quality of life in Tamil Nadu. In her view, his programs and

8 – See, e.g., Kalpana Parikh and Sumiya Yasmeen, *Groundswell for Mid-day Meal Scheme*, India Together (January 2004), http://www.indiatogether.org/2004/jan/pov-midmeal.htm. For a more critical view of the program's effectiveness, see Chandra Bhan Prasad, *Midday Meals Don't Work for Dalit Children*, Infochange News and Features (April 2005), http://www.infochangeindia.org/analysis66.jsp.

9 – Similar programs have been modelled on this one in other states since 1995, after Manmohan Singh, then Finance Minister of India, applauded the Tamil Nadu program and encouraged its implementation nationwide. Now, as Prime Minister, Singh has included a nationwide noon meals program in his Central budget proposal.

ideologies have improved health, decreased child mortality, and increased literacy; they have decreased family size and enabled women to enter paid employment, thus adding to family resources, and making families more able to purchase the consumer goods that ease labor, add pleasure and serve as status markers. While Dravidian parties have governed Tamil Nadu before and after MGR, in an unbroken hegemony since 1967, and while the initiation of each of the social policies she mentions actually preceded the DMK and ADMK, Darshini brings all these social improvements back to MGR. Like other fans, Darshini saw MGR's film roles, personal character, and political goals as intimately related. She told me about accounts she had read of his generosity when he was a film star, and explained, 'We observed no differences between his life and his characters'. Darshini first saw *Ayirathil Oruvan* when she was 6 or 7 years old, and I asked whether her favorite film had taught her anything about what MGR was like. "Yes", she said, adding reflectively,

> "In that film he was working for the liberation of his friends. He gives up his chance of a luxurious life with Punkodi to be with his [poor] friends. He is always with the poor, though he has a chance to live a sophisticated and easy life. The message is this: Though he has a crown to wear, though he has the power to rule the people, he doesn't want that – he wants to take care of the sick. He doesn't want to be identified with the ruling authority – he is the representative of the poor and the sick".

But it is not just the poor whom he represents – Darshini sees MGR as the leader of *all* the people, not just the poor or the rich, unlike the Communists who (in her words) 'grab from the rich to give to the poor', or other political parties who favor the wealthy. Her view contrasts with those of a wide array of analysts, who see MGR essentially as having stolen from the poor to give to the rich. Holding to the latter opinion myself, I was also perplexed by Darshini's argument as I recalled the many film characters MGR had played who fought for the uplift of the poor. When I pointed out these roles, Darshini replied, 'Oh, but MGR never says the poor will become rich. They have to be treated kindly, they have to be paid well, they have to be honored. But he doesn't say anything against the rich. In the film *Nadodi Mannan* (*Vagabond King*, 1966), someone says to MGR, "If the poor become rich, there won't be any rich people!" and MGR answers, "No, there won't be any poor people"'. Similarly, she noted, in *Ayirathil Oruvan* MGR takes only the ill-gotten booty of pirates and distributes it to the common people; he does not 'grab from the rich'. While it is critical to Darshini that MGR supported the poor, she also feels included among the people he represented. This is in part because, as she told me, the slaves in *Ayirathil Oruvan* stand for 'any poor man, any bonded laborer, any laborer', and 'naturally, their liberation is something any oppressed group loves to see, it is a longing that any oppressed group would have – whether they are oppressed by caste, by class, racially, or anything else'. But it is also because, she believes, his films and propaganda cast a wide net around the 'common people' without alienating those few who might have felt outside that group. To her mind, the liberation he offered was inclusive.

As MGR's men prepare to return to their native land after MGR has defeated the pirate chief, they sing joyfully on the ship:

> *"We should live like that bird over there*
> *We should dance like these waves*
> *On the same earth, in the same sky*
> *We sing the one song, the song of rights".*

Darshini adamantly believes that MGR and his parties have substantially improved the lives of people in Tamil Nadu, bringing freedom from poverty, caste and gender inequality, and injustice. She contends that economic liberalization, on the other hand, has hurt the people. In holding both these views, Darshini is somewhat unusual among middle-class people. In particular, she is both vocal and articulate about certain government policies that have accompanied liberalization. She is especially critical of policies related to education, finance, and expansion of the private sector:

> "Economic liberalization did not improve the standard of living. Really, it hurt higher education. Research, arts, language, and literature education were hurt. Professional education [e.g., business and information technologies] was increased but value-based education started deteriorating".

Such policies, along with the loosening of import restrictions and encouragement of international investment in Indian ventures that accompanied liberalization, encouraged the growth of the private sector in the Indian economy. Darshini was directly affected by these policies because her Ph.D. cohort was one of the first to face monumental difficulty in attaining university appointments. Conversely, she has benefited less from new consumer opportunities than have many other people. The sole support for her family since her husband died 15 years ago, Darshini owns no vehicle and lives in a sparsely furnished rented house, and all her spare money seems to be sent to her children in weekly bank drafts. But her criticisms were much broader than this; she saw new financial trends as having a devastating impact on cultural attitudes. As she said,

> "Since then [1991], only the private sector expanded. Private sectors [banks and finance companies] introduced loan schemes. They made the people debtors – lifetime debtors. This made the people work – work work work work, that's all. The people started running after work. It's like holding the tiger's tail – if you let go the tail, the tiger kills you.
>
> The exchange offers [from private lending institutions] made people financially dependent. For example, it used to be only the rich had a vehicle. Now so many people not only have them, they are always getting a new model. To trade in an old vehicle for a new vehicle, you need not pay new money – just keep paying a

loan for another ten years. What has happened is, the private sector took over the financial management of individuals. Now every month, instead of budgeting, people's salary goes to loans... There is no savings anymore – loans are seen as saving, that is the brainwash of consumers. It used to be that taking out a loan was very shameful. And now, a person's status is determined by loan eligibility. If you don't have it, it is a shame – it means you don't have proper employment".

Darshini, an exceptionally well educated woman who values learning in its own right, was highly chagrined at this turn in values. She finds it deeply ironic that banks used to be about saving and now are about debt, that debt used to be stigmatized and now demonstrates prestige, that money has displaced education and character, and that economic 'liberalization' has brought dependence rather than freedom. In short, Darshini regrets the loss of MGR, who worked to bring people freedom.

CONSUMPTION, MORALITY AND GENDER

Punkodi is an ideal young woman, a modest and beautiful virgin who values her good name as her life. When the pirate chief captures her, he puts her up for auction, intending to buy her for himself. Punkodi is forced to dance on the auction platform. Every time she wearies, she is whipped. Wearing a revealing costume and grimacing with pain and shame, Punkodi laments that she is searching helplessly for her lord. Forcing her to dance, she sings, is like asking a cuckoo to sing after its wings are broken, or asking a peacock to dance after its legs are broken.

'Decentness' is a key middle-class value in urban Tamil Nadu. It encompasses both neatness and modesty, qualities that are imbued with moral value and are often difficult to disentangle. When I asked Darshini for her definition of the word, she said, 'Decent means being modest in speech, in activity, in the way they look and smile. A person shouldn't laugh loudly at other people's problems. They should be decently dressed, not exposing themselves. Not shouting to express themselves, especially girls. Those who don't want to be hygienic and healthy, they wear dirty clothes.' Darshini pointed out that dirtiness is often assumed by high-caste people to be inversely proportionate to caste rank. I added that neatness and decentness are also associated with class. She agreed, and confirmed my impression that these values have a wider spread than they used to, especially when linked with consumption:

"Nowadays all the poor, with maybe one or two exceptions, they dress up neatly. There are cheaper textiles available now. Construction workers used to have dry skin and hair, but now they have oiled hair and skin, pinned-up saris. When I was in college [25-30 years previously], no one did. They wear neat blouses, not torn, not faded. 20 years ago, they didn't mind wearing these... And the poor and middle class people all have some minimal jewelry now".

Darshini was noting not only the narrowing material gap between the lower and middle classes, but also the increasingly shared values associated with consumption, grooming, and hygiene. Thus even those in stereotypically lower class jobs, such as construction workers, take care with their personal appearance – skin, hair, clothing, and accessories – in ways that surpass what even college students did 20 to 30 years ago. Being 'neat' in this way is a part of being 'decent'. Both terms have moral connotations, since poverty itself is a moral issue (some Hindus, for example, assume it results from sins in past lives), and avoidance of public dishevelment is seen as a laudable character quality. But the moral issues involved go further than this; being 'decent' also means dressing and behaving modestly ('not exposing', 'not shouting').

Both women and men should be modest in their appearance and behavior, but achieving modesty places greater constraints on women than on men. This includes the use of new technologies as well. Darshini pointed out the gender differences in rights to technology one day when we were talking about how certain luxury items have now become 'basic commodities'. Televisions, for example, have replaced the metal bureau as one of the first material signs of status in a lower – or lower-middle-class household (though it is likely to be a second-hand, black-and-white TV). Recently cell phone ownership has burgeoned, thanks to a promotional scheme by the Reliance Company. But holding up her own cell phone, Darshini observed,

> "Cell phones are not common among women. I am criticized for carrying a cell phone in my hand. A man can have it, but a woman? She has to keep it inside her purse. One (auto rickshaw) driver asked me, 'Why do you want to keep it in your hand? Why can't you keep it in your bag?' I said, 'Why *can't* I have it in my hand?' and finally he kept quiet. My sister's husband challenges me also. They think it is something like women's equality. They don't want women to speak anything in the public, other than with their relatives or their husband".

To some extent, Darshini's brother-in-law is right – Darshini does challenge gender roles. She supports her family without help from a man, she has a tutoring business, she is highly educated. But she also has relatively conservative views about modesty and morality, and believes that liberalization encourages excessive spending and promotes immoral behaviors – such as prostitution among women of all classes – to satisfy the desire for money. Darshini has deep respect for Jayalalithaa, a woman who like her is also unmarried, and who has stepped out of traditional women's roles while maintaining a modest image. It is very important for her to see Jayalalithaa as a moral person; she does not believe the claims, for example, that Jayalalithaa is divorced and had a daughter out of wedlock, saying that if such a daughter existed anywhere on this earth, surely the media would have unearthed her by now. I never asked what she thought of the corruption charges that Jayalalithaa had been acquitted of.

CONCLUSION

MGR died in 1987, but neither his films nor his regime have faded from people's understandings of the social world. Darshini pointed out that MGR always has two to three movies showing in the theatres everyday, in all the cities of Tamil Nadu. 'No other actor has that many showing at the same time', she said, 'not even Rajnikanth and Kamalhasan'. She had a point. And each of those films has posters plastered on city walls, reminding people of the roles that MGR played in films and politics alike.

Darshini is one of the many people who respond to those posters by talking about what MGR and his personal and political ideals mean to her. Like the working-class fans I first spoke with twenty years ago, she praises his liberation of and generosity to the people. Those fan club members, who differed from Darshini in gender as well as class, also recounted (and still recount) the fighting skills and virility with which MGR quashed his enemies and elevated the poor. Some of these fans are as supportive of Jayalalithaa as Darshini is, and others are not. Jayalalithaa has long been distrusted by some MGR loyalists, in part because her ascension to power challenged gender norms. But like Darshini, most fans are unimpressed by the economic changes instituted at the national level in recent years.

Glorification of MGR's reign is one means for expressing dissatisfaction with the changes brought by economic liberalization – which is more widespread, especially among the middle class, than most popular literature suggests. Conversely, my talks with Darshini began to dispel the stereotype I had held that few middle and upper-class people had supported MGR's and Jayalalithaa's politics. These conversations, and those I had later with other well educated and economically secure people, helped me to understand their views that the early DMK and the ADMK social programs had served as models for the nation, making Tamil Nadu a national leader in advancing education, literacy, and health, and in decreasing fertility – policies that, in their broadest strokes, are valued by lower and middle classes alike. Perhaps MGR and his reign are also coming to stand for the values of what has already been telescoped as a "simpler" and more "traditional" time: when social ties were more important than business ones, and when education, generosity, and good character mattered more than money and new cars. Posters of his films condense those values onto a single plane.

Ayirathil Oruvan itself continues to play a role in the social imaginary, including in fairly elite spheres. It recently received a tribute from renowned filmmaker Mani Ratnam in *Iruvar* (*The Duo*, an examination of the relationship among MGR, Karunanidhi, and Jayalalithaa), with a song titled *Aayirathil Naan Oruvan* (*I Am One Among A Thousand*). And then there is the July 2000 posting about a nuclear warhead on Bharat Rakshak, a venue for current affairs discussions organized by the Consortium of Indian Defence Websites:[10] 'I suppose it will hit one target, then get up and reconstitute itself like MGR in *Aayirathil Oruvan* (translation: one missile against 1,000 targets)'. MGR the hero plays on.

10 – http://www.bharat-rakshak.com/phpBB2/viewtopic.php?t=257& (viewed 14 March 2005).

PATRICIA UBEROI
THE PAIN OF LOVE AND THE LOVE OF PAIN [1]

The *Times of India* used to be a grave and portentous newspaper. It carried grave and portentous news. And it was read by grave and portentous people – the makers of national policy and enlightened public opinion. Disconcertingly, front-page news early in August 2004 was a Reuters' dispatch with the punning headline: "It takes toe to tango, but Dutch law refuses to bite". According to the report, the Netherlands Parliament was debating the introduction of a law to criminalize unsolicited toe-licking in public places. This followed the detention of a 35 year old man who was purportedly in the habit of sneaking up to women on beaches and park benches and licking their toes. Dutch parliamentarians were incensed that the man had later been released without charge: "Licking a stranger's toes is rather unusual but there is nothing criminal about it", a police spokesman clarified. [2]

The appearance of this particular item as front-page international news must have convinced many readers (if indeed more convincing were required) that the *Times* is now little better than the local tabloid press – laced with *filmi* gossip, celebrity scandal, "believe-it-or-not" trivia and pin-ups of half-naked women; alas, many Indian starlets and beauty queens among them these days. But to leave the matter there would be to ignore the subtle omnipresence of visual foot-fetishism in the contemporary public sphere in India – in popular cinema, in particular. Not unexpectedly, since India is rivalled only by China as a civilizational crucible of podo-erotica, [3] the erotic has a big place in this complex semiotics. But it is certainly not all of it.

In the South Asian cultural context, a touch to the feet indexes the asymmetrical relations of the weak to the strong, of junior to senior, of servant to master, of wife to husband, and also – on the spiritual plane – of devotee to guru and worshipper to god. The feet are in constant touch with polluting substances and must be ritually cleansed before approach to the sacred. Yet, for the devotee as for the lover, the dross of everyday materiality is the purist of substances, to be reverently ingested in token of the abjection that is unconditional and uncontaminated love.

1 - I am grateful to a number of interlocutors – among them Urvashi Butalia, Nasreen Kabir, Veena Naregal, Jit Uberoi, Safina Uberoi, Ravi Vasudevan and, mediatedly, Akbar – none of whom can be held responsible for my final interpretation.

2 - *Times of India* (Delhi Edition), 8 August 2004.

3 - William A. Rossi, *The Sex Life Of The Foot and The Shoe*, London: Routledge & Kegan Paul, 1977.

4 - See Patricia Uberoi, *Dharma and Desire, Freedom and Destiny: Rescripting the Man-Woman Relationship in Popular Hindi Cinema* in Meenakshi Thapan (Ed.), *Embodiment: Essays in Gender and Identity*, Delhi: Oxford University Press, 1997, p. 147-73. Though the direction of this film was formally attributed to Guru Dutt's long-term script-writer and good friend, Abrar Alvi, the film is usually treated as a Guru Dutt film. See Nasreen Munni Kabir, *Guru Dutt: A Life in Cinema*, Delhi: Oxford University Press, 1996, Ch. 7 and *Tribute to Guru Dutt* in Osian's *Cinefan Sixth Festival of Asian Cinema*, New Delhi, July 2004.

5 - A social reform movement in late 19th century Bengal.

6 - See Reena Mohan's short documentary, *In High Places* (2000), dealing with the work of Laxman and Vincent, two Chennai (Madras) hoarding painters. Chennai is the recognized epicentre of billboard paintings and giant "cut-outs", setting standards for the whole country in making film stars of politicians, and politicians of film stars. See Preminda Jacob, *From Co-Star To Deity: Popular Representations of Jayalalitha Jayaram* in Vidya Dehejia (Ed.), *Representing the Body: Gender Issues in Indian Art*, New Delhi: Kali for Women, p. 140-65.

I first began to think along these lines some time ago when I was assigned the task of explaining Guru Dutt's classic *Sahib, Bibi aur Ghulam* (*Master, Mistress and Servant/ King, Queen and Knave*, 1962) to Australian Film Studies students.[4] This was in the days before Bollywood cinema had really "caught on" in the West, and I tried to put myself in mind of what had struck me when I first saw the film, newly arrived in India from Australia. What stuck in my mind, as I recalled the experience some thirty years later, was the amazing rendering of the erotically-charged first encounter of the film's male protagonist, Bhoothnath (played by Guru Dutt), with the beautiful but neglected wife (played by "tragedy queen" Meena Kumari) of the wealthy landlord in whose mansion he was temporarily quartered. An educated but poor young man from the village, Bhoothnath had found work in a nearby factory, owned by a rich Brahmo[5] social reformer. The factory manufactured a renowned love-inducing *sindur* (vermilion powder) which Chhoti Bahu, the landlord's young wife, wanted Bhoothnath to procure for her. She believed it might help enchant her errant husband, who spent all his nights in company with the most beautiful and talented of the city's courtesans. There was quite a build-up of erotic tension around this meeting. Escorted conspiratorially by the man-servant, Bansi, Bhoothnath enters Chhoti Bahu's bedchamber; his eyes track to a pair of painted and ornamented feet across the room; a mat is placed for him to sit on; the feet walk step-by-step towards him over the chequered tile floor; the person settles in a chair in front of him; and slowly he looks up – at her eyes, her mouth, her face. She smiles and leans forward as though to confide. Such was the beginning of the "servant's" transgressive relationship with the mistress of the great house, a beginning memorably condensed in the gaze of a man at a woman's beautiful feet. Simultaneously, in the bazaar, the wayward landlord is peremptorily roused from his drunken stupor by the ringing anklets of the dancing girl who sings of the intoxication of the night to come: yet another first encounter visually encoded in the language of feet.

Remarkably, the podo-semiotic register of *Sahib, Bibi aur Ghulam* extends even further to encapsulate the two other male-female relationships that the film explores against the background of the decline of the old feudal system and the rise of a rapacious new commercial class. Thus, Chhoti Bahu's sterile relationship with her uncaring husband is signalled in the tragic-comic efforts of her proxy, the manservant Bansi, to persuade the inebriated landlord to dip his big toe into a glass of water. Without ritually consuming this "toe-water", the young wife refuses to break her fast, and she had remained hungry since the previous day while her husband was busy with his mistress in the brothel. To complete the matrix, the fourth man-woman relationship – between the hero and the Brahmo reformer's daughter Jabba (played by Waheeda Rehman), whom he finally marries – is also initiated through the language of feet. The rustic hero's arrival in the presence of the sophisticated Jabba is heralded by the loud squeaking of his brand new patent-leather shoes. Tongue-tied and embarrassed, he quickly removes the shoes, hugging them clumsily to his breast as he gazes into her eyes. The squeaky shoes parsimoniously index the social and cultural difference between them, a difference which finally turns out to be illusory for, unbeknown to either of them, they had actually been married in their childhood and were thus cosmologically and narratively destined for re-union.

THE BODY LANGUAGE OF THE FILM POSTER

The Indian film poster has always invited public scandal. This is partly because it is subject to a different regime of state censorship, control and certification to the film itself; and partly because its localized production by small-scale off-set printing companies and ateliers of bill-board painters has – at least until the recent introduction of computer digitalization – encouraged the imaginative and colourful embellishment of film publicity stills and press-handouts. "It is more interesting to paint *the heroines*", two Chennai-based hoarding painters observed in conversation with documentary filmmaker, Reena Mohan. "We use… only soft strokes and pink fluorescent colours … lips should look like guavas, the teeth perfect and pearly. As for the anatomy, we concentrate on the softer areas – the stomach and cleavage." Apparently, many stars require the strategic enhancement of these assets.[6]

Arbiters of public taste and moral vigilantes are intermittently provoked to protest against "obscene" film posters and hoardings, occasionally effecting their removal, and the Indian Women's Movement counts among its early successes a series of campaigns against obscene, pornographic and degrading advertising and film imagery, resulting in the passing of the Indecent Representation of Women (Prohibition) Act (1986).[7] Expectedly, public concern around film posters and hoardings is focused on the degree and manner of exposure of the female body, on suggestive postures, simulated copulation and – most worryingly – graphic scenes of female abjection. What with blood-dripping knives, smoking pistols, glaring eyes, fury and torture, let alone boobs and bottoms, the podo-semiotic motif, erotic or otherwise, is relatively muted in the film poster. One domain where it is conspicuous, however, is that of the *mujra*, the erotic-poetic performance of the professional dancing girl (*tawaif*), who is characteristically presented in seated salutation to her patrons – *feet*-first, as it were.[8] The iconic poster of Rekha playing the eponymous courtesan of Lucknow, *Umrao Jaan** (Muzaffar Ali, 1981) is a memorable example. The *tawaif's* body-posture condenses the "Islamicate" *nawabi* culture of pre-colonial Lucknow, a stereotype of leisured decadence nostalgically-recalled in innumerable Muslim "socials" and historical romances. But beyond this, as Mukul Kesavan has observed, the *tawaif* figure – or her transformation in the persona of the westernized "vamp" – is a *structural necessity* in the semiotic register of popular cinema, where she is required to function as the "other" of the chaste wife or untouched virgin.[9]

While the *tawaif's* teasing salutation is, so to speak, a "conventional" gesture in the podo-semiotic register, one finds relatively unconventional images, too. If anything, these are all the more striking for their inversion of social expectations. One such is the poster for another Guru Dutt film, *Mr & Mrs 55** (1955), starring Guru Dutt along with the fabulous Madhubala, regarded as the most beautiful actress of the 1950s.[10] The poster shows a rather rakish-looking Guru Dutt, wearing a weather-beaten brown

7 – The initial exhilaration on this account was short-lived, however. Not only does the legislation give unduly wide powers to state officials to decide on whether or not a depiction "is indecent or derogatory to women or… likely to deprave or injure public morality" but – as was very visibly demonstrated during the fraught 1996 Miss World competition in Bangalore – the issue of indecency tends to push feminists and ultra-conservatives uncomfortably into the same political camp. See Nandita Gandhi and Nandita Shah, *The Issues At Stake: Theory and Practice in the Contemporary Women's Movement in India*, New Delhi: Kali for Women, p. 67-80, 224-27; also Mary John, *Globalization, Sexuality and the Visual Field: Issues and Non-Issues For Cultural Critique* in Mary E. John and Janaki Nair, (Eds.), *A Question of Silence? The Sexual Economies of Modern India*, New Delhi: Kali for Women, p. 368-96.

8 – The other ubiquitous representation of the *tawaif* is in the skirt-swirling pirouette: passion contained, then passion released.

* *Umrao Jaan*, see illustration on page 200.

9 – See Mukul Kesavan, *Urdu, Awadh and The Tawaif: The Islamicate Roots of Hindi Cinema* in Zoya Hasan, (Ed.), *Forging Identities: Gender, Communities and The State*, New Delhi: Kali for Women, 1994, p. 244-57.

* *Mr & Mrs 55*, see illustrations on pages 85, 100.

10 – The triumph of Madhubala's career was her role as Anarkali in K. Asif's *Mughal-e-Azam* (1960). Her death in 1969 at the early age of 36 has added to the mystique surrounding her persona.

felt hat and casual western attire, kneeling at the feet of Madhubala to tie the ankle-strap of her black court shoes (a type known in those days as "bellies" or "belleys").[11] Madhubala, in "western" dress (long skirt, laced belt and sleeveless blouse) and holding a striped umbrella, glances superciliously down at him over her shoulder. The kneeling pose notwithstanding, Guru Dutt appears anything but abject as he looks up at Madhubala with a rather cheeky smile. Come to think of it, he is almost caressing her leg.

MODERN MARRIAGE: 'MR & MRS 55'

Typed as a "social" or "romantic comedy", *Mr & Mrs 55* is the story of a naïve young heiress, Anita, bequeathed a huge fortune by her father on the condition that she get married within a month of her 20th birthday. Her overbearing aunt, Sita Devi (Lalita Pawar), a staunch feminist and man-hater, contracts with Preetam, an indigent cartoonist (Guru Dutt), to marry Anita on the condition that they get divorced immediately afterwards. As it happens, however, the couple had already met and been attracted to each other, and this complicates matters.

Anita is hurt and furious when she learns that Preetam has married her for money. Desperate to explain his side of the story, Preetam poses as her chauffeur, kidnaps Anita and carries her off to his village. She is kindly received by his sister-in-law, through whom she begins to appreciate the qualities of a "traditional" wife and the real meaning of conjugal love. Indeed, Anita seems on the point of falling genuinely in love with Preetam, when aunt Sita Devi turns up to reclaim her ward. Convinced that Anita doesn't care for him after all, Preetam provides Sita Devi with faked evidence to clinch the case for divorce, and decides to leave Bombay for Delhi. Meanwhile, awaiting the court decision on the divorce case, Anita has a change of mind, finally telling her aunt that a woman's happiness lies in marriage and family, and not in the false freedom promised by the feminists. Anita's aunt locks her up in her room but Anita escapes, aided by Preetam's loyal friend and confidant (Johnny Walker), to be melodramatically united with Preetam at the airport just in the nick of time.

The scene of Preetam's abjection, down on his knees tying up the haughty Anita's ankle-strap, is not, as far as I can see, part of the film. True, the skirt-blouse ensemble (or something like it)[12] is worn by Anita in several scenes, including at the tennis match when Anita and Preetam first meet. The striped umbrella motif also appears intermittently in the film. In one scene, the elderly maidservant chases after Anita with an umbrella as she escapes to meet her tennis-star idol, Ramesh, warning her not to let her complexion get darkened by the sun: otherwise, who will marry her? And a scene set at the Mahatma Gandhi swimming pool in Bombay has a parade of girls with umbrellas (and some very inept divers) providing the background to Anita's song, "Blue skies, black clouds". Anita's footwear also figures conspicuously in her first meeting with Preetam. Anita has sneaked out of her home to watch Ramesh at the tennis courts, but is pursued by her aunt's telltale secretary. Trying to escape detection by crawling out through the stands, Anita throws her high-heeled sandals – no, *not* black "belleys" – down on to Preetam, who is coincidentally sleeping underneath the stands, oblivious to

11 – Etymology unknown, but perhaps denoting "ballet" shoes: rather appropriate, in this case, as the leg position evokes a Western ballet position.

12 – The blouse is usually "sleeveless". This sartorial preference, read as a sign of an upper-class, relatively Westernized, life-style, or of the Anglo-Indian, is regarded as rather daring in the north Indian context even today (though it is the notorious "spaghetti straps" that are now the focus of public comment and tussles between parents and their teenage children). Aunt Sita Devi, exposed to progressive western thought on the women's question, also wears sleeveless blouses – and never covers her head, of course.

the match on centre-court. Preetam, whose first view of Anita is of dangling legs and feet, is instantaneously love-struck. He wordlessly hands her back her sandals, one by one, gazing into her eyes and retrieving her dropped handkerchief for future savouring. All these little details are in place in the cinematic text, but nowhere do we see the scene of Preetam's ironic abjection, kneeling at Anita's feet to buckle her shoe. The nearest we get to that posture is when Preetam, attempting to woo his haughty captive wife in a sylvan setting en route to the village, sinks briefly to his knees in a parody of the chivalrous western-style "proposal": you trickster-Cupid, don't think you can get fresh with me, is her songful retort.

Of course, the shoe-tying scene might have been edited out of the film, but more likely – as Chris Pinney's account here suggests – the poster would have derived from an independent studio publicity photo, devised to emphasize the classic "woman-on-top" situation of Hollywood romantic comedy, in this case the class difference between the penniless cartoonist and the spoilt heiress.[13] Indeed, it is a very apt illustration of Preetam's response to Sita Devi: "You 'decent' people just want to make the husband the wife's 'servant' (*ghulam*)."

Preetam's gallant-abject gesture, kneeling at Anita's feet, is in any case deceptive. No wonder he is smirking. From the moment of their formal marriage (even without the sacrament of Hindu marriage), Preetam was effectively "on top", though his material circumstances undergo a change only somewhat later. He repeatedly claims the "rights" of a husband over his wife and, finally disappointed, takes the initiative to divorce her. He also tames the rich shrew by contriving to make her push the stalled car, coolly lighting up a cigarette as she does so; after this he allows her to share the front seat with him so that they arrive in the village looking like the new middle-class *Mr & Mrs '55*, not like chauffeur and mistress. Though he is determined to woo her love rather than press himself upon her, he demonstrates his male power of possession by effortlessly carrying the petulant heiress in his arms across the door-step of his village home, and up into the bedroom: "She's just strained her ankle", he tells his sister-in-law by way of explanation. Emotionally, too, Preetam has already conquered Anita's heart, despite her attempts to suppress and deny her feelings. This is brilliantly rendered in a scene, soon after their registry marriage, when Anita and Preetam coincidentally meet up in a nightclub. As Preetam watches Anita dancing with her smartly togged escort, their eyes meet and avoid each other, meet and avoid each other, through a whole dance number. His ultimate victory is Anita's voluntary choice of the wifely "subjection" (*ghulami*) that her feminist aunt so vociferously deplores.

COLLATION AND CITATION[14]: 'GUIDE'

When I first came across the film poster of *Mr & Mrs 55*,[15] I was convinced that I had seen the picture before – though I recalled that in that instance the woman was wearing a bridal or dancing girl's costume, not western (or Anglo-Indian) dress, a detail which I had immediately discounted.[16] Specifically, my husband and I had acquired the print I had in mind in 1966/67 from a prominent Delhi off-set printer whose inventory of

13 – Another publicity still for *Mr & Mrs 55*, published in the Osian's-Cinefan catalogue (op. cit., p. 65), has Madhubala and Guru Dutt sharing a bench but facing in opposite directions. Madhubala, gorgeously dressed, is putting on lipstick; Guru Dutt (in hat, again) is holding up a newspaper, but actually looking at her disapprovingly over his shoulder. The intention seems to be to emphasize the contrast between *her* modern frivolity, and *his* modern professionalism, thereby gendering the "threat" of modernity.

14 – The phrase, borrowed from art historian Jyotindra Jain, to emphasize the intertextual, cross-media *bricolage* so typical of Indian popular culture.

15 – Osian-Cinefan catalogue, op. cit., p. 65.

16 – Changes of costume are so common in *filmi* song-sequences that one tends to ignore them.

prints included Hindu deities, patriotic posters (this was just after the 1965 Indo-Pak war), maps, and boring school charts of alphabet letters, "leaders", fruits and vegetables, and what have you.[17] I remembered that we had once displayed the print – No. 10 in their "Film Stars" series for that year – at an exhibition of Indian calendar art in 1996,[18] using it as both a "filler" on a nondescript column, and also to illustrate the give-and-take relationship between popular cinema and calendar art. The sight of a man in hat kneeling at a woman's feet in some sort of ritual of reversal evoked immediate mirth and amazement; apparently it challenged the general feminist expectation of the Indian woman's abjection before the object of her love.[19]

As it turned out, Film Stars No. 10 was not the *Mr & Mrs 55* poster after all, despite the striking similarity of body image (kneeling man in hat at the feet of haughty woman). First of all, the image was *laterally inverted* – though perhaps this formal transfiguration is semiotically of no consequence. Moreover, on closer inspection, the debonair kneeling man in hat didn't have a moustache like Guru Dutt; his hat was a white panama, not a brown felt one; his gaze was downcast, not cheekily upwards; and he was carrying some sort of staff or baton. Indeed, he was quite recognizably Dev Anand, coincidentally, the male lead in several Guru Dutt films, including *Baazi* (1951) and *C.I.D.** (1956), where he appropriately wears a brown felt hat, though the female figure appeared to be more a generic "type" of the era, a composite of Sadhana, Vijayanthimala, Mala Sinha and Waheeda Rehman in the opinion of my informants. Also, the man was not so much putting *on* the woman's high-heeled gold lamé mules, but tying (in fact, probably *un*-tying) her anklets, which were clearly the anklets of a dancer, not of a respectable married woman. A little sleuthing (the clues: the year, ca. 1966, and the male star) revealed the film to be *Guide* (Vijay Anand, 1965), starring Dev Anand and Waheeda Rehman in the lead roles.[20]

Guide, based on a novel by R.K. Anand, tells the story of Raju (Dev Anand), an impecunious tourist guide who takes up with the rejected and unhappy Rosie, a girl from a courtesan background married off in a marriage of convenience to a nasty and pedantic old archeologist, Marco. Marco will not allow Rosie to disgrace him by dancing in public, and her first act on attaining her freedom from him is to rush to the bazaar to buy herself a set of dancer's anklets. Delightedly, she runs through the bazaar in her high-heeled mules, anklets jingling, to the snide remarks and stares of loitering men, until Raju begs her not to make a spectacle of herself (and him) and to take off her anklets. She then teases him to help her do so, which he embarressedly does, to the scathing comments of onlookers: "Look what sort of a woman Raju's got now". Thereafter, Raju launches Rosie on a very successful national and international dancing career. Having tasted success and recognition (and in a sense socially rehabilitated herself as the custodian of a national cultural tradition), Rosie in due course longs for marriage and children, but Raju is unwilling to forsake the high living to which he has now become addicted. A gambler, he is jailed for forging Rosie's signature; indeed, he was set up by the vengeful and jealous Marco. On his release from jail, he becomes a wanderer, eventually settling in a far-away village where he is mistaken by the superstitious villagers for a holy man. Tragically, he is compromised

17 - Indian Book House, Map House, Delhi. See Shirish Rao, et al., compiled, *An Ideal Boy: Charts From India* (Chennai: Tara Publishers) for many examples of Indian school charts of the type published by this press.

18 - Eicher Gallery, New Delhi, *From Goddess to Pin-Up*, 1996.

19 - A famous example may be found in Meena Kumari's *Na Jao Saiyan* (*Don't Leave, Beloved*) song in *Sahib Bibi aur Ghulam*.

* *C.I.D.*, see illustration on page 103.

20 - On *Guide*, see Sumita S. Chakravarty, *National Identity in Indian Popular Cinema, 1947-1987*, Delhi: Oxford University Press, 1996, p. 46-52; and Ashish Rajadhyaksha & Paul Willemen, (Eds.), *Encyclopaedia of Indian Cinema*, Delhi: Oxford University Press (Rev. ed.), 1999, p. 384-85.

into undertaking a fast for rains – and the rains *do* come to the parched village lands – but Raju dies in the end, with his mother and the forgiving Rosie at his side.

We recall that the poster for *Mr & Mrs 55* did not appear to be a reproduction of any particular scene from the film, but was rather an enactment (possibly based on a publicity still) contrived to summate the guiding *idea* of the film – namely, the ironic abjection of a poor man in love with, or married to, a wealthy woman. The situation is rather different with the image featured in Indian Book House's Film Stars No. 10, for the scene concerned effectively appears in the film itself, when Rosie demands that Raju untie her anklets, in full public view. There are some differences, though. First, Film Stars No. 10 is a lateral inversion of the composition of the film scene, which actually follows the template of the poster for *Mr & Mrs 55*. Second, the public space of the bazaar has been replaced with a flower-strewn meadow, a more suitable setting in fact for Indian Book House gods and goddesses. And Raju is not wearing the distinctive red shirt of the film scene, but smart western casuals more like Guru Dutt's costume in *Mr & Mrs 55*. Most noticeably, Waheeda Rehman is wearing a striking red and yellow embroidered *lehnga* – bridal or dance attire – rather than the genteel (if somewhat overdressed) pale blue sequined chiffon sari befitting her film scripted status as the wife of a rich man and pillar of bourgeois society. The changed colour and design of Rosie's costume align her with the dancing girl that she truly is by birth. The dancing girl (Rosie), as well as the Anglo-Indian or westernised upper-class woman (Anita), are both, in their different ways, an antitheses of postcolonial middle-class respectabllity.

LEFT – Poster for Guru Dutt's film *Mr & Mrs 55*.

RIGHT – *Film Stars No. 10*, Indian Book House, Map House, Delhi.

Let us not get lost in the minor details of the transformations and reconfigurations of images from poster to poster and film to poster, but simply observe the serendipity (or sheer opportunism) of the *double* citation. First, there is the citation of one film poster by another, a practice common enough in the calendar art industry; and then, rather more curiously, the citation by Vijay Anand's *film* (*Guide*) of the film *poster* of an earlier film (Guru Dutt's *Mr & Mrs 55*) – albeit with lateral inversions and re-inversions. While we may take it from Chris Pinney that a publicity still or poster may sometimes end up being literally enacted in the film for which it is contrived, it is certainly a challenge to account for one director's film sequence bringing to life a poster created some ten years earlier for another director's film (but never in fact part of the latter film's text!).

21 - See Nasreen Munni Kabir, op. cit., p. 61. Jyotika Virdi is particularly harsh in her comments on this film. Describing the film as a "heavy-handed caricature of upper-class Indian women, their obsession with women's rights, and the spectre of the 'divorce bill'", she presents the film as effectively the postcolonial, middle-class male's projection of the "threat" posed by the economically independent woman to the institution of Hindu marriage. See Jyotika Virdi, *The Cinematic ImagiNation: Indian Popular Films As Social History*, New Delhi: Permanent Black, 2004, p. 75-85.

22 - This is a point that has been made by many writers: see, e.g., Sumita Chakravarty, *National Identity in Indian Popular Cinema*, op. cit.; Rosie Thomas, *Melodrama and the Negotiation of Morality in Mainstream Hindi Film*. In Carol A. Breckenride, (Ed.), *Consuming Moderning: Public Culture in Contemporary India*, Delhi: Oxford University Press, 1996, p. 157-82; and Ravi Vasudevan, *You Cannot Live in Society – And Ignore It: Nationhood and Female Modernity in 'Andaz'*; In Patricia Uberoi, (Ed.), *Social Reform, Sexuality and The State*, New Delhi: Sage Publications, 1996, p. 83-108.

Serendipity or intentional citation, the two posters illustrate the situation common to both films, that is, the compromised relationship of a poor man with a rich woman. At a deeper level, both films explore the dilemmas of post-colonial Indian modernity through the figure of the woman, utilizing the stock oppositions of popular cinema: the good Indian wife versus the "free", westernized woman; and the wife *versus* the courtesan. (As noted, the westernized woman and the courtesan are often condensed into the role of the "vamp".) *Mr & Mrs 55* reputedly derives from a play, entitled *Modern Marriage*, written earlier by the film's script-writer, Abrar Alvi, and touched up at Guru Dutt's suggestion with a situation (that is, a marriage of convenience to be followed by divorce) borrowed from a Cary Grant-Bette Davis film. To this, the Director/Script-writer duo added the "feminist" angle, topical at the time of the passing of the Hindu Marriage Act (1955), a gesture for which they have been roundly criticized by some contemporary critics.[21] In this exploration of the tensions of modernity, the male figure, whether cartoonist or tourist guide, is scripted as "modern" – the *hat* (of whatever kind) is surely the clinching sign – while the burden of modernity and cultural alienation is transposed on to the woman as the bearer of Indian tradition.[22] For her, it is an awesome responsibility.

Both Anita (in *Mr & Mrs 55*) and Rosie (in *Guide*) – the one rich and westernized, the other from a stigmatized courtesan background – eventually indicate their desire to become true Indian wives and mothers, but *narratively speaking* it appears much easier to tame a rich shrew and restore the "man-on-top", than to redeem a courtesan to postcolonial social respectability. One can possibly read this latter observation off the contrast between Guru Dutt's cheeky smile, and Dev Anand's downcast gaze: a happy ending in the case of *Mr & Mrs 55*, but tragic closure for *Guide*.

THE PAIN OF LOVE AND CINEMATIC PODO-SADOMASOCHISM: 'PAKEEZAH'

Retracing our steps to *Sahib, Bibi aur Ghulam*, we saw a schema of man-woman relationships encoded in a podo-semiotic register: love as longing; love as duty;

love as passion; love as foregone conclusion, cosmologically predetermined; and love compromised by mismatched social status. An important motif is missing, however: the *pain* of love and of the "wounded heart".[23] Podo-semiotically, this is nowhere more exquisitely expressed than in *Pakeezah* (Kamal Amrohi, 1971), coincidentally, a film that also stars Meena Kumari.

Pakeezah, meaning "the Pure One" (played by Meena Kumari), is the daughter of a Muslim nobleman, Shahabuddin (Ashok Kumar) and a beautiful courtesan, Nargis (Meena Kumari again) who, rejected by her husband's family, dies while giving birth to her daughter in a deserted cemetery. The girl is brought up by her aunt to be a courtesan, unaware of her noble lineage. One night, travelling in a train, a young man, Salim (Raj Kumar) – who happens to be her father's nephew – enters her compartment and is enthralled by the sight of her feet, peeking out from under the coverlets. Before he gets off the train, he leaves a note between her toes: "I entered your compartment by mistake. Your feet are beautiful. Don't let them ever touch the ground. They will get soiled." Apart from being a citation from the Urdu poet Ghalib, the message is ironic for, as a professional dancing girl, her feet are destined to touch the ground. Pakeezah falls in love with the unknown writer of the note, who has signed himself simply as a "fellow traveller".

Eventually, Pakeezah meets up with her "fellow traveler" when he rescues her from drowning, but her aunt forces her back into the courtesan's life. In this capacity she is invited to sing and dance at Salim's marriage. Her song challenges Salim to allow their eyes to meet, and the wounds of her broken heart to be revealed, but when she looks up for him, he has disappeared. Crazed by love, Pakeezah hurls a chandelier to the ground, her blood tracing gruesome footprints as she dances over the shattered glass.[24] The aunt then reveals Pakeezah's true parentage to her father, Shahabuddin, who is among the wedding guests. Rushing to claim her, he is shot dead by his own father. In the melodramatic finale of contrition and attrition, Shahabuddin is brought on a funeral bier to attend the wedding of his nephew Salim with Pakeezah (who, as first cousin, is incidentally the spouse of choice in the Muslim kinship system). Pakeezah's aristocratic blood wipes out the stigma of her courtesan upbringing, enabling her to claim the status of legitimate "wife", tragically denied to her mother. The final and exceedingly graphic display of podo-sadomasochism brings to a closure both the drama of betrayal initiated in the previous generation, and the drama set in motion by the glance of the "fellow traveler" at Pakeezah's painted and ornamented feet.[25] It memorably indexes the pain of love – "the wounds of the heart we shall see" – in the lacerated feet. And it painfully charts the infinite distance between the roles of courtesan and of wife, on whose separation rests the respectability of Indian modernity. How else to explain the ubiquity and resilience of the "courtesan" theme in the Indian cinematic imagination?[26]

An enormously popular film, the success of *Pakeezah* was no doubt augmented by the tragic off-screen personality of Meena Kumari, who completed the film despite the breakdown of her marriage to director, Kamal Amrohi, and who eventually died of

23 - A phrase commonly emblazoned as a graffito on trucks and three-wheeler scooters.

24 - The scene was used in film hoardings of the time, if not in the Pakeezah film posters *per se*. I have seen seasoned Australian film technicians, inured to the pyrotechnical display of Hollywood action films, positively wince while watching Pakeezah's dance on glass.

25 - "How I used to wish I had feet as beautiful as Pakeezah's!" a Delhi feminist once confessed to me in an unguarded moment.

26 - See Sumita Chakravarty, op. cit., Chapter 8; Fareed Kazmi, *Muslim Socials and the Female Protagonist: Seeing a Dominant Discourse At Work*. In Zoya Hasan, (Ed.), *Forging Identities*, op. cit., p. 226-43; Mukul Kesavan, *Urdu, Awadh and The Tawaif*, op. cit.; among many others.

alcoholism just before the film's release. But the podo-sadomasochistic exhibition of the pain of love was cited very shortly afterwards in the blockbuster Bollywood "curry western", Sholay (Ramesh Sippy, 1975), a film that starred Amitabh Bachchan, Dharmendra, Hema Malini and Jaya Bhaduri, with the inimitable Amjad Khan as the fearsome dacoit, Gabbar Singh.

In a memorable scene, small-time crook Veeru (Dharmendra) is captured by Gabbar Singh and tied to a post, while his girl-friend Basanti is challenged at gun-point to keep on dancing for the dacoit gang: the moment she stops, Gabbar commands, Veeru will be executed. "As long as there is life", she sings, "I will continue to dance; love is immortal, and fears not even death." The trial continues as the dacoits break liquor bottles in her path – "Let my anklets fall, my feet be wounded", she continues, plucking the glass pieces from her bleeding feet and staggering under the burning sun. It is a dramatic scene, drawn out to its full length. Gabbar Singh performs his full repertoire of sadistic sneers; Veeru grimaces helplessly in witness of Basanti's agony; and Basanti, after a brilliant exhibition of endurance, collapses on Veeru, neatly ripping his vest open from neck to groin! [27] Just then, Veeru is rescued by his friend Jaidev (Amitabh), to gallop off with Basanti on a white horse.

Admittedly, the podo-sadomasochistic scene of Basanti's dance on shattered glass is rather a sideshow to the main action in a film which presaged a decade or more of hero-focused action films. The Sholay film posters (as far as I know) focus on the two male protagonists and the theme of revenge, leaving the women, and surprisingly even the villain, as mere insets. All the same, the tiny inset of the Sholay poster unmistakably alludes to Basanti's trail. Her dance on shattered glass is etched in the collective mind as the epitome of the idea, even the ideal, of painful love: perhaps love's highest form.

In themselves, film posters are a relatively impoverished form of Indian popular print culture, perhaps better for a good laugh than for grave sociological deconstruction. In itself, the podo-semiotic register may be of greater interest to foot fetishists than to serious commentators on contemporary Indian culture. Yet, the podo-semiotic motif is surely a running thread in Indian popular cinema, rarely acknowledged in the public focus on decorous and indecorous body-exhibition. Occasionally cited and collated into the film poster and the film hoarding, especially with respect to the performed salutation of the tawaif, the podo-semiotic register provides an entrée into more serious reflections: on love and sex and the general relations of the sexes in the first instance, but also on the underlying dilemmas of postcolonial nationhood and modernity. Here, the symbolic burden of post-coloniality is to be borne by the woman, even when the modern male citizen in felt hat kneels abjectly at her feet.

27 - An amazing number of women of my acquaintance remember the last scene with great clarity, speculating that Dharmendra's vest must have been made of tissue paper to disintegrate so efficiently.

KING KONG
1933
ENGLISH (DUBBED IN
HINDI) – B&W
FILM GENRE **ADVENTURE**
DIRECTOR **MERIAN C. COOPER
& ERNEST B. SCHOEDSACK**
PRODUCER **MERIAN C. COOPER
& ERNEST B. SCHOEDSACK**
PRODUCTION **RKO RADIO
PICTURES INC.**
CAST **FAY WRAY,
ROBERT ARMSTRONG**
MUSIC **MAX STEINER**
POSTER SIZE **100.6 X 74.5 CM**

TOOFANI TIRANDAAZ
1947
HINDI – B&W
FILM GENRE **ACTION**
DIRECTOR **BOMAN SHROFF**
PRODUCER **HOMI WADIA**
PRODUCTION **BASANT PICTURES**
CAST **NADIA, PRAKASH, SAYANI, BOMAN SHROFF, DALPAT, SONA CHATERJEE, RANJAN**
MUSIC **A. KARIM**
LYRICS **BEGUM AZIZ MINAAI**
POSTER PRINTER **MEENA TRADERS, BOMBAY**
POSTER SIZE **76.3 X 52 CM**

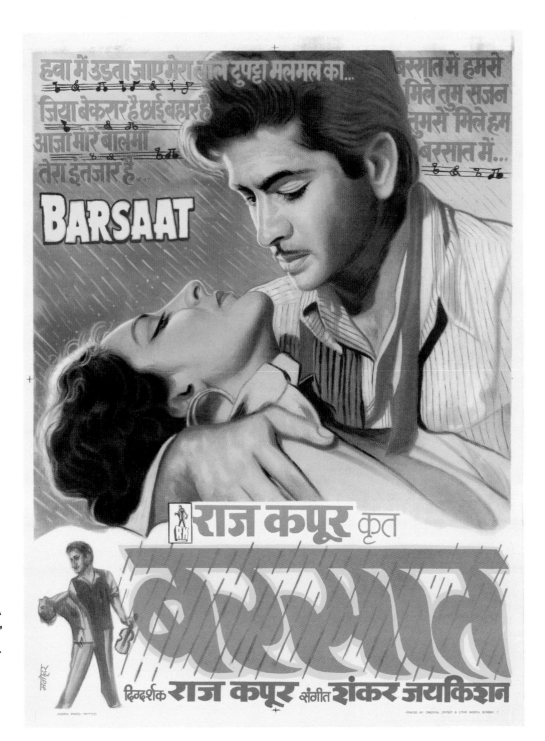

BARSAAT
1949
HINDI – COLOUR
FILM GENRE **SOCIAL**
DIRECTOR **YASH CHOPRA**
PRODUCER **B.R. CHOPRA**
PRODUCTION **B.R. FILMS**
CAST **SUNIL DUTT, SHARMILA TAGORE, SHASHI KAPOOR, RAJ KUMAR, SADHANA, BALRAJ SAHANI, MOTILAL**
MUSIC **RAVI**
LYRICS **SAHIR LUDHIANVI**
POSTER ARTIST **TUILKA**
POSTER PRINTER **NENSEY OFFSET PVT. LTD., BOMBAY**
POSTER SIZE **100.6 X 75 CM**

SANT NAMDEV
1949
MARATHI – B&W
FILM GENRE **DEVOTIONAL**
DIRECTOR **KESHAV TALPADE**
PRODUCER **KESHAV TALPADE**
PRODUCTION **SURAMYA PICTURES**
CAST **JAIRAM SHILEDAR, LALITA PAWAR, SUMATI GUPTE, SHAHU MODAK**
MUSIC **DADA CHANDEKAR**
LYRICS **G.R. AZGAONKAR, VYANKATESH MADGULKAR**
POSTER ARTIST **KUMKUM SAI STUDIO**
POSTER PRINTER **MEENA TRADERS, BOMBAY**
POSTER SIZE **76 X 51 CM**

DILRUBA
1950
HINDI – B&W
FILM GENRE **SOCIAL**
DIRECTOR **DWARKA KHOSLA**
PRODUCTION **LOTUS ORIENT FILMS**
CAST **DEV ANAND, REHANA,
YAKUB, CUCKOO,
ACHLA SACHDEV**
MUSIC **GYAN DUTT**
LYRICS **P.L. SANTOSHI,
D.N. MADHOK,
RAJENDRA KRISHAN,
NEELKANTH TIWARI,
BOOTA RAM SHARMA,
S.H. BIHARI**
POSTER ARTIST **BOMBAY LAB**
POSTER PRINTER **ADVANCE
LITHOGRAPHERS, BOMBAY**
POSTER SIZE **102 X 76.2 CM**

95

DEEDAR
1951
HINDI – B&W
FILM GENRE **SOCIAL**
DIRECTOR **NITIN BOSE**
PRODUCER **FILMKAR**
PRODUCTION **RAJSHREE FILMS**
CAST **ASHOK KUMAR, DILIP
KUMAR, NARGIS, NIMMI**
MUSIC **NAUSHAD**
LYRICS **SHAKIL BADAIYUNI**
POSTER ARTIST **VISHNU**
POSTER SIZE **97.5 X 72.9 CM**

TARANA
1951
HINDI – B&W
FILM GENRE **SOCIAL**
DIRECTOR **RAM DARYANI**
PRODUCER **K.S. DARYANI**
PRODUCTION **KRISHIN MOVIETONE**
CAST **MADHUBALA,
DILIP KUMAR, SHYMA,
KUMAR, JEEVAN, GOPE**
MUSIC **ANIL BISWAS**
LYRICS **D.N. MADHOK,
KAIF IRFANI,
PREM DHAWAN**
POSTER ARTIST **T.D. KAR**
POSTER PRINTER **MASTER
PRINTERS, BOMBAY**
POSTER SIZE **102 X 76 CM**

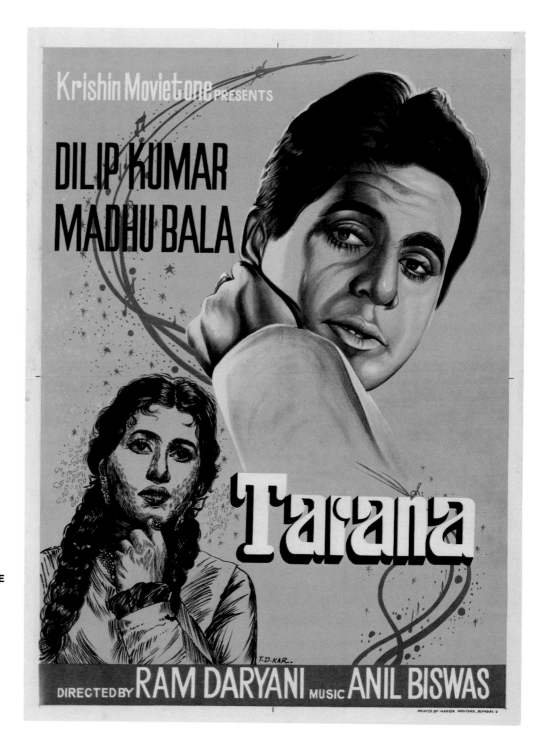

MADHOSH
1951
HINDI – B&W
FILM GENRE **SOCIAL**
DIRECTOR **J.B.H. WADIA**
PRODUCER **J.B.H. WADIA**
PRODUCTION **WADIA FILMS**
CAST **MEENA KUMARI, USHA KIRAN, MANHAR DESAI, JILLOO, S. NASIR, MUBARAK**
MUSIC **MADAN MOHAN**
LYRICS **RAJA MEHDI ALI KHAN**
POSTER ARTIST **MIRAJKAR**
POSTER PRINTER **JAI-MA ARTS**
POSTER SIZE **76.1 X 51.3 CM**

AAH
1953
HINDI – B&W
FILM GENRE **SOCIAL**
DIRECTOR **RAJA NAWATHE**
PRODUCER **RAJ KAPOOR**
PRODUCTION **R.K. FILMS**
CAST **NARGIS, RAJ KAPOOR,
PRAN, MUKESH,
LEELA MISRA**
MUSIC **SHANKER JAIKISHEN**
LYRICS **HASRAT JAIPURI,
SHAILENDRA**
POSTER PRINTER **ORIENTAL OFFSET
LITHO WORKS, BOMBAY;
JAGDISH PHOTO PROCESS,
BOMBAY**
POSTER SIZE **102.3 X 76 CM**

MR & MRS 55
1955
HINDI – B&W
FILM GENRE **SOCIAL**
DIRECTOR **GURU DUTT**
PRODUCER **GURU DUTT**
PRODUCTION **GURU DUTT FILMS**
CAST **GURU DUTT,
MADHUBALA,
LALITA PAWAR, KUMKUM,
JOHNNY WALKER**
MUSIC **O.P. NAYYAR**
LYRICS **MAJROOH SULTANPURI**
POSTER PRINTER **DNYANSAGAR
LITHO PRESS, BOMBAY**
POSTER SIZE **101** X **74.8 CM**

KAVERI
1955
TAMIL – B&W
MOVIE GENRE **SOCIAL**
DIRECTOR **YOGANAND**
PRODUCTION **KRISHNA PICTURES**
CAST **SIVAJI GANESAN,**
PADMINI, NAMBIAR,
LALITHA, P.S. VEERAPPA
MUSIC **G. RAMANATHAN,**
RAMAMOORTHY
VISWANATHAN
LYRICS **T.N. RAMIAH DOSS,**
NARAYANA KAVI,
UDUMALA
POSTER PRINTER **THE SAFIRE**
PRINTOGRAPH, SIVAKASI
POSTER SIZE **100.9 X 76.6 CM**

SHREE 420
1955
HINDI – B&W
FILM GENRE **SOCIAL**
DIRECTOR **RAJ KAPOOR**
PRODUCER **RAJ KAPOOR**
PRODUCTION **R.K. FILMS**
CAST **RAJ KAPOOR, NARGIS,**
NADIRA, LALITA PAWAR
MUSIC **SHANKER-JAIKISHEN**
LYRICS **SHAILENDRA,**
HASRAT JAIPURI
POSTER ARTIST **MADAN**
POSTER SIZE **98.7 X 73.5 CM**

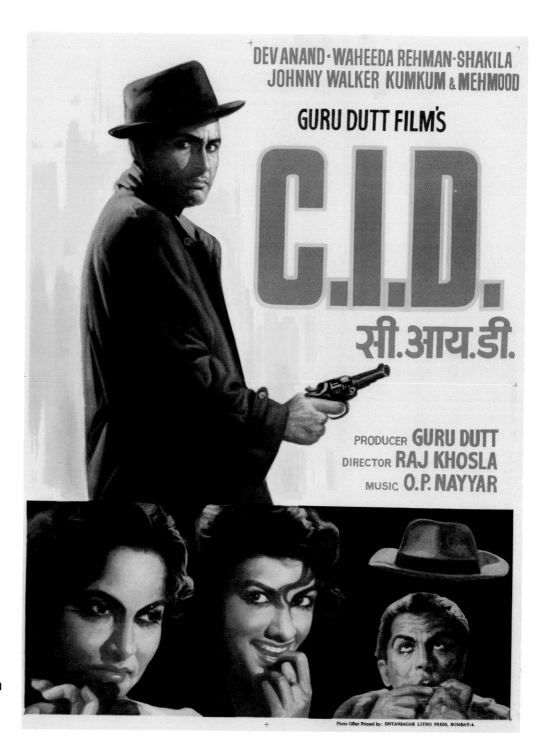

C.I.D.
1956
HINDI – B&W
FILM GENRE **DETECTIVE**
DIRECTOR **RAJ KHOSLA**
PRODUCER **GURU DUTT**
PRODUCTION **GURU DUTT FILMS**
CAST **DEV ANAND,
WAHEEDA REHMAN,
SHAKILA,
JOHNNY WALKER,
KUMKUM, MEHMOOD**
MUSIC **O.P. NAYYAR**
LYRICS **MAJROOH SULTANPURI**
POSTER PRINTER **DNYANSAGAR
LITHO PRESS, BOMBAY**
POSTER SIZE **100.5 X 74.5 CM**

TALWAR KA DHANI

1956
HINDI – B&W
FILM GENRE **COSTUME DRAMA**
DIRECTOR **DWARKA KHOSLA**
PRODUCTION **VIKAS**
PRODUCTIONS
CAST **NADIRA, ANWAR,**
MANHAR DESAI, B.M. VYAS
MUSIC **CHITRAGUPTA**
LYRICS **G.S. NEPALI,**
ANJUM JAIPURI
POSTER ARTIST **TALISHALKAR**
POSTER PRINTER **ORIENTAL OFFSET**
LITHO WORKS, BOMBAY
POSTER SIZE **76.4 X 50.8 CM**

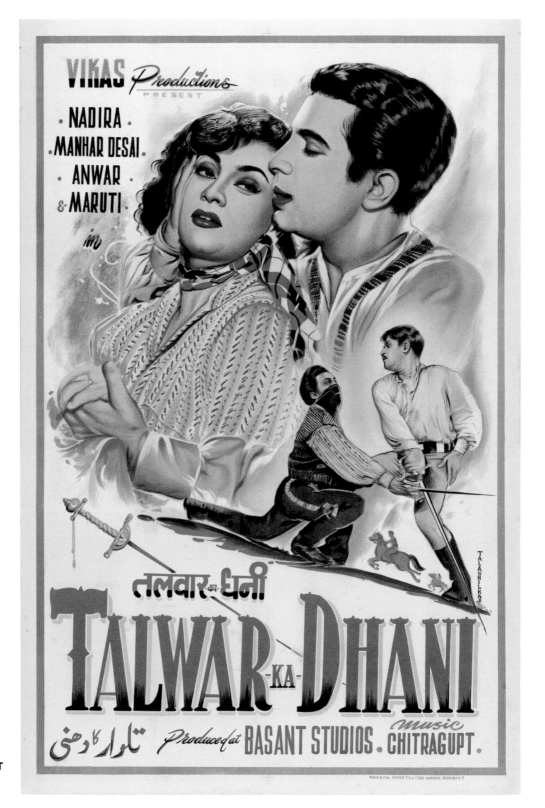

MOTHER INDIA
1957
HINDI – COLOUR
FILM GENRE **SOCIAL**
DIRECTOR **MEHBOOB KHAN**
PRODUCER **MEHBOOB KHAN**
PRODUCTION **MEHBOOB PRODUCTIONS**
CAST **NARGIS, SUNIL DUTT, RAAJ KUMAR, RAJENDRA KUMAR**
MUSIC **NAUSHAD**
LYRICS **SHAKEEL BADAIYUNI**
POSTER ARTIST **BALKRISHNA VAIDYA – SETH STUDIO**
POSTER PRINTER **DNYANSAGAR LITHO PRESS, BOMBAY**
POSTER SIZE **101 X 73 CM**

SONE KI CHIDIYA
1958
HINDI – B&W
FILM GENRE **SOCIAL**
DIRECTOR **SHAHID LATEEF**
PRODUCER **ISMAT CHUGTAI**
PRODUCTION **FILM INDIA CORPORATION**
CAST **BALRAJ SAHNI, NUTAN, TALAT MEHMOOD**
MUSIC **O.P. NAYYAR**
LYRICS **SAHIR LUDHIANVI, MAJROOH SULTANPURI, KAIFI AZMI**
POSTER ARTIST **SIRISH**
POSTER PRINTER **SHAKTHI OFFSET WORKS, NAGPUR**
POSTER SIZE **76.2 X 57 CM**

MAYA BAZAAR

1958
HINDI – **B&W**
FILM GENRE **MYTHOLOGICAL**
DIRECTOR **BABUBHAI MISTRI**
PRODUCER **HOMI WADIA**
PRODUCTION **BASANT PICTURES
& WADIA BROTHERS**
CAST **ANITA GUHA, MAHIPAL,
VASANT PAHELWAN,
RAAJ KUMAR**
MUSIC **CHITRAGUPTA**
LYRICS **GOPAL SINGHNEPALI,
SARASWATI KUMAR
DEEPAK, INDIVAR**
POSTER PRINTER **PRASAD PROCESS
PVT. LTD., MADRAS**
POSTER SIZE **38 X 50.4 CM**

THANGAPATUMAI

1959
TAMIL – B&W
FILM GENRE **FOLKLORE**
DIRECTOR **A.S.A. SWAMY**
PRODUCER **M. SOMASUNDARAM**
PRODUCTION **JUPITER PICTURES**
CAST **SIVAJI GANESHAN,**
PADMINI, T.R. RAJAKUMARI,
M.N. NAMBIAR
MUSIC **VISHWANATHAN**
RAMAMOORTHY
LYRICS **UDUMALAI NARAYANA**
KAVI, PATTUKKOTTAI
KALYANASUNDARAM,
KANNADASAN,
MARUDAKASI
POSTER PRINTER **JAYARAMAN**
LITHO PRESS, CHENNAI
POSTER SIZE **102** X **150.8 CM** 2 SHEET

THANGAPATUMAI
1959
TAMIL – B&W
FILM GENRE **FOLKLORE**
DIRECTOR **A.S.A. SWAMY**
PRODUCER **M. SOMASUNDARAM**
PRODUCTION **JUPITER PICTURES**
CAST **SIVAJI GANESHAN,
PADMINI, T.R. RAJAKUMARI,
M.N. NAMBIAR**
MUSIC **VISHWANATHAN
RAMAMOORTHY**
LYRICS **UDUMALAI NARAYANA
KAVI, PATTUKKOTTAI
KALYANASUNDARAM,
KANNADASAN,
MARUDAKASI**
POSTER PRINTER **JAYARAMAN
LITHO PRESS, CHENNAI**
POSTER SIZE **99.8** X **73.6 CM**

MANZIL
1960
HINDI – B&W
FILM GENRE **SOCIAL**
DIRECTOR **MANDI BURMAN**
PRODUCER **MANDI BURMAN**
PRODUCTION **KALPANA PICTURES**
CAST **DEV ANAND, NUTAN, K.N. SINGH**
MUSIC **S.D. BURMAN**
LYRICS **MAJROOH SULTANPURI**
POSTER PRINTER **J.P. PRINTERS, DELHI**
POSTER SIZE **76** X **51 CM**

111

SARHAD
1960
HINDI – B&W
FILM GENRE **SOCIAL**
DIRECTOR **SHANKAR MUKERJEE**
PRODUCER **K.H. KAPADIA**
PRODUCTION **ALANKAR CHITRA**
CAST **DEV ANAND,
SUCHITRA SEN, RAGINI,
LALITA PAWAR, SAJJAN**
MUSIC **C. RAMCHANDRA**
LYRICS **MAJROOH SULTANPURI**
POSTER ARTIST **D.R. BHOSLE**
POSTER PRINTER **PRASAD PROCESS
PVT. LTD., MADRAS**
POSTER SIZE **101 X 75.3 CM**

JAB PYAR KISISE HOTA HAI

1961
HINDI – B&W
FILM GENRE **SOCIAL**
DIRECTOR **NASIR HUSAIN**
PRODUCER **NASIR HUSAIN**
PRODUCTION **NASIR HUSAIN FILMS PVT. LTD.**
CAST **DEV ANAND, ASHA PAREKH, PRAN, MUBARAK**
MUSIC **SHANKER JAIKISHEN**
LYRICS **HASRAT JAIPURI, SHAILENDRA**
POSTER ARTIST **ADIL**
POSTER PRINTER **NENSEY OFFSET PVT. LTD., BOMBAY**
POSTER SIZE **101.4 X 73.7 CM**

113

HALF TICKET
1962
HINDI – B&W
FILM GENRE **COMEDY**
DIRECTOR **KALIDAS**
PRODUCTION **CINE TECHNICIANS PRODUCTIONS**
CAST **KISHORE KUMAR, MADHUBALA, PRAN**
MUSIC **SALIL CHOUDHURY**
LYRICS **SHAILENDRA**
POSTER PRINTER **APSARA ART, BOMBAY**
POSTER SIZE **102.1 X 76.3 CM**

REPORTER RAJU
1962
HINDI – B&W
FILM GENRE **SOCIAL**
DIRECTOR **DWARKA KHOSLA**
PRODUCER **HOMI WADIA**
PRODUCTION **BASANT PICTURES**
CAST **FEROZ KHAN, CHITRA, SULOCHANA CHATTERJEE, INDIRA**
MUSIC **MOHINDER SINGH**
LYRICS **RAJA MEHNDI ALI KHAN, SHAKEEL NOMANI, ANJAAN, ANAND BAKSHI**
POSTER ARTIST **EVER GREEN PUBLICITY**
POSTER PRINTER **VIR MILAP PRESS, HYDERABAD**
POSTER SIZE **76 X 51 CM**

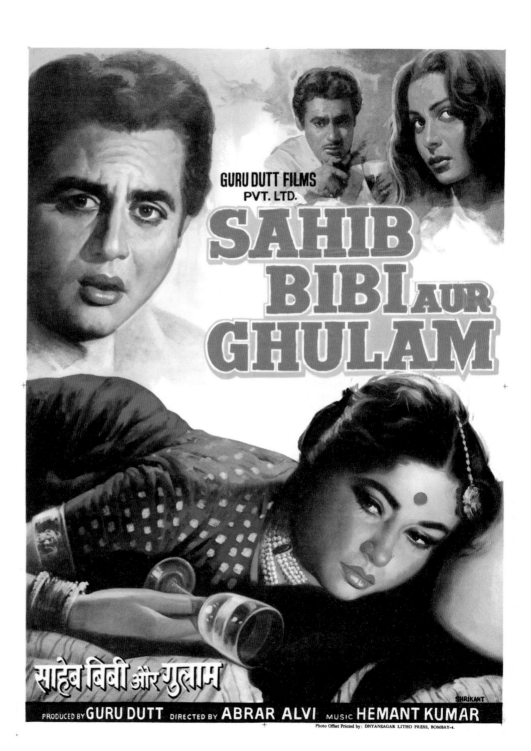

SAHIB BIBI AUR GULAM
1962
HINDI – B&W
FILM GENRE **SOCIAL**
DIRECTOR **ABRAR ALVI**
PRODUCER **GURU DUTT**
PRODUCTION **GURU DUTT FILMS**
CAST **GURU DUTT,
MEENA KUMARI,
WAHEEDA REHMAN,
SAPRU, REHMAN**
MUSIC **HEMANT KUMAR**
LYRICS **SHAKEEL BADAIYUNI**
POSTER ARTIST **SHRIKANT**
POSTER PRINTER **DNYANSAGAR
LITHO PRESS, BOMBAY**
POSTER SIZE **101.3** X **74.5 CM**

FAULAD
1963
HINDI – B&W
FILM GENRE **SOCIAL**
DIRECTOR **MOHAMMED HUSSAIN**
PRODUCER **VINOD DOSHI**
PRODUCTION **BROADWAY PICTURES**
CAST **DARA SINGH, MUMTAZ, SHYAM KUMAR, RANDHIR, MINU MUMTAZ, KAMAL MEHRA**
MUSIC **G.S. KOHLI**
LYRICS **FAROOKH KAISER**
POSTER ARTIST **UDAYKUMAR**
POSTER PRINTER **MASTER PRINTERS, BOMBAY**
POSTER SIZE **76.7 X 50.7 CM**

117

FAULAD
1963
HINDI – B&W
FILM GENRE **SOCIAL**
DIRECTOR **MOHAMMED HUSSAIN**
PRODUCER **VINOD DOSHI**
PRODUCTION **BROADWAY**
PICTURES
CAST **DARA SINGH, MUMTAZ,**
SHYAM KUMAR
MUSIC **G.S. KOHLI**
LYRICS **FAROOKH KAISER**
POSTER ARTIST **MANOHAR**
POSTER PRINTER **MASTER**
PRINTERS, BOMBAY
POSTER SIZE **102 X 76 CM**

FAULAD
1963
HINDI – B&W
FILM GENRE **SOCIAL**
DIRECTOR **MOHAMMED HUSSAIN**
PRODUCER **VINOD DOSHI**
PRODUCTION **BROADWAY**
PICTURES
CAST **DARA SINGH, MUMTAZ,**
SHYAM KUMAR
MUSIC **G.S. KOHLI**
LYRICS **FAROOKH KAISER**
POSTER ARTIST **MANOHAR**
POSTER PRINTER **MASTER**
PRINTERS, BOMBAY
POSTER SIZE **102.3 X 76 CM**

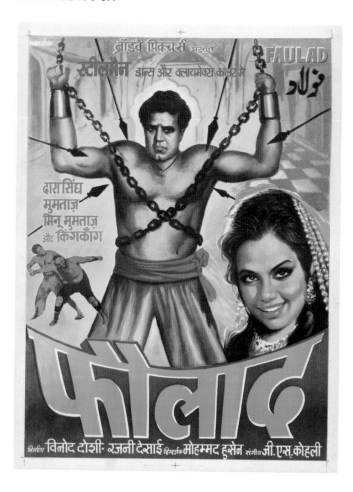

EN KADAMAI
1964
TAMIL – B&W
FILM GENRE **DRAMA**
DIRECTOR **M. NATESAN**
PRODUCER **M. NATESAN**
PRODUCTION **NATESH ART PICTURES**
CAST **M.G. RAMACHANDRAN, SAROJA DEVI, M.R. RADHA, NAMBIAR, NAGESH, MANORAMA**
MUSIC **VISHWANATHAN RAMAMURTHY**
LYRICS **KANNADASAN**
POSTER ARTIST **N.B. GURUSWAMY**
POSTER PRINTER **ACM PROCESS, SIVAKASI**
POSTER SIZE **96.2 X 71.2 CM**

THE SAFIRE CINE PRINTERS, SIVAKASI. Ph: 72071, 72942

PUDHIYA PARAVAI
1964
TAMIL – B&W
FILM GENRE **DRAMA**
DIRECTOR **DADA MIRASI**
PRODUCER **SIVAJI GANESAN**
PRODUCTION **SIVAJI FILMS**
CAST **SIVAJI GANESAN,
SAROJA DEVI, NAGESH,
SOWCAR JANAKI**
MUSIC **VISWANATHAN
RAMAMURTHY**
LYRICS **DADA MIRASI**
POSTER PRINTER **SAFIRE CINE
PRINTERS, SIVAKASI**
POSTER SIZE **96.7 X 71 CM**

121

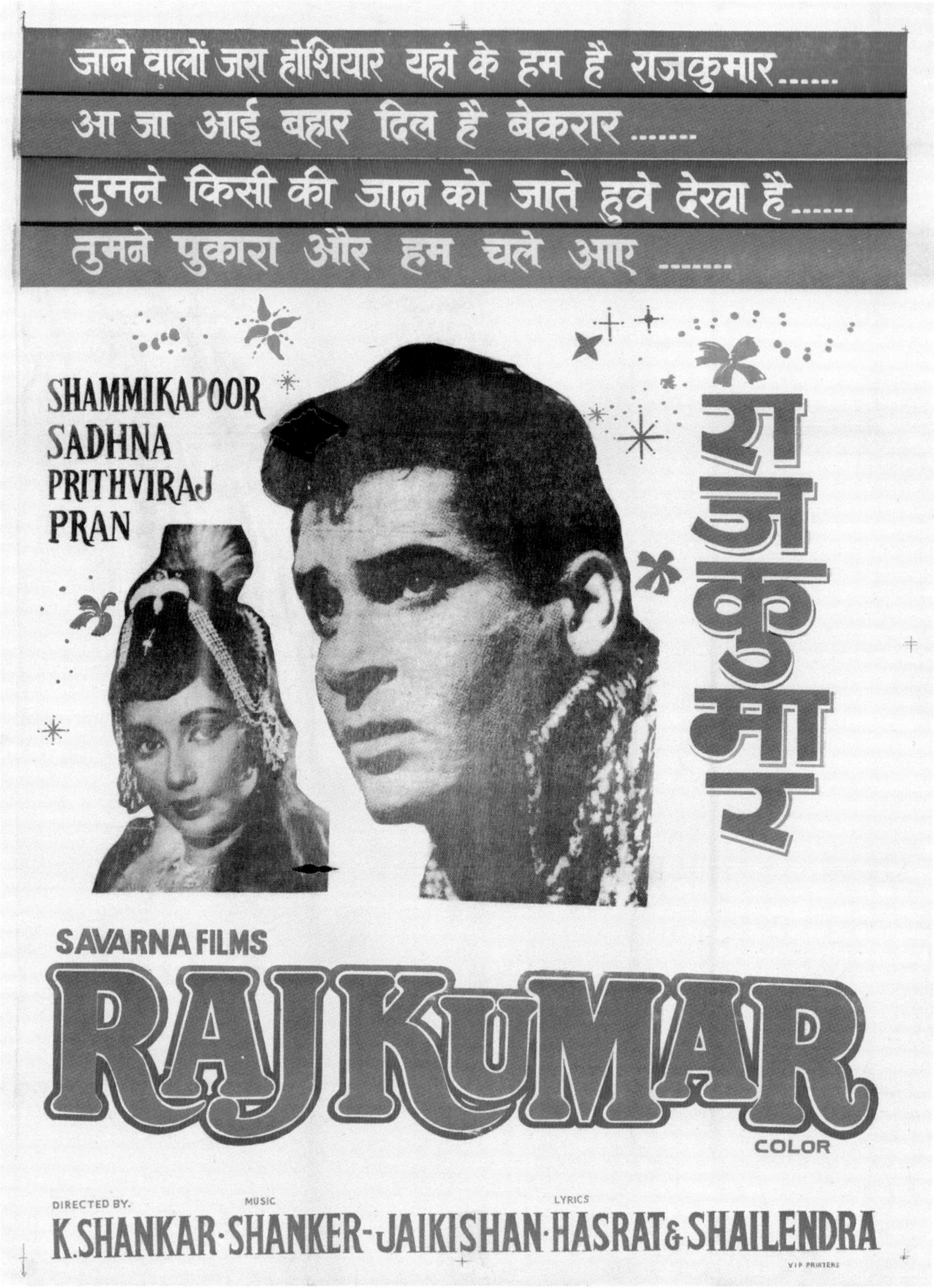

RAJKUMAR
1964
HINDI – COLOUR
FILM GENRE **COSTUME DRAMA**
DIRECTOR **K. SHANKAR**
PRODUCER **VELLU MANI**
PRODUCTION **SARAVANA FILMS**
CAST **SHAMMI KAPOOR,**
SADHANA, PRAN,
PRITHVIRAJ KAPOOR,
MUSIC **SHANKER-JAIKISHEN**
LYRICS **SHAILENDRA,**
HASRAT JAIPURI
POSTER PRINTER **VIP PRINTERS**
POSTER SIZE **102 X 76.4 CM**

SANGAM
1964
HINDI – COLOUR
FILM GENRE **SOCIAL**
DIRECTOR **RAJ KAPOOR**
PRODUCER **RAJ KAPOOR**
PRODUCTION **R.K. FILMS**
CAST **RAJ KAPOOR,
VYJAYANTHIMALA,
RAJENDRA KUMAR,
LALITA PAWAR**
MUSIC **SHANKER-JAIKISHEN**
LYRICS **SHAILENDRA**
POSTER SIZE **97.2 X 71.5 CM**

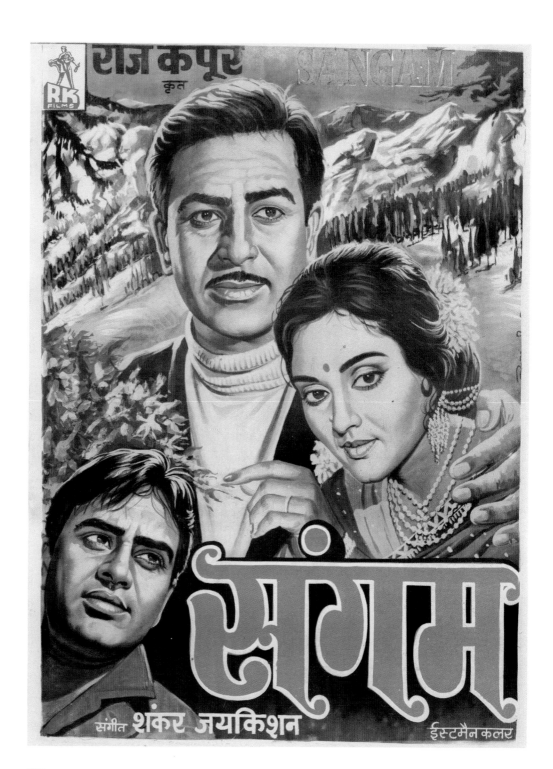

VETTAIKARAN

1964

TAMIL – B&W

FILM GENRE **ACTION**

DIRECTOR **M.A. THIRUMUGAM**

PRODUCER **M.M.A. CHINNAPPA THEVAR**

PRODUCTION **DEVAR FILMS**

CAST **M.G. RAMACHANDRAN, SAVITRI, M.R. RADHA, NAMBIAR, NAGESH, RAJAMMA**

MUSIC **K.V. MAHADEVAN**

LYRICS **KANNADASAN**

POSTER ARTIST **ESHWAR**

POSTER PRINTER **STANDARD LITHOGRAPHERS, CHENNAI**

POSTER SIZE **97 X 138.7 CM** 2 SHEET

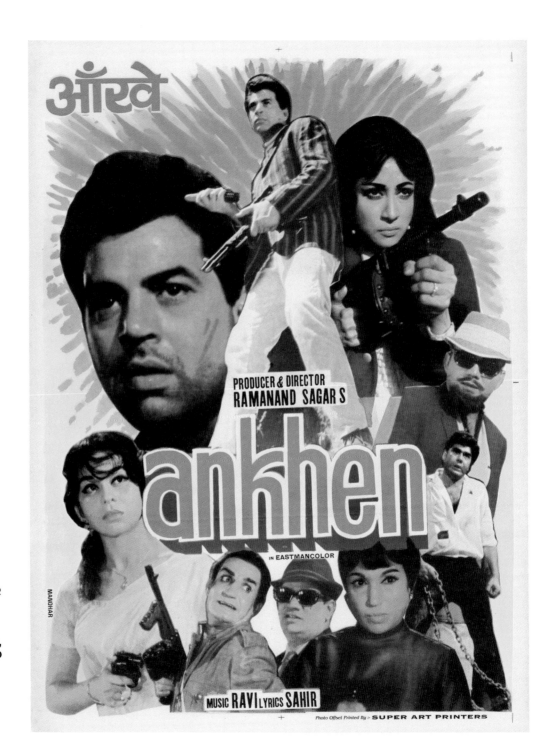

ANKHEN
1964
HINDI – COLOUR
FILM GENRE **DETECTIVE**
DIRECTOR **RAMANAND SAGAR**
PRODUCTION **SAGAR ART
INTERNATIONAL**
CAST **MALA SINHA,
DHARMENDRA, KUMKUM,
SUJIT KUMAR, MEHMOOD**
MUSIC **RAVI**
LYRICS **SAHIR LUDHIANVI**
POSTER ARTIST **MANOHAR**
POSTER PRINTER **SUPER ART
PRINTERS**
POSTER SIZE **101.4 X 75.7 CM**

125

BHEEGI RAAT
1965
HINDI – COLOUR
FILM GENRE **SOCIAL**
DIRECTOR **KALIDAS**
PRODUCTION **MAYA MOVIES**
CAST **ASHOK KUMAR,**
MEENA KUMARI,
PRADEEP KUMAR,
KAMINI KAUSHAL,
I.S. JOHAR, SHASHIKALA
MUSIC **ROSHAN**
LYRICS **MAJROOH SULTANPURI**
POSTER PRINTER **JAPAN ART**
PRESS, DELHI
POSTER SIZE **102.3 X 76.2 CM**

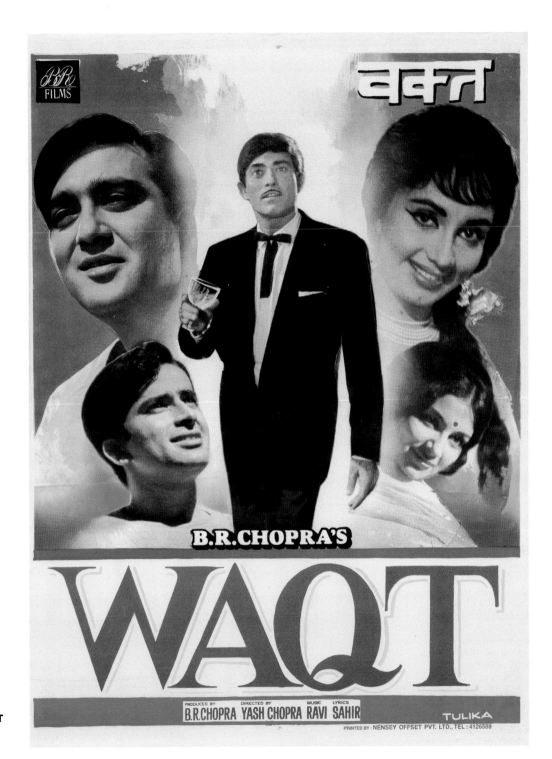

WAQT
1965
HINDI – COLOUR
FILM GENRE **SOCIAL**
DIRECTOR **YASH CHOPRA**
PRODUCER **B.R. CHOPRA**
PRODUCTION **B.R. FILMS**
CAST **SUNIL DUTT,**
RAAJ KUMAR, SADHANA
SHARMILA TAGORE,
SHASHI KAPOOR,
BALRAJ SAHANI
MUSIC **RAVI**
LYRICS **SAHIR LUDHIANVI**
POSTER ARTIST **TULIKA**
POSTER PRINTER **NENSEY OFFSET**
PVT. LTD., BOMBAY
POSTER SIZE **101 X 73 CM**

127

DO BADAN
1966
HINDI – COLOUR
FILM GENRE **SOCIAL**
DIRECTOR **RAJ KHOSLA**
PRODUCER **HUDA BIHARI**
PRODUCTION **J.B. PRODUCTIONS**
CAST **MANOJ KUMAR,
ASHA PAREKH, PRAN,
SIMI GAREWAL**
MUSIC **RAVI**
LYRICS **SHAKEEL BADAIYUNI**
POSTER ARTIST **YASHWANT**
PRINTER **NENSEY OFFSET
PVT. LTD., BOMBAY**
POSTER SIZE **107 X 75.3 CM**

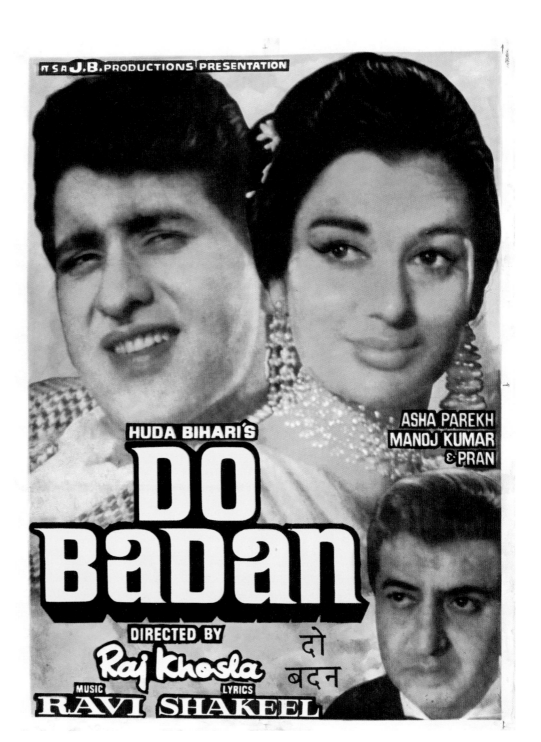

LOVE IN TOKYO
1966
HINDI – COLOUR
FILM GENRE **SOCIAL**
DIRECTOR **PRAMOD**
CHAKRAVORTY
PRODUCER **PRAMOD**
CHAKRAVORTY
PRODUCTION **PRAMOD FILMS**
CAST **JOY MUKERJI,**
ASHA PAREKH, MEHMOOD,
PRAN, LALITA PAWAR
MUSIC **SHANKER-JAIKISHAN**
LYRICS **HASRAT JAIPURI**
POSTER ARTIST **PAM ART**
POSTER SIZE **102.2 X 75.9 CM**

129

ZIMBO FINDS A SON

1966
HINDI – B&W
FILM GENRE **ACTION**
DIRECTOR **JOHN CAVAS**
PRODUCER **HOMI WADIA**
PRODUCTION **BASANT PICTURES**
CAST **AZAD, TABASSUM, INDIRA, SHERRY, SUNDER, PRINCE ARJUN, RANI, DALPAT, SAMSON**
MUSIC **SAPAN JAGMOHAN**
LYRICS **NAQSH LYALPURI**
POSTER ARTIST **GULATI ARTS**
POSTER PRINTER **JAPAN ART PRESS, DELHI**
POSTER SIZE **76 X 51 CM**

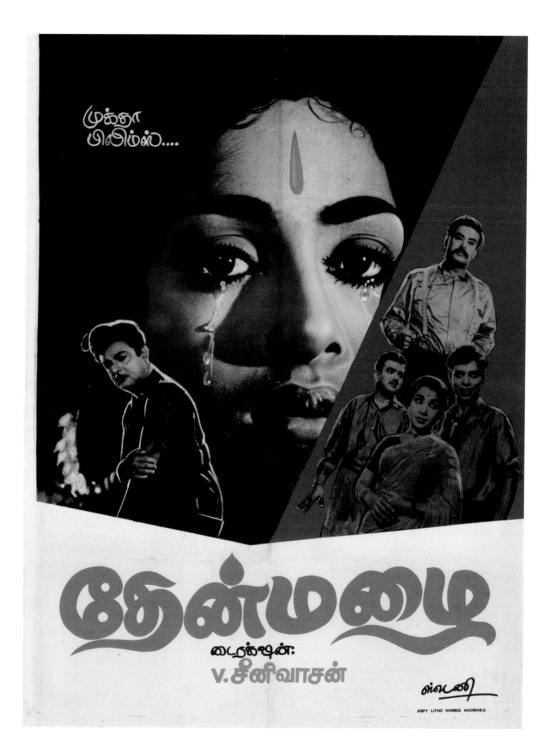

THEN MAHZI
1966
TAMIL – B&W
FILM GENRE **SOCIAL**
DIRECTOR **V. SRINIVASAN**
PRODUCER **V. RAMASAMI**
PRODUCTION **MUKTHA FILMS**
CAST **GEMINI GANESAN,**
K.R. VIJAYA, DEVIKA,
NAGESH, MANORAMA
MUSIC **T.K. RAMAMURTHY**
LYRICS **ALANGUDI**
POSTER PRINTER **ASPY LITHO**
WORKS, MADRAS
POSTER SIZE **102.4 X 76.3 CM**

131

SHRI KRISHNA PANDAVIYAM

1966
TELUGU – B&W
FILM GENRE **MYTHOLOGICAL**
DIRECTOR **N.T. RAMA RAO**
PRODUCER **TRIVIKRAMA RAO**
PRODUCTION **N.A.T. COMBINES &
RAMAKRISHNA COMBINES**
CAST **N.T. RAMA RAO,
K.R. VIJAYA, KANTA RAO,
S. VARALAKSHMI,
UDAY KUMAR**
MUSIC **T.V. RAJU**
LYRICS **C. NARAYANA REDDY**
POSTER ARTIST **P.A. RANGA**
POSTER PRINTER **NATIONAL LITHO
PRINTERS, VIJAYAWADA**
POSTER SIZE **96.8 X 139.4 CM** 2 SHEET

DAADI MAA
1967
HINDI – COLOUR
FILM GENRE **DRAMA**
DIRECTOR **L.V. PRASAD**
PRODUCER **L.V. PRASAD**
PRODUCTION **PRASAD
PRODUCTIONS, MADRAS**
CAST **DILIP RAJ, MUMTAZ,
MEHMOOD, DAVID,
ASHOK KUMAR,**
MUSIC **ROSHAN**
LYRICS **MAJROOH**
POSTER PRINTER **POSTER CENTRE,
BOMBAY**
POSTER SIZE **102 X 76.4 CM**

DIWANA

1967
HINDI – B&W
FILM GENRE **SOCIAL**
DIRECTOR **MAHESH KAUL**
PRODUCER **MAHESH KAUL,
PANDIT MUKHRAM SHARMA**
PRODUCTION **ANUPAM CHITRA**
CAST **RAJ KAPOOR,
SAIRA BANU,
LALITA PAWAR,
KAMAL KAPOOR, ULHAS**
MUSIC **SHANKER JAIKISHEN**
LYRICS **HASRAT JAIPURI,
SHAILENDRA**
POSTER ARTIST **MARIOBAR**
POSTER PRINTER **ORIENTAL OFFSET
LITHO WORKS, BOMBAY**
POSTER SIZE **100 X 75 CM**

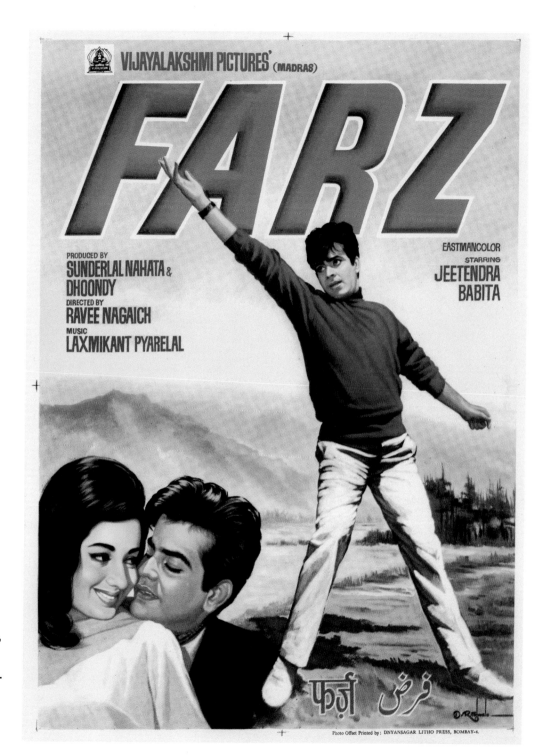

FARZ
1967
HINDI – COLOUR
FILM GENRE **SOCIAL**
DIRECTOR **RAVI NAGAICH**
PRODUCTION **VIJAYALAXMI
PICTURES**
CAST **JEETENDRA, BABITA,
SAJJAN, KANCHAN, AGHA,
MUKRI, MEHAN CHOTI,
DAVID, ARUNA IRANI**
MUSIC **LAXMIKANT PYARELAL**
LYRICS **ANAND BAKSHI**
POSTER ARTIST **D.R. BHOSLE**
POSTER PRINTER **DNYANSAGAR
LITHO PRESS, BOMBAY**
POSTER SIZE **99.7 X 72.6 CM**

KHILARI
1968
HINDI – B&W
FILM GENRE **SOCIAL**
DIRECTOR **HOMI WADIA**
PRODUCER **HOMI WADIA**
PRODUCTION **BASANT PICTURES**
CAST **NADIA, DILEEP RAJ,
UMA SUJATA, SHEIKH**
MUSIC **SAPAN JAGMOHAN**
LYRICS **FAROOQ KAISER**
POSTER SIZE **101.5** X **68.2 CM**

KUDDI IRRINDA KOIL

1968

TAMIL – COLOUR

FILM GENRE **DRAMA**
DIRECTOR **K. SANKAR**
PRODUCER **T.S. RAJASUNDARESAN**
PRODUCTION **SARAVANA SCREENS**
CAST **M.G. RAMACHANDRAN, JAYALALITHA**
MUSIC **M.S. VISHWANATHAN**
LYRICS **VALI-ALANGUDI SOMU, PULAMAI PITHAN, ROSHANARA BEGAN**
POSTER ARTIST **STOMI**
POSTER PRINTER **SAFIRE INDUSTRIES, SIVAKASI**
POSTER SIZE **96.8** X **138 CM** 2 SHEET

NEEYUM NAANUM

1968
TAMIL – B&W
MOVIE GENRE **SOCIAL**
DIRECTOR **RAMANNA**
PRODUCER **KANNAN,**
B.S. MOORTHY
PRODUCTION **IRIS MOVIES**
CAST **RAVICHANDRAN,**
RAJSRI, NAGESH,
SRIRANJINKI, VASANTHA
MUSIC **M.S. VISWANATHAN**
LYRICS **KANNADASAN**
POSTER PRINTER **VINAYAGA LITHO,**
MADRAS
POSTER SIZE **76.1 X 102 CM** 2 SHEET

JEENE KI RAAH
1969
HINDI – COLOUR
FILM GENRE **SOCIAL**
DIRECTOR **L.V. PRASAD**
PRODUCER **L.V. PRASAD**
PRODUCTION **PRASAD
PRODUCTIONS**
CAST **JEETENDRA, ANJALI,
TANUJA, DURGA KHOTE,
MANMOHAN KRISHNA,**
MUSIC **LAXMIKANT PYARELAL**
LYRICS **ANAND BAKSHI**
POSTER PRINTER **JAPAN ART
PRESS, DELHI**
POSTER SIZE **97.7 X 72 CM**

SHATRANJ

1969
HINDI – COLOUR
FILM GENRE **SOCIAL**
DIRECTOR **S.S. VASAN**
PRODUCTION **N.N. SIPPY
& GEMINI PRODUCTIONS**
CAST **RAJENDRA KUMAR,
WAHEEDA REHMAN,
MEHMOOD,
SHASHIKALA, HELEN,
ACHLA SACHDEV, AGHA,
MANMOHAN KRISHNA**
MUSIC **SHANKER-JAIKISHEN**
LYRICS **HASRAT JAIPURI,
S.H. BIHARI, INDIVAR,
KIRAN KALYANI**
POSTER PRINTER **DEEPTI ARTS,
BOMBAY**
POSTER SIZE **102.3 X 76 CM**

INSAAN AUR SHAITAN

1970
HINDI – COLOUR
FILM GENRE **ACTION**
DIRECTOR **ASPI IRANI**
PRODUCER **ASPI IRANI**
PRODUCTION **SUPER PICTURES**
CAST **SANJEEV KUMAR,
FARYAL HIRALAL,
SHAIKH MUKHTAR,
ARJUNA IRANI**
MUSIC **USHA KHANNA**
LYRICS **INDEEVAR,
ASAD BHOPALI**
POSTER ARTIST **WAMAN MISTRY**
POSTER PRINTER **REGIMENTAL
PRESS, BOMBAY**
POSTER SIZE **102 X 76 CM**

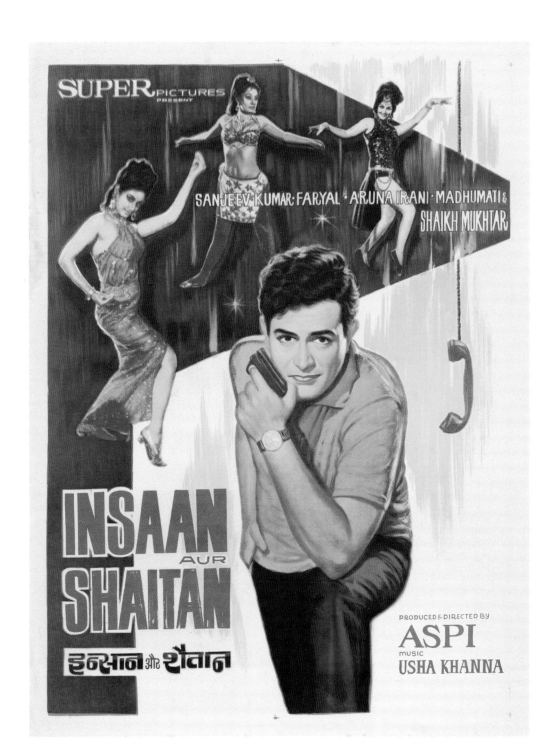

**JULIE MY
DARLING**
MALAYALAM–COLOUR
FILM GENRE **LOVE STORY**
PRINTER **DEVI BALA LITHO
PRESS, MADRAS**
POSTER SIZE **100** X **72.2 CM**

143

KATI PATANG
1970
HINDI – COLOUR
FILM GENRE **SOCIAL**
DIRECTOR **SHAKTI SAMANTA**
PRODUCER **SHAKTI SAMANTA**
PRODUCTION **SHAKTI FILMS**
CAST **RAJESH KHANNA,**
ASHA PAREKH,
PREM CHOPRA, BINDU
MUSIC **R.D. BURMAN**
LYRICS **ANAND BAKSHI**
POSTER ARTIST **C. MOHAN,**
D.R. BHOSLE, SHILPA
STUDIO GAMANJAN
POSTER PRINTER **NENSEY OFFSET**
PVT. LTD., BOMBAY
POSTER SIZE **101.4 X 75.5 CM**

KATI PATANG
1970
HINDI – COLOUR
FILM GENRE **SOCIAL**
DIRECTOR **SHAKTI SAMANTA**
PRODUCER **SHAKTI SAMANTA**
PRODUCTION **SHAKTI FILMS**
CAST **RAJESH KHANNA,
ASHA PAREKH,
PREM CHOPRA, BINDU**
MUSIC **R.D. BURMAN**
LYRICS **ANAND BAKSHI**
POSTER ARTIST **C. MOHAN,
D.R. BHOSLE, SHILPA
STUDIO GAMANJAN**
POSTER PRINTER **NENSEY OFFSET
PVT. LTD., BOMBAY**
POSTER SIZE **100.5 X 73.3 CM**

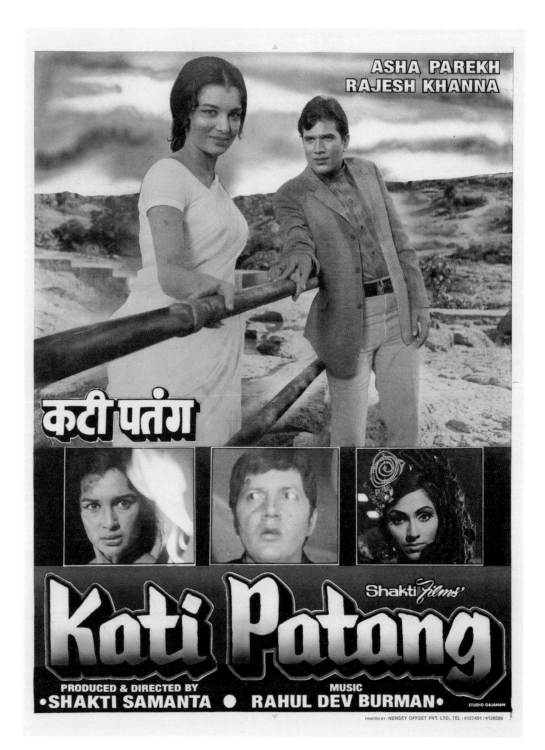

145

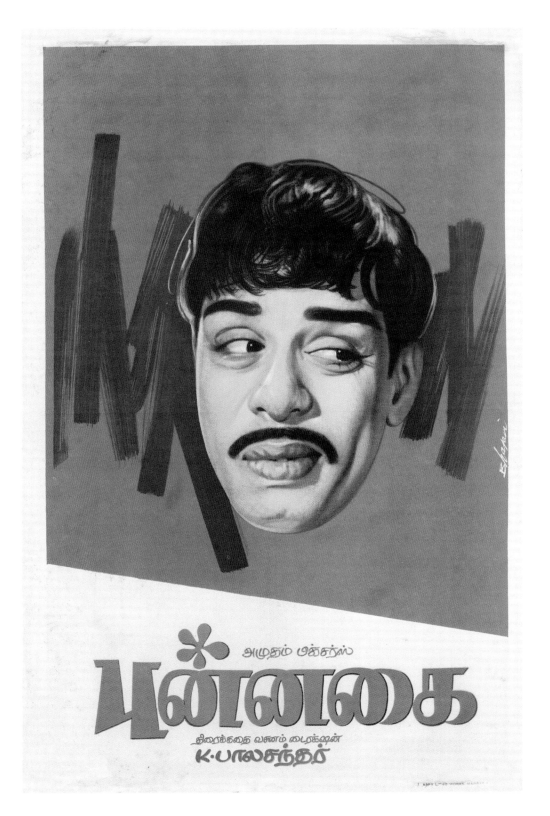

PUNNAGAI
1971
TAMIL – COLOUR
FILM GENRE **COMEDY**
DIRECTOR **K. BALACHANDER**
PRODUCER **R. VENKATRAHMAN**
PRODUCTION **AMUDHAM PICTURES**
CAST **GEMINI GANESH, JAYANTHI, M.R. RADHA, NAGESH, VASU**
MUSIC **M.S. VISWANATHAN**
LYRICS **KANNADASAN**
POSTER ARTIST **BHAPRI**
POSTER PRINTER **J. ASPRY LITHO WORKS, MADRAS**
POSTER SIZE **75.1 X 51.2 CM**

MEHBOOB KI MEHNDI
1971
HINDI – COLOUR
FILM GENRE **SOCIAL**
DIRECTOR **H.S. RAWAIL**
PRODUCER **H.S. RAWAIL**
PRODUCTION **SUPER FILM MAKERS**
CAST **RAJESH KHANNA, LEENA CHANDAVARKAR, PRADEEP KUMAR**
MUSIC **LAXMIKANT PYARELAL**
LYRICS **ANAND BAKSHI**
POSTER SIZE **102.3 X 76.5 CM**

MELA
1971
HINDI – COLOUR
FILM GENRE **SOCIAL**
DIRECTOR **PRAKASH MEHRA**
PRODUCER **A.A. NADIADWALA**
PRODUCTION **A.G. FILMS**
CAST **SANJAY KHAN,**
FEROZ KHAN, MUMTAZ,
LALITA PAWAR
MUSIC **R.D. BURMAN**
LYRICS **MAJROOH SULTANPURI**
POSTER ARTIST **LAXMAN RANJEET**
POSTER PRINTER **JAPAN ART**
PRESS, DELHI
POSTER SIZE **102.3 X 76.1 CM**

MELA

1971
HINDI – COLOUR
FILM GENRE **SOCIAL**
DIRECTOR **PRAKASH MEHRA**
PRODUCER **A.A. NADIADWALA**
PRODUCTION **A.G. FILMS**
CAST **SANJAY KHAN,**
FEROZ KHAN, MUMTAZ,
LALITA PAWAR
MUSIC **R.D. BURMAN**
LYRICS **MAJROOH SULTANPURI**
POSTER ARTIST **LAXMAN RANJEET**
POSTER PRINTER **NENSEY OFFSET**
PVT. LTD., BOMBAY
POSTER SIZE **95.2 x 70 CM**

PAKEEZAH
1971
HINDI – COLOUR
FILM GENRE **SOCIAL**
DIRECTOR **KAMAL AMROHI**
PRODUCER **KAMAL AMROHI**
PRODUCTION **MAHAL PICTURES**
CAST **ASHOK KUMAR,
MEENA KUMARI,
RAAJ KUMAR**
MUSIC **GHULAM MOHAMMED,
NAUSHAD**
LYRICS **KAIF BHOPALI,
MAJROOH SULTANPURI,
KAIFI AZMI**
POSTER ARTIST **NARAYAM**
POSTER SIZE **94 X 68.5 CM**

**SAMPOORNA
DEVI DARSHAN**
1971
HINDI – COLOUR
FILM GENRE **DEVOTIONAL**
DIRECTOR **SHANTILAL SONI**
PRODUCER **S.J. RAJDEO**
PRODUCTION **SARGAM CHITRA,
BOMBAY**
CAST **SUSHAMA, SHABNAM,
ASHISH KUMAR,
PADMA RANI, B.M. VYAS**
MUSIC **S.N. TRIPARTI**
LYRICS **B.D. MISHRA**
POSTER ARTIST **G.T. ARTS**
POSTER PRINTER **JAPAN ART
PRESS, DELHI**
POSTER SIZE **102 X 76.4 CM**

APNA DESH

1972
HINDI – COLOUR
FILM GENRE **DRAMA**
DIRECTOR **JAMBU**
PRODUCER **A.V. SUBRAMANIAM**
& T.M. KITTU
PRODUCTION **VENUS PICTURES**
& OLYMPIC PICTURES
CAST **RAJESH KHANNA,**
MUMTAZ, MADAN PURI
MUSIC **R.D. BURMAN**
LYRICS **ANAND BAKSHI**
POSTER PRINTER **MADRAS SAFIRE**
LITHOGRAPHERS, MADRAS
POSTER SIZE **98.7** X **70.7 CM**

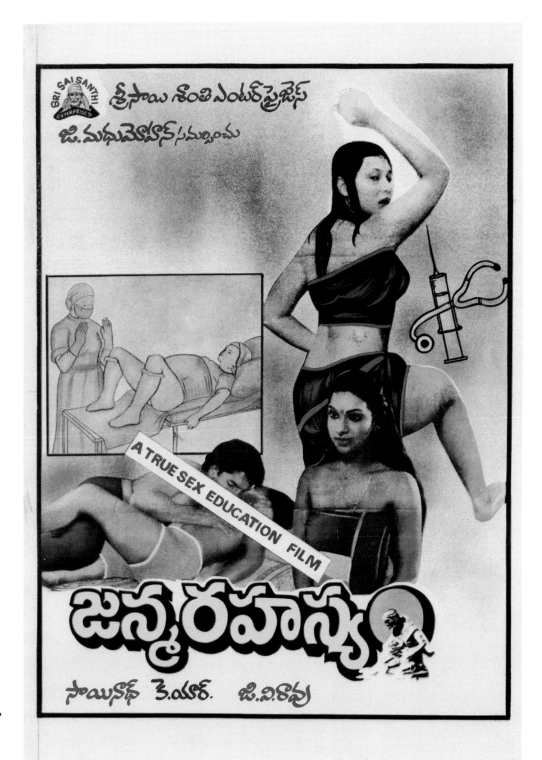

JANMA RAHASYA
1972
KANNADA – COLOUR
FILM GENRE **ADULT SEX**
DIRECTOR **S.P.N. KRISHNA**
PRODUCTION **SHRIKANT &**
SHRIKANT ENTERPRISES
CAST **RAJKUMAR, BHARATHI,**
ASWATH
MUSIC **M. RANGARAO**
LYRICS **R.N. JAYAGOPAL**
POSTER SIZE **101.6 X 70.4 CM**

KAANCH AUR
HEERA

1972
HINDI – COLOUR
FILM GENRE **SOCIAL**
DIRECTOR **CHARANDAS SHOKH**
PRODUCER **DWARKA DAS**
PRODUCTION **SUDARSHAN CHITRA**
CAST **PANKAJ, SHAMIM,
RAJAN HAKSAR,
KAMAL KAPOOR**
MUSIC **RAVINDRA JAIN**
LYRICS **RAVINDRA JAIN**
POSTER ARTIST **JAMAN**
POSTER PRINTER **CHAWAN CINE
ARTS STUDIO, BOMBAY**
POSTER SIZE **102 X 75.8 CM**

NALLA NERAM

1972
TAMIL – COLOUR
FILM GENRE **SOCIAL**
DIRECTOR **M.A. THIRUMUGAM**
PRODUCER **M.M.A. CHINNAPPA THEVAR**
PRODUCTION **DEVAR FILMS**
CAST **M.G. RAMACHANDRAN, K.R. VIJAYA, NAGESH**
MUSIC **K.V. MAHADEVAN**
LYRICS **KANNADASAN, AVINASHI MANI, PULAMAI PITHAN**
POSTER ARTIST **ESHWAR**
POSTER PRINTER **MADRAS SAFIRE LITHOGRAPHERS, MADRAS**
POSTER SIZE **98.6 X 70.6 CM**

PATTIKADA PATTANANA

1972
TAMIL – COLOUR
FILM GENRE **SOCIAL**
DIRECTOR **P. MADHAVAN**
PRODUCER **P. MADHAVAN**
PRODUCTION **ARUN PRASAD MOVIES**
CAST **SIVAJI GANESHAN, JAYALALITHA**
MUSIC **M.S. VISHWANATHAN**
POSTER ARTIST **ESHWAR**
POSTER PRINTER **ELEGANT PRINTERS, MADRAS**
POSTER SIZE **99** X **143.5 CM** 2 SHEET

**BEES SAAL
PAHELE**
1972
HINDI – COLOUR
FILM GENRE **SUSPENSE**
DIRECTOR **PRABIR ROY**
PRODUCER **HEMANT KUMAR**
PRODUCTION **GEETANJALI
PICTURES PVT. LTD.**
CAST **ANUPAMA,
FARIDA JALAL,
RAMESH DEO, RITESH**
MUSIC **HEMANT KUMAR**
LYRICS **SHAILENDRA**
POSTER PRINTER **REDIJ PUBLICITY
CONCERN, BOMBAY**
POSTER SIZE **102.2 X 76 CM**

DEIVAM

1972

TAMIL – COLOUR

FILM GENRE **SOCIAL**

DIRECTOR **M.A. THIRUMUGAM**

PRODUCER **SANDOW,**
M.M.A. CHINAPPA DEVAR

PRODUCTION **DEVAR FILMS,**
DHANDAYUTHAPANI FILMS

CAST **GEMINI GANESAN,**
SIVAKUMAR, K.R. VIJAYA,
SOWKAR JANAKI,
MUTHURAMAN, NAGESH

MUSIC **KUNNAKUDI**
VAIDYANATHAN

LYRICS **G.V. RAMANAN,**
A.R. SWAMINATHAN,
T.S. RANGASWAMI

POSTER ARTIST **BABU**

POSTER SIZE **96.7** X **140.3 CM** 2 SHEET

**RAAMPUR KA
LAKSHMAN**
1972
HINDI – COLOUR
FILM GENRE **DRAMA**
DIRECTOR **MANMOHAN DESAI**
PRODUCER **A.A. NADIADWALA**
PRODUCTION **A.G. FILMS PVT. LTD.**
CAST **RANDHIR KAPOOR,
SHATRUGHAN SINHA,
REKHA**
MUSIC **R.D. BURMAN**
LYRICS **MAJROOH SULTANPURI**
POSTER PRINTER **NENSEY OFFSET
PVT. LTD., BOMBAY**
POSTER SIZE **102.5 X 77 CM**

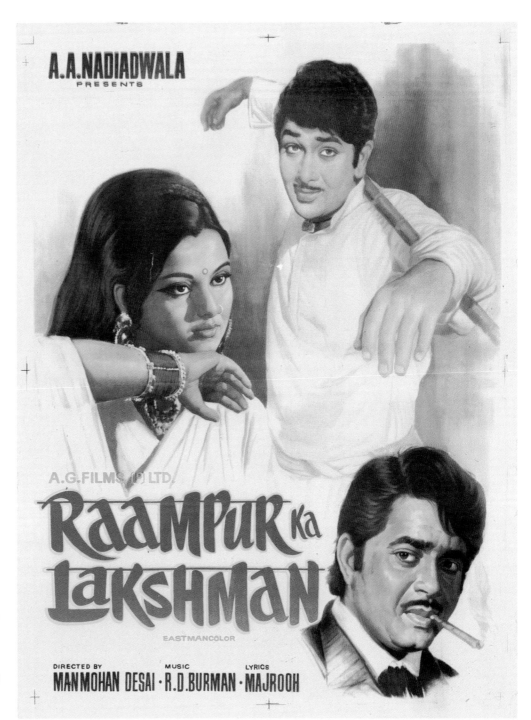

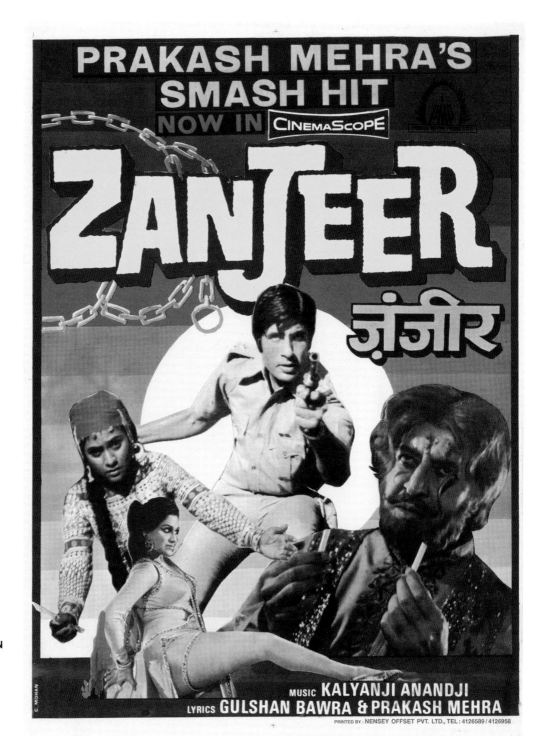

ZANJEER
1973
HINDI – COLOUR
FILM GENRE **SOCIAL**
DIRECTOR **PRAKASH MEHRA**
PRODUCER **PRAKASH MEHRA**
PRODUCTION **PRAKASH MEHRA**
CAST **AMITABH BACHCHAN,
JAYA BHADURI, AJIT, PRAN**
MUSIC **KALYANJI-ANANDJI**
LYRICS **PRAKASH MEHRA &
GULSHAN BAWRA**
POSTER ARTIST **C. MOHAN**
POSTER PRINTER **NENSEY OFFSET
PVT. LTD., BOMBAY**
POSTER SIZE **101** X **73.2 CM**

160

THE RETURN OF THE DRAGON

1973
CHINESE (DUBBED IN ENGLISH) – COLOUR
FILM GENRE **ACTION**
DIRECTOR **BRUCE LEE**
PRODUCER **GOLDEN HARVEST GROUP**
PRODUCTION **INDO-OVERSEAS FILMS**
CAST **BRUCE LEE, NORA MIAO, CHUCK NORRIS**
POSTER ARTIST **KETHA ARTS**
POSTER PRINTER **MANIMEGALAI LITHO WORKS, MADRAS**
POSTER SIZE **100 X 73 CM**

ULAGAM SUTRUM VALIBAN

1973
TAMIL – COLOUR
FILM GENRE **DRAMA**
DIRECTOR **M.G. RAMACHANDRAN**
PRODUCER **M.G. RAMACHANDRAN**
PRODUCTION **EMGEEYAR PICTURES**
CAST **M.G. RAMACHANDRAN,
M.N. NAMBIAR,
S.A. ASHOKAN, MANJULA,
NAGESH, CHANDRAKALA,
V. GOPALAKRISHNAN**
MUSIC **M.S. VISHWANATHAN**
LYRICS **KANNADASAN,
VALI PULAMAI PITHAN**
POSTER PRINTER **MADRAS SAFIRE
LITHOGRAPHERS, CHENNAI**
POSTER SIZE **96.3 X 71 CM**

ULAGAM SUTRUM VALIBAN

1973
TAMIL – COLOUR
FILM GENRE **DRAMA**
DIRECTOR **M.G. RAMACHANDRAN**
PRODUCER **M.G. RAMACHANDRAN**
PRODUCTION **EMGEEYAR PICTURES**
CAST **M.G. RAMACHANDRAN,**
M.N. NAMBIAR,
S.A. ASHOKAN, MANJULA,
NAGESH, CHANDRAKALA,
V. GOPALAKRISHNAN
MUSIC **M.S. VISHWANATHAN**
LYRICS **KANNADASAN,**
VALI PULAMAI PITHAN
POSTER PRINTER **MADRAS SAFIRE**
LITHOGRAPHERS, CHENNAI
POSTER SIZE **98.6 X 70.6 CM**

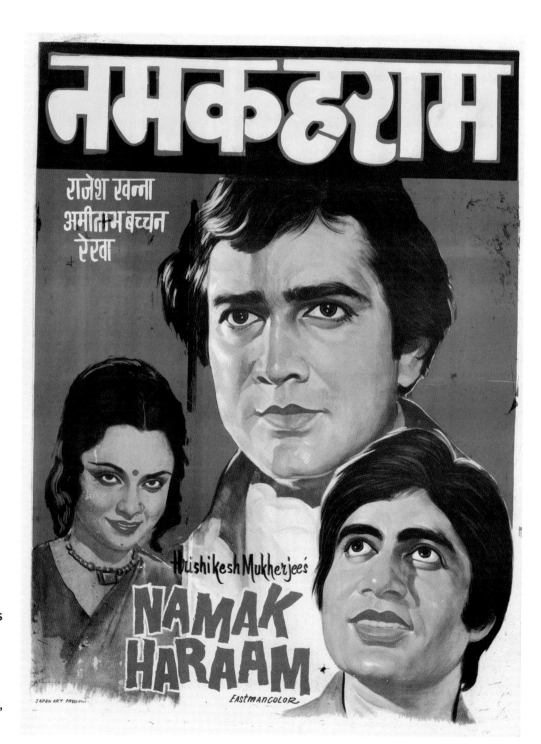

NAMAK HARAAM
1973
HINDI – COLOUR
FILM GENRE **SOCIAL**
DIRECTOR **HRISHIKESH MUKHERJEE**
PRODUCER **RAJA RAM, SATISH WAGLE, JAYENDRA PANDYA**
PRODUCTION **R.S.J. PRODUCTIONS**
CAST **RAJESH KHANNA, AMITABH BACHCHAN, REKHA, SIMI GAREWAL, DURGA KHOTE**
MUSIC **R.D. BURMAN**
LYRICS **ANAND BAKSHI**
POSTER PRINTER **JAPAN ART PRESS, DELHI**
POSTER SIZE **97.8 X 71.8 CM**

HEERA
1973
HINDI – COLOUR
FILM GENRE **SOCIAL**
DIRECTOR **SULTAN AHMED**
PRODUCER **SULTAN AHMED**
PRODUCTION **SULTAN
PRODUCTIONS, BOMBAY**
CAST **SUNIL DUTT,
ASHA PAREKH,
FARIDA JALAL,
SHATRUGHAN SINHA**
MUSIC **KALYANJI ANANDJI**
LYRICS **INDIVAR, ANJAAN**
POSTER ARTIST **BALKRISHNA**
POSTER PRINTER **V. PRINT WADALA,
BOMBAY**
POSTER SIZE **102 X 76 CM**

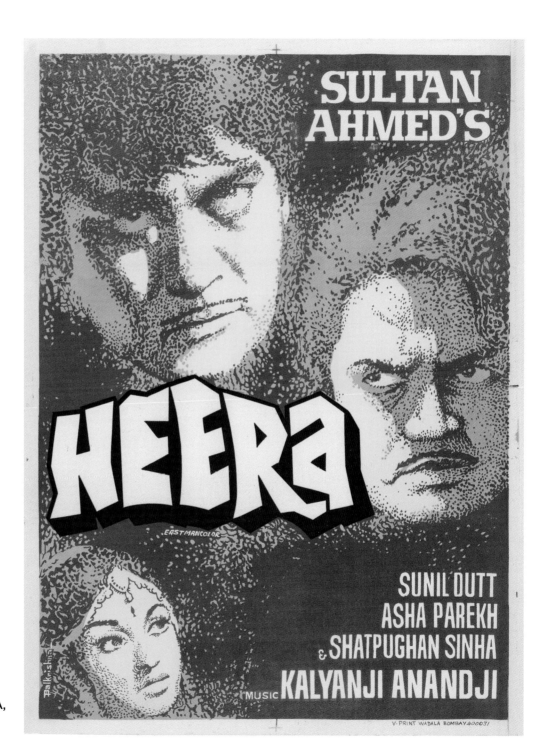

**PRAN JAYE PER
VACHAN NA JAYE**
1973
HINDI – COLOUR
FILM GENRE **SOCIAL**
DIRECTOR **ALI RAZA**
PRODUCER **RATAN MOHAN**
PRODUCTION **R.M. ART
PRODUCTIONS**
CAST **SUNIL DUTT, REKHA,
PREMNATH, BINDU**
MUSIC **O.P. NAYYAR**
LYRICS **S.H. BIHARI
& AHMED WASI**
POSTER ARTIST **DHARAMDAS SAGA**
POSTER PRINTER **DNYANSAGAR
LITHO PRESS, BOMBAY**
POSTER SIZE **102 X 76 CM**

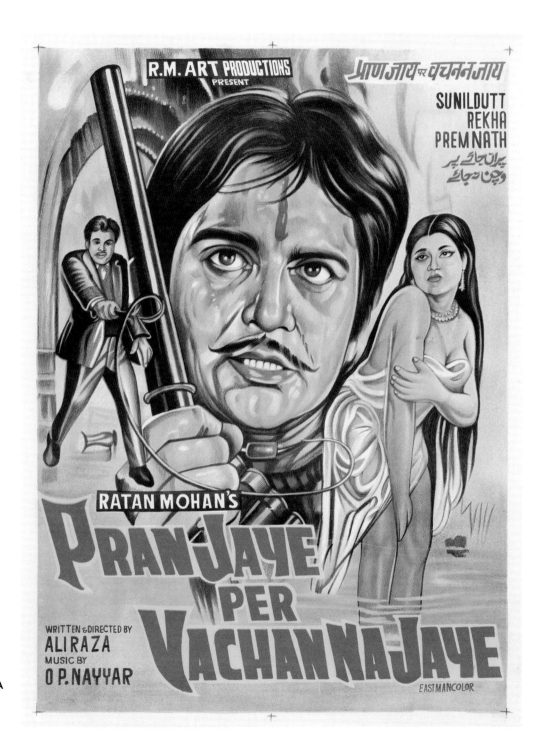

**PRAN JAYE PER
VACHAN NA JAYE**
1973
HINDI – COLOUR
FILM GENRE **SOCIAL**
DIRECTOR **ALI RAZA**
PRODUCER **RATAN MOHAN**
PRODUCTION **R.M. ART
PRODUCTIONS**
CAST **SUNIL DUTT, REKHA,
PREMNATH, BINDU**
MUSIC **O.P. NAYYAR**
LYRICS **S.H. BIHARI
& AHMED WASI**
POSTER ARTIST **DHARAMDAS SAGA**
POSTER PRINTER **DNYANSAGAR
LITHO PRESS, BOMBAY**
POSTER SIZE **96.3 X 70.7 CM**

VADA TERA VADA
1974
HINDI – COLOUR
FILM GENRE **DRAMA**
DIRECTOR **MOHINDER BATRA**
PRODUCER **VASUDEO SHROFF**
PRODUCTION **THAKKAR FILMS INTERNATIONAL**
CAST **VINOD MEHRA, ASHA SACHDEV, DANNY DENZONGPA, RADHA SALUJA**
MUSIC **LAXMIKANT PYARELAL**
POSTER ARTIST **NIRU**
POSTER PRINTER **SAURASTRA KUCH CHITRAN, RAJKOT**
POSTER SIZE **56.5 X 44.2 CM**

DHARMATMA
1975
HINDI – COLOUR
FILM GENRE **ACTION**
DIRECTOR **FEROZ KHAN**
PRODUCER **FEROZ KHAN**
PRODUCTION **FEROZ KHAN**
PRODUCTIONS PVT. LTD.
CAST **REKHA, PREMNATH,**
HEMA MALINI,
FEROZ KHAN
MUSIC **KALYANJI ANANDJI**
LYRICS **MAJROO SULTANPURI**
POSTER ARTIST **S. NAMGEKAR**
POSTER SIZE **101 X 75 CM**

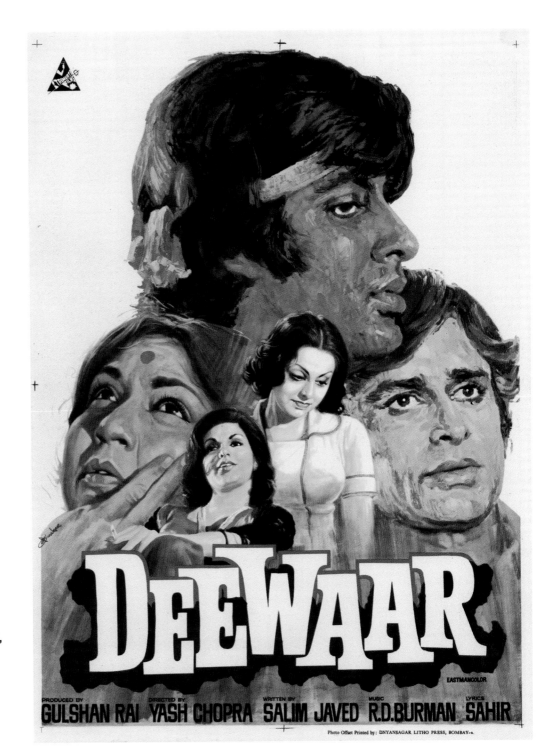

DEEWAAR
1975
HINDI – COLOUR
FILM GENRE **DRAMA**
DIRECTOR **YASH CHOPRA**
PRODUCER **GULSHAN RAI**
PRODUCTION **TRIMURTI FILMS**
CAST **AMITABH BACHCHAN,**
SHASHI KAPOOR,
NIRUPA ROY
MUSIC **R.D. BURMAN**
LYRICS **SAHIR LUDHIANVI**
POSTER ARTIST **SIVAKAR**
POSTER PRINTER **DNYANSAGAR**
LITHO PRESS, BOMBAY
POSTER SIZE **100.7** X **73 CM**

SHOLAY
1975
HINDI – COLOUR
FILM GENRE **SOCIAL**
DIRECTOR **RAMESH SIPPY**
PRODUCER **G.P. SIPPY**
PRODUCTION **SIPPY FILMS**
CAST **DHARMENDRA,
SANJEEV KUMAR,
AMITABH BACHCHAN,
HEMA MALINI,
JAYA BHADURI,
AMJAD KHAN**
MUSIC **R.D. BURMAN**
LYRICS **ANAND BAKSHI**
POSTER ARTIST **MOIE**
POSTER PRINTER **BHARAT LITHO
PRESS, MUMBAI**
POSTER SIZE **76.7 X 51.5 CM**

172

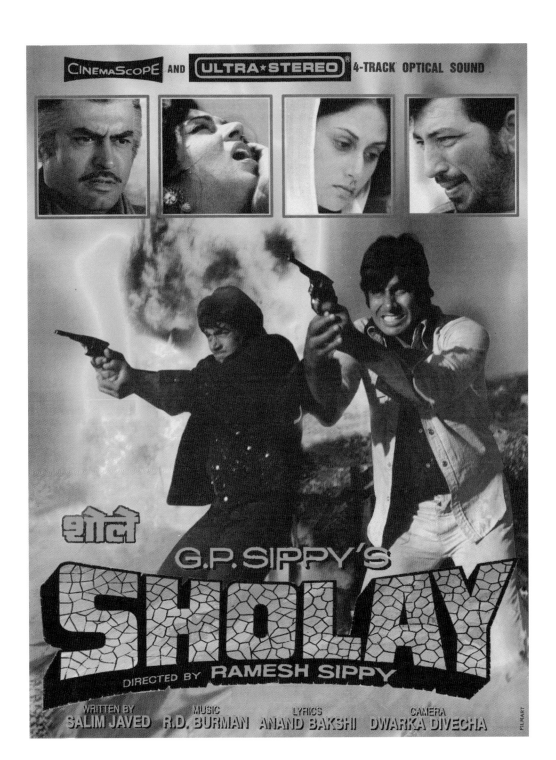

SHOLAY
1975
HINDI – COLOUR
FILM GENRE **SOCIAL**
DIRECTOR **RAMESH SIPPY**
PRODUCER **G.P. SIPPY**
PRODUCTION **SIPPY FILMS**
CAST **DHARMENDRA,
SANJEEV KUMAR,
AMITABH BACHCHAN,
HEMA MALINI,
JAYA BHADURI,
AMJAD KHAN**
MUSIC **R.D. BURMAN**
LYRICS **ANAND BAKSHI**
POSTER ARTIST **C. MOHAN –
FILMART**
POSTER PRINTER **GLAMOUR,
BOMBAY**
POSTER SIZE **92.5 X 69.5 CM**

YASHODA KRISHNA

1976
TELUGU (DUBBED IN HINDI) – COLOUR
FILM GENRE **MYTHOLOGICAL**
DIRECTOR **C.S. RAO**
PRODUCER **C.H. PRAKASA RAO**
PRODUCTION **VENUS MAHEEJAA PICTURES**
CAST **S.V. RANGA RAO, GUMMADI, RAMAKRISHNA, JAMUNA**
MUSIC **S. RAJESWARA RAO**
POSTER ARTIST **KATHA ARTS**
POSTER PRINTER **PRASAD PROCESS PVT. LTD., MADRAS**
POSTER SIZE **101.5 x 75.4 CM**

175

UZHAIKUM KARANGAL

1976
TAMIL – COLOUR
FILM GENRE **SOCIAL**
DIRECTOR **K. SHANKAR**
PRODUCER **KOVAI CHEZHIAN**
PRODUCTION **KAY CEE FILMS**
CAST **M.G. RAMACHANDRAN, LATHA, THANGAVELU, NAGESH, KANNAN**
MUSIC **M.S. VISWANATHAN**
LYRICS **VALI, PULAMAI PITHAN, MUTHULINGAM**
POSTER PRINTER **VIGNESH PRINTING SYSTEMS, SIVAKASI**
POSTER SIZE **76.3 X 75 CM**

HAIWAN
1977
HINDI – COLOUR
FILM GENRE **HORROR**
DIRECTOR **RAM MUKERJI,**
RONO MUKERJI,
SUBHASH MUKERJI
PRODUCER **S. MUKERJI**
PRODUCTION **FAMILY FILM CLUB**
CAST **DEV MUKERJI, NAZNEEN,**
PREMA NARAYAN,
PADMA KHANNA
MUSIC **BAPPI LAHIRI**
LYRICS **HASRAT JAIPURI,**
AMIT KHANNA,
GAUHAR KANPURI,
P.N. CHOUDHURY
POSTER ARTIST **GLAMOUR**
POSTER PRINTER **PERFECT**
PRINTERS, BOMBAY
POSTER SIZE **76.2 X 50.5 CM**

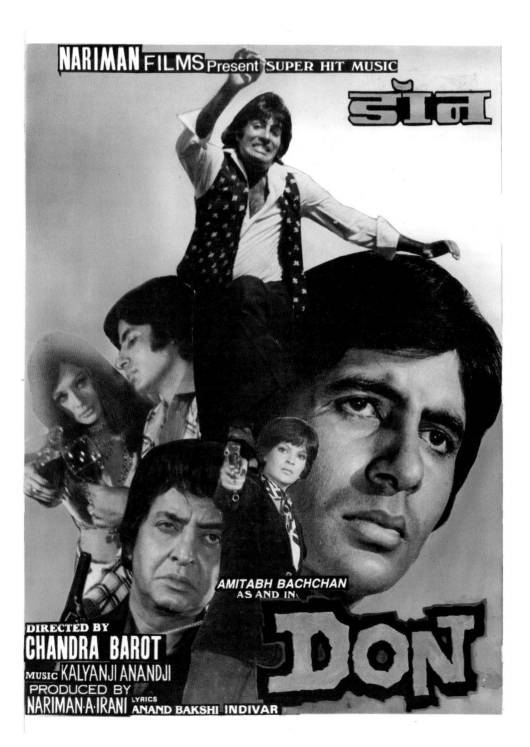

DON
1978
HINDI – COLOUR
FILM GENRE **ACTION**
DIRECTOR **CHANDRA BAROT**
PRODUCER **NARIMAN A. IRANI**
PRODUCTION **NARIMAN FILMS**
CAST **AMITABH BACHCHAN,**
ZEENAT AMAN, PRAN
MUSIC **KALYANJI ANANDJI**
LYRICS **ANAND BAKSHI**
INDIVAR
POSTER SIZE **96.5 X 71 CM**

DON
1978
HINDI—COLOUR
FILM GENRE **ACTION**
DIRECTOR **CHANDRA BAROT**
PRODUCER **NARIMAN A. IRANI**
PRODUCTION **NARIMAN FILMS**
CAST **AMITABH BACHCHAN,**
ZEENAT AMAN, PRAN
MUSIC **KALYANJI ANANDJI**
LYRICS **ANAND BAKSHI**
INDIVAR
POSTER SIZE **100.2 X 75 CM**

SWARAG NARAK

1978
HINDI – COLOUR
FILM GENRE **SOCIAL**
DIRECTOR **DASARI**
NARAYAN RAO
PRODUCER **B. NAGI REDDI**
PRODUCTION **VIJAYA**
PRODUCTIONS
CAST **SANJEEV KUMAR,**
JEETENDRA,
VINOD MEHRA,
MOUSHUMI CHATTERJEE,
SHABANA AZMI
MUSIC **RAJESH ROSHAN**
LYRICS **GULZAR**
POSTER PRINTER **PRASAD PROCESS**
PVT. LTD. MADRAS
POSTER SIZE **75.7** X **49.5 CM**

SWARAG NARAK

1978
HINDI – COLOUR
FILM GENRE **SOCIAL**
DIRECTOR **DASARI**
NARAYAN RAO
PRODUCER **B. NAGI REDDI**
PRODUCTION **VIJAYA**
PRODUCTIONS
CAST **SANJEEV KUMAR,**
JEETENDRA,
VINOD MEHRA,
MOUSHUMI CHATTERJEE,
SHABANA AZMI
MUSIC **RAJESH ROSHAN**
LYRICS **GULZAR**
POSTER ARTIST **ESHWAR**
POSTER PRINTER **PRASAD PROCESS**
PVT. LTD. MADRAS
POSTER SIZE **73.9** X **50.5 CM**

SWARAG NARAK

1978
HINDI – COLOUR
FILM GENRE **SOCIAL**
DIRECTOR **DASARI NARAYAN RAO**
PRODUCER **B. NAGI REDDI**
PRODUCTION **VIJAYA PRODUCTIONS**
CAST **SANJEEV KUMAR, JEETENDRA, VINOD MEHRA, MOUSHUMI CHATTERJEE, SHABANA AZMI**
MUSIC **RAJESH ROSHAN**
LYRICS **GULZAR**
POSTER ARTIST **O.P. BANGALI**
POSTER PRINTER **JAPAN ART PRESS, DELHI**
POSTER SIZE **76 X 51 CM**

181

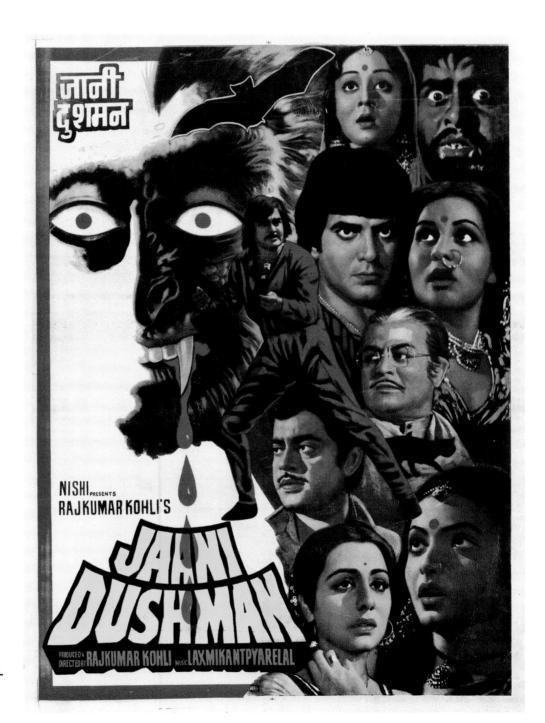

JAANI DUSHMAN
1979
HINDI – COLOUR
FILM GENRE **HORROR**
DIRECTOR **RAJKUMAR KOHLI**
PRODUCTION **SHANKAR MOVIES**
CAST **SUNIL DUTT,**
SANJEEV KUMAR, REKHA,
SHATRUGHAN SINHA,
VINOD MEHRA,
JEETENDRA, REENA ROY
MUSIC **LAXMIKANT PYARELAL**
LYRICS **VARMA MALIK**
POSTER ARTIST **PARDUMAN**
POSTER SIZE **95.2 X 72.7 CM**

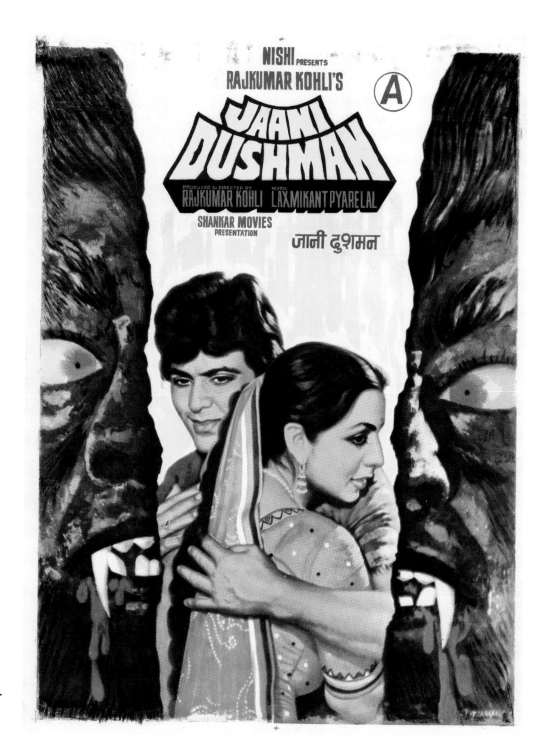

JAANI DUSHMAN

1979
HINDI – COLOUR
FILM GENRE **HORROR**
DIRECTOR **RAJKUMAR KOHLI**
PRODUCTION **SHANKAR MOVIES**
CAST **SUNIL DUTT,**
SANJEEV KUMAR, REKHA,
SHATRUGHAN SINHA,
VINOD MEHRA,
JEETENDRA, REENA ROY
MUSIC **LAXMIKANT PYARELAL**
LYRICS **VARMA MALIK**
POSTER ARTIST **PARDUMAN**
POSTER SIZE **101.3 X 74.5 CM**

KAALA PATTHAR

1979

HINDI – COLOUR

FILM GENRE **SOCIAL**

DIRECTOR **YASH CHOPRA**

PRODUCER **YASH CHOPRA**

PRODUCTION **YASH RAJ FILMS**

CAST **SHASHI KAPOOR,
RAAKHEE, NEETU SINGH,
AMITABH BACHCHAN,
SHATRUGHAN SINHA,
PARVEEN BABI,
POONAM DHILLON**

MUSIC **RAJESH ROSHAN,
SALIL CHOUDHURY**

LYRICS **SAHIR LUDHIANVI**

POSTER ARTIST **SIVAKAR**

POSTER PRINTER **ORIENTAL OFFSET
LITHO WORKS, BOMBAY**

POSTER SIZE **102.2 X 76 CM**

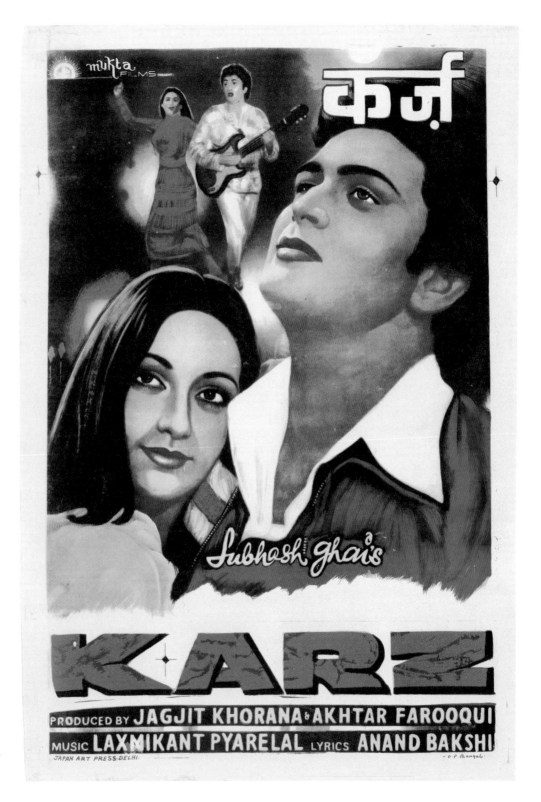

KARZ
1980
HINDI – COLOUR
FILM GENRE **SOCIAL**
DIRECTOR **SUBHASH GHAI**
PRODUCER **JAGJIT KHORANAN AKHTAR**
PRODUCTION **MUKTA FILMS**
CAST **RISHI KAPOOR, TINA MUNIM, SIMI, RAJ KIRAN, PREMNATH, PRAN, DURGA KHOTE**
MUSIC **LAXMIKANT PYARELAL**
LYRICS **ANAND BAKSHI**
POSTER SIZE **76 X 51.5 CM**

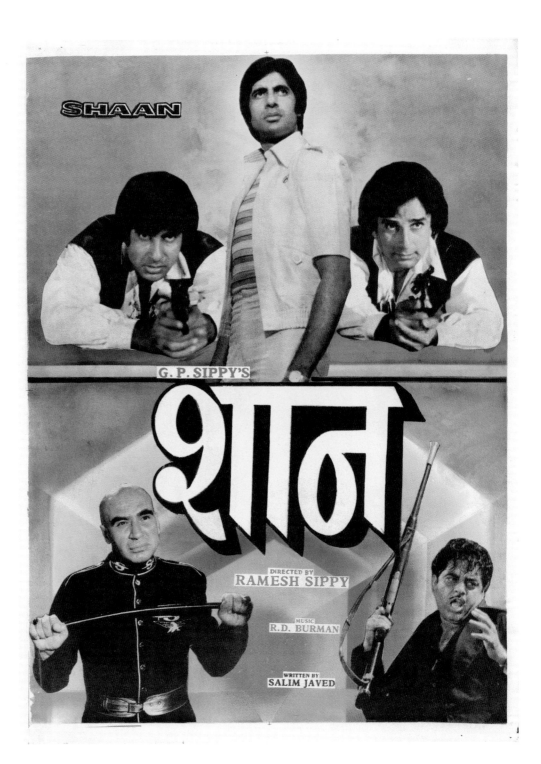

SHAAN
1980
HINDI – COLOUR
FILM GENRE **ACTION**
DIRECTOR **RAMESH SIPPY**
PRODUCER **G.P. SIPPY**
PRODUCTION **SIPPY FILMS**
CAST **AMITABH BACHCHAN,**
SHASHI KAPOOR,
SHATRUGHAN SINHA,
RAKHEE, SUNIL DUTT
MUSIC **R.D. BURMAN**
LYRICS **ANAND BAKSHI**
POSTER SIZE **96.2** X **70.5 CM**

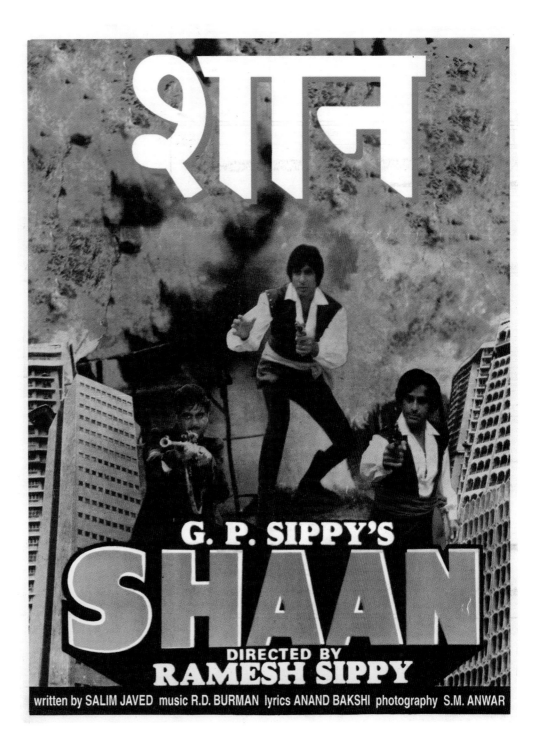

SHAAN
1980
HINDI – COLOUR
FILM GENRE **ACTION**
DIRECTOR **RAMESH SIPPY**
PRODUCER **G.P. SIPPY**
PRODUCTION **SIPPY FILMS**
CAST **AMITABH BACHCHAN,
SHASHI KAPOOR,
SHATRUGHAN SINHA,
RAKHEE, SUNIL DUTT**
MUSIC **R.D. BURMAN**
LYRICS **ANAND BAKSHI**
POSTER SIZE **96.4 X 70.7 CM**

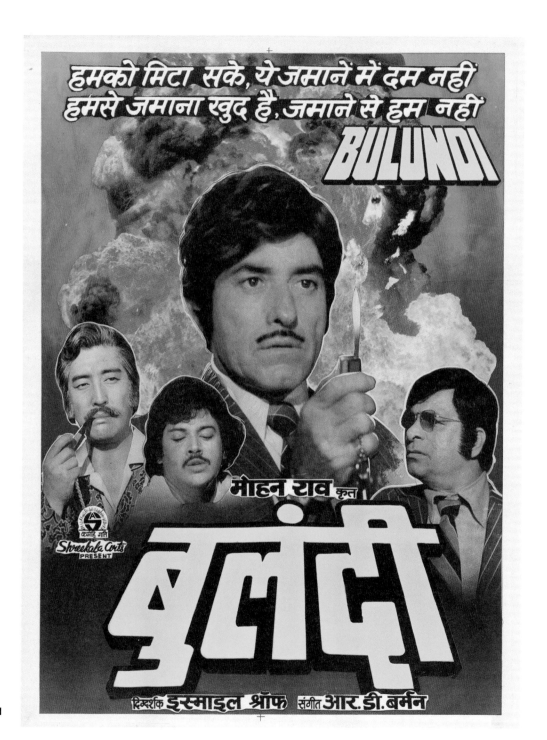

BULUNDI

1980
HINDI – COLOUR
FILM GENRE **SOCIAL**
DIRECTOR **ESMAYEEL SHROFF**
PRODUCER **MOHAN RAO**
PRODUCTION **SHREEKALA ARTS**
CAST **RAAJ KUMAR, KIM, ASHA PAREKH, DANNY, RAJ KIRAN, KULBHUSHAN KHARBANDA**
MUSIC **R.D. BURMAN**
LYRICS **MAJROOH SULTANPURI**
POSTER SIZE **99.6 x 74.5 CM**

AHIMSA
1981
MALAYALAM – B&W
FILM GENRE **SOCIAL**
DIRECTOR **I.V. SASI**
PRODUCER **P.V. GANGADHARAN**
PRODUCTION **GRIHALAXMI**
PRODUCTIONS
CAST **SUKUMARAN, SEEMA,**
MAMMOOTY
MUSIC **A.T. UMMER**
LYRICS **BICHU THIRUMALA**
POSTER ARTIST **S.A. NAIR**
POSTER PRINTER **MADURAI**
PRINTING SYNDICATE,
MADURAI
POSTER SIZE **101.3 X 73 CM**

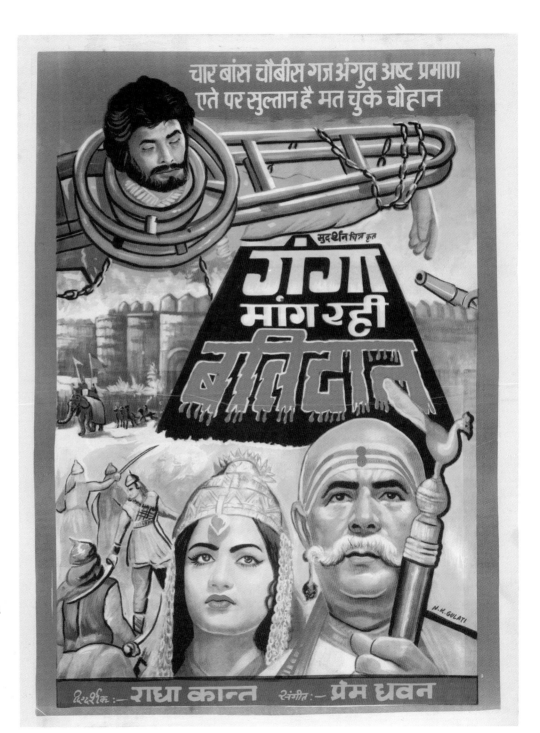

**GANGA MAANG
RAHI BALIDAAN**
1981
HINDI – COLOUR
FILM GENRE **SOCIAL**
DIRECTOR **RADHAKANT**
PRODUCER **DWARKADAS,
SHRINATHDAS**
PRODUCTION **SUDARSHAN CHITRA**
CAST **SOHRAB MODI,
DEV KUMAR,
HEENA KAUSAR,
ABHI BHATTACHARYA,
JAYSHREE T**
MUSIC **PREM DHAWAN**
LYRICS **PREM DHAWAN**
POSTER ARTIST **N.K. GULATI**
POSTER SIZE **102 X 76.2 CM**

GHUNGROO KI AWAAZ

1981
HINDI – COLOUR
FILM GENRE **SOCIAL**
DIRECTOR **TULSI RAMSAY,
SHYAM RAMSAY**
PRODUCER **VIJAY ANAND**
PRODUCTION **NAVKETAN
PRODUCTIONS**
CAST **VIJAY ANAND, REKHA,
DR. SHRIRAM LAGOO,
DHEERAJ, PADMA KHANNA,
LEELA MISHRA,
IFTEKHAR, RATANMALA**
MUSIC **R.D. BURMAN**
POSTER ARTIST **VIJAY ANAND**
POSTER PRINTER **PERFECT
PRINTERS, BOMBAY**
POSTER SIZE **102.3 X 75.8 CM**

192

GHUNGROO KI AWAAZ

1981
HINDI — COLOUR
FILM GENRE **SOCIAL**
DIRECTOR **TULSI RAMSAY,
SHYAM RAMSAY**
PRODUCER **VIJAY ANAND**
PRODUCTION **NAVKETAN
PRODUCTIONS**
CAST **VIJAY ANAND, REKHA,
DR. SHRIRAM LAGOO,
DHEERAJ, PADMA KHANNA,
LEELA MISHRA,
IFTEKHAR, RATANMALA**
MUSIC **R.D. BURMAN**
POSTER ARTIST **VIJAY ANAND**
POSTER PRINTER **PERFECT
PRINTERS, BOMBAY**
POSTER SIZE **101.9 X 76 CM**

193

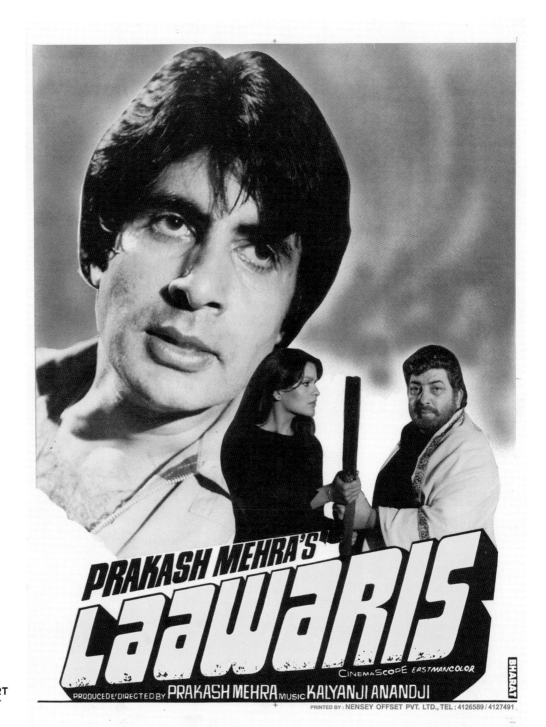

LAAWARIS

1981

HINDI – COLOUR

FILM GENRE **SOCIAL**

DIRECTOR **PRAKASH MEHRA**

PRODUCER **PRAKASH MEHRA**

PRODUCTION **PRAKASH MEHRA PRODUCTIONS**

CAST **AMITABH BACHCHAN, ZEENAT AMAN, AMJAD KHAN, RANJEET, BINDU**

MUSIC **KALYANJI ANANDJI**

LYRICS **ANJAAN, PRAKASH MEHRA**

POSTER ARTIST **BHARAT – PAM ART**

POSTER PRINTER **NENSEY OFFSET PVT. LTD., BOMBAY**

POSTER SIZE **100.9 X 73.3 CM**

NAKHUDA
1981
HINDI – COLOUR
FILM GENRE **SOCIAL**
DIRECTOR **DILIP NAIK**
PRODUCER **YASH CHOPRA**
PRODUCTION **YASH RAJ FILMS**
CAST **RAJ KIRAN,**
SWAROOP SAMPAT,
KULBHUSHAN KHARBANDA
JAVED KHAN
MUSIC **KHAYYAM**
LYRICS **NIDA FAZLI**
POSTER ARTIST **SIVAKAR**
POSTER PRINTER **JAGDISH PHOTO**
PROCESS, BOMBAY
POSTER SIZE **101 X 75 CM**

RAMAYAN
1981
GUJARATI – COLOUR
FILM GENRE **MYTHOLOGICAL**
DIRECTOR **GIRISH MANUKANT**
PRODUCER **RAVJIBHAI J. PATEL**
PRODUCTION **R.J. FILMS**
CAST **MANHAR DESAI,
RANJITRAJ, ANJANA**
MUSIC **DHEERAJ DHANAK**
POSTER ARTIST **GOLARTS**
PRINTER **SHILPI-SARVODAYA**
POSTER SIZE **102 x 76 CM**

SATTE PE SATTA
1981
HINDI – COLOUR
FILM GENRE **SOCIAL**
DIRECTOR **RAJ N. SIPPY**
PRODUCER **N.C. SIPPY**
PRODUCTION **UTTAM CHITRA**
CAST **AMITABH BACHCHAN,
HEMA MALINI, RANJEETA,
AMJAD KHAN**
MUSIC **R.D. BURMAN**
LYRICS **GULSHAN BAWRA**
POSTER ARTIST **SAKHI THAKUR,
COLOUR LAB**
POSTER PRINTER **NENSEY OFFSET
PVT. LTD., BOMBAY**
POSTER SIZE **98.9 X 72.5 CM**

197

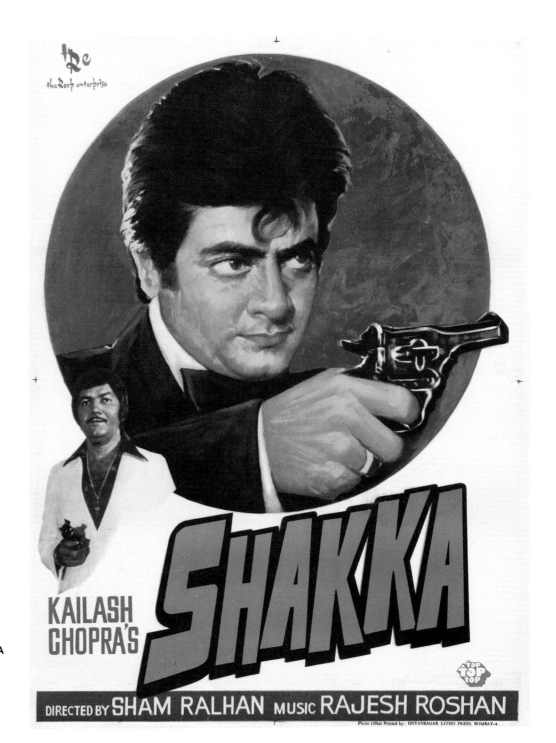

SHAKKA
1981
HINDI – COLOUR
FILM GENRE **DRAMA**
DIRECTOR **SHAM RALHAN**
PRODUCER **KAILASH CHOPRA**
PRODUCTION **THE ROOP
ENTERPRISE**
CAST **JEETENDRA, HELEN,
PREM CHOPRA,
ZAHIRA, SIMPLE KAPADIA**
MUSIC **RAJESH ROSHAN**
LYRICS **VERMA MULLICK**
POSTER ARTIST **TOP TOP TOP**
POSTER PRINTER **DNYANSAGAR
LITHO PRESS, BOMBAY**
POSTER SIZE **99.7 X 74.3 CM**

SILSILA
1981
HINDI – COLOUR
FILM GENRE **LOVE STORY**
DIRECTOR **YASH CHOPRA**
PRODUCER **YASH CHOPRA**
PRODUCTION **YASH RAJ FILMS**
CAST **AMITABH BACHCHAN,**
SHASHI KAPOOR,
JAYA BHADURI, REKHA,
SANJEEV KUMAR
MUSIC **SHIV HARI**
LYRICS **JAVED AKHTAR**
POSTER ARTIST **SIVAKAR**
POSTER SIZE **100 X 75 CM**

UMRAO JAAN

1981
URDU – COLOUR
FILM GENRE **DRAMA**
DIRECTOR **MUZAFFAR ALI**
PRODUCER **MUZAFFAR ALI**
PRODUCTION **INTEGRATED FILMS**
CAST **REKHA,
FAROOQUE SHAIKH,
NASEERUDDIN SHAH**
MUSIC **KHAYYAM**
LYRICS **SHAHRYAR**
POSTER ARTIST **MANJULA
PADMANABHAN,
ANJOLIE ELA MENON,**
POSTER PRINTER **DNYANSAGAR
LITHO PRESS, BOMBAY**
POSTER SIZE **100.4 X 74.6 CM**

INSAAN
1982
HINDI – COLOUR
FILM GENRE **DRAMA**
DIRECTOR **NARINDER BEDI**
PRODUCER **VED KHANNA**
PRODUCTION **MUKESH MOVIES**
CAST **JEETENDRA,
VINOD KHANNA,
AMJAD KHAN, REENA ROY**
MUSIC **LAXMIKANT PYARELAL**
LYRICS **ANAND BAKSHI**
POSTER PRINTER **ORIENTAL
OFFSET LITHO WORKS,
BOMBAY; JAGDISH PHOTO
PROCESS, BOMBAY**
POSTER SIZE **76 X 51 CM**

SAWAAL
1982
HINDI – COLOUR
FILM GENRE **SOCIAL**
DIRECTOR **RAMESH TALWAR**
PRODUCER **YASH CHOPRA**
PRODUCTION **YASH RAJ FILMS**
CAST **SANJEEV KUMAR,
SHASHI KAPOOR,
POONAM DHILLON,
WAHEEDA REHMAN**
MUSIC **KHAYYAM**
LYRICS **MAJROOH**
POSTER ARTIST **SIVAKAR**
POSTER PRINTER **ORIENTAL OFFSET
LITHO WORKS, BOMBAY,
JAGDISH PHOTO PROCESS,
BOMBAY**
POSTER SIZE **100.7** X **74.5 CM**

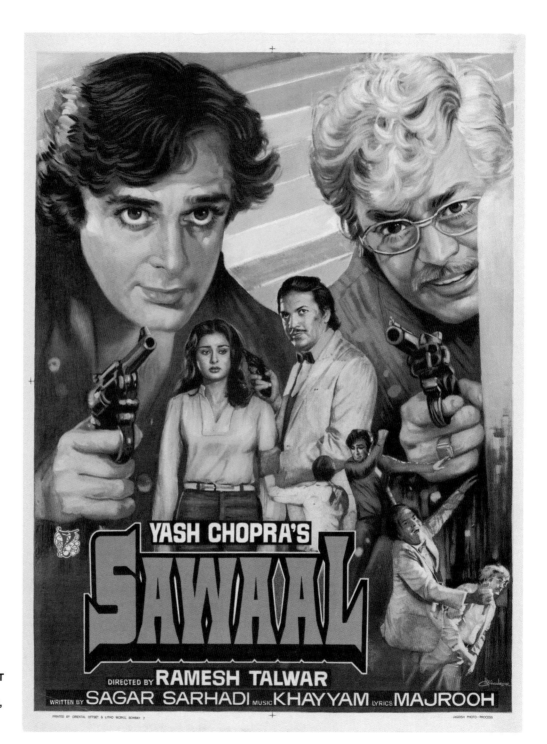

SAWAAL
1982
HINDI – COLOUR
FILM GENRE **SOCIAL**
DIRECTOR **RAMESH TALWAR**
PRODUCER **YASH CHOPRA**
PRODUCTION **YASH RAJ FILMS**
CAST **SANJEEV KUMAR,**
SHASHI KAPOOR,
POONAM DHILLON,
WAHEEDA REHMAN
MUSIC **KHAYYAM**
LYRICS **MAJROOH**
POSTER ARTIST **SIVAKAR**
POSTER PRINTER **ORIENTAL OFFSET**
LITHO WORKS, BOMBAY;
JAGDISH PHOTO PROCESS,
BOMBAY
POSTER SIZE **101.2** X **75 CM**

SAWAAL
1982
HINDI – COLOUR
FILM GENRE **SOCIAL**
DIRECTOR **RAMESH TALWAR**
PRODUCER **YASH CHOPRA**
PRODUCTION **YASH RAJ FILMS**
CAST **SANJEEV KUMAR,**
SHASHI KAPOOR,
POONAM DHILLON,
WAHEEDA REHMAN
MUSIC **KHAYYAM**
LYRICS **MAJROOH**
POSTER ARTIST **SIVAKAR**
POSTER PRINTER **IMPRESSIONS,**
NEW DELHI
POSTER SIZE **101.6** X **75.4 CM**

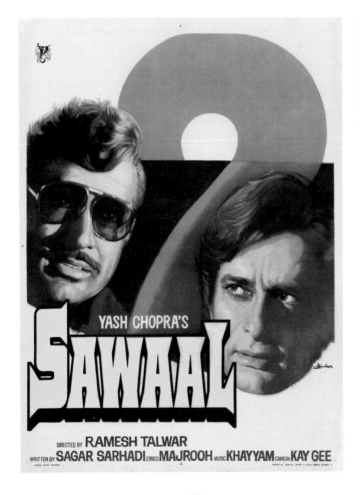

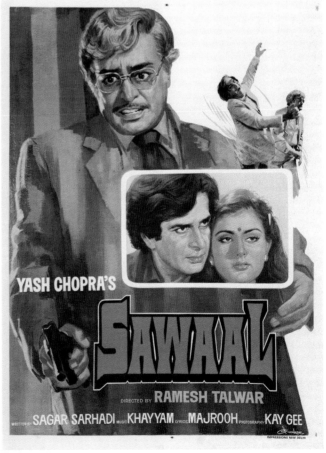

**PAKADAI
PANIRENDHU**
1982
TAMIL – COLOUR
FILM GENRE **SOCIAL**
DIRECTOR **M. SANTHINARAYANAN**
PRODUCER **N. DHAMODHARAN**
PRODUCTION **SWARNAMBIKA
PRODUCTIONS**
CAST **KAMALAHASAN,
SUNDARRAJAN, SRIPRIYA
KANCHANA, MAHENDRAN,**
MUSIC **CHAKRAVARTHI**
LYRICS **KANNADASAN, VAALI**
POSTER ARTIST **DEENIN**
POSTER SIZE **102.4 X 73.1 CM**

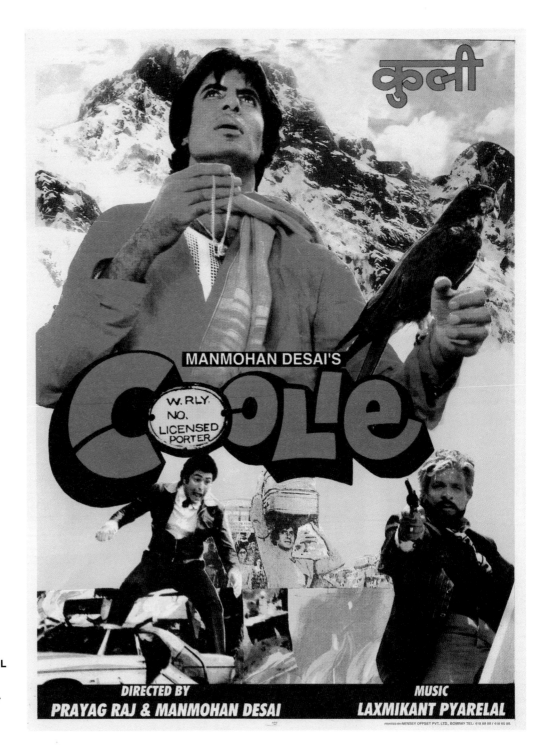

COOLIE
1983
HINDI – COLOUR
FILM GENRE **SOCIAL**
DIRECTOR **MANMOHAN DESAI**
& PRAYAG RAJ
PRODUCER **KETAN DESAI**
PRODUCTION **M.K.D. FILMS**
COMBINE
CAST **AMITABH BACHCHAN,**
WAHEEDA REHMAN,
RISHI KAPOOR,
RATI AGNIHOTRI
MUSIC **LAXMIKANT PYARELAL**
LYRICS **ANAND BAKSHI**
POSTER ARTIST **SAILESH SHAH**
POSTER PRINTER **NENSEY OFFSET**
PVT. LTD., BOMBAY
POSTER SIZE **97 X 71 CM**

TUCKER BABY
1983
TAMIL (DUBBED IN
TELUGU) – COLOUR
FILM GENRE **ACTION**
DIRECTOR **J. WILLIAMS**
PRODUCER **S.V. RAMANAN**
PRODUCTION **NITHYASRI
PRODUCTIONS**
CAST **RAJKUMAR,
SANKAP, MADHAVI,
POORNIMA JAYARAM**
MUSIC **GANGAI AMARAN**
POSTER SIZE **100 X 71 CM**

JAGIR
1984
HINDI – COLOUR
FILM GENRE **ACTION**
DIRECTOR **PRAMOD CHAKRAVORTY**
PRODUCER **PRAMOD CHAKRAVORTY**
PRODUCTION **PRAMOD FILMS**
CAST **DHARMENDRA, MITHUN CHAKRAVORTY, DANNY, ZEENAT AMAN**
MUSIC **R.D. BURMAN**
LYRICS **ANAND BAKSHI**
POSTER ARTIST **PAM ART**
POSTER PRINTER **DEEPTI ARTS, BOMBAY**
POSTER SIZE **102 X 76 CM**

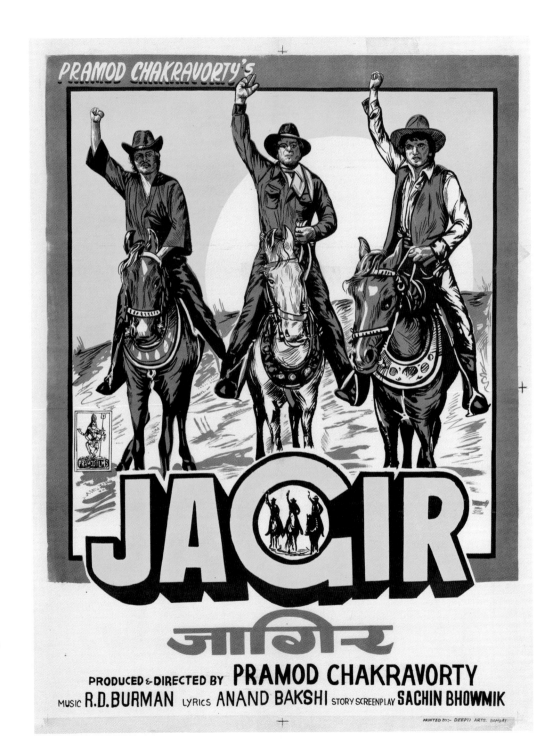

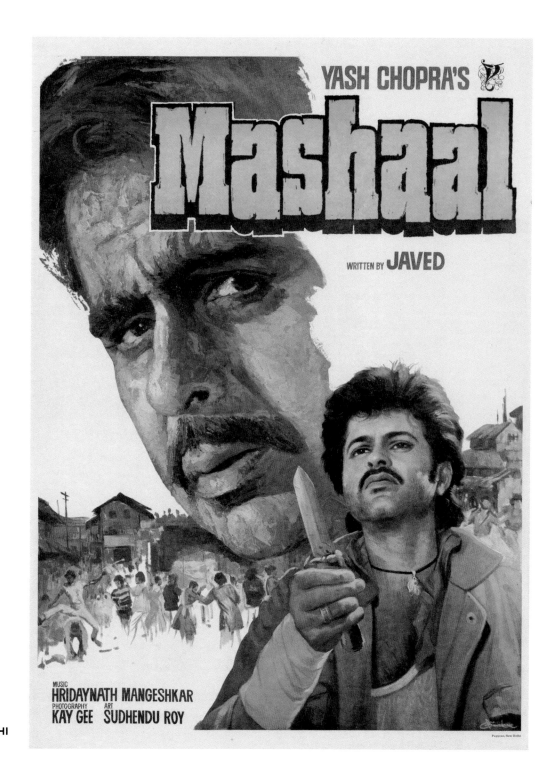

MASHAAL
1984
HINDI – COLOUR
FILM GENRE **SOCIAL**
DIRECTOR **YASH CHOPRA**
PRODUCER **YASH CHOPRA**
PRODUCTION **YASH RAJ FILMS**
CAST **DILIP KUMAR,
WAHEEDA REHMAN,
ANIL KAPOOR,
RATI AGNIHOTRI**
MUSIC **HRIDAYNATH
MANGESHKAR**
LYRICS **JAVED AKHTAR**
POSTER ARTIST **SHIVAKAR**
PRINTER **PAPYRUS, NEW DELHI**
POSTER SIZE **97.5 X 71 CM**

MASHAAL
1984
HINDI – COLOUR
FILM GENRE **SOCIAL**
DIRECTOR **YASH CHOPRA**
PRODUCER **YASH CHOPRA**
PRODUCTION **YASH RAJ FILMS**
CAST **DILIP KUMAR,**
WAHEEDA REHMAN,
ANIL KAPOOR,
RATI AGNIHOTRI
MUSIC **HRIDAYNATH**
MANGESHKAR
LYRICS **JAVED AKHTAR**
POSTER ARTIST **SHIVAKAR**
POSTER PRINTER **PAPYRUS, NEW**
DELHI
POSTER SIZE **100.8 X 71.2 CM**

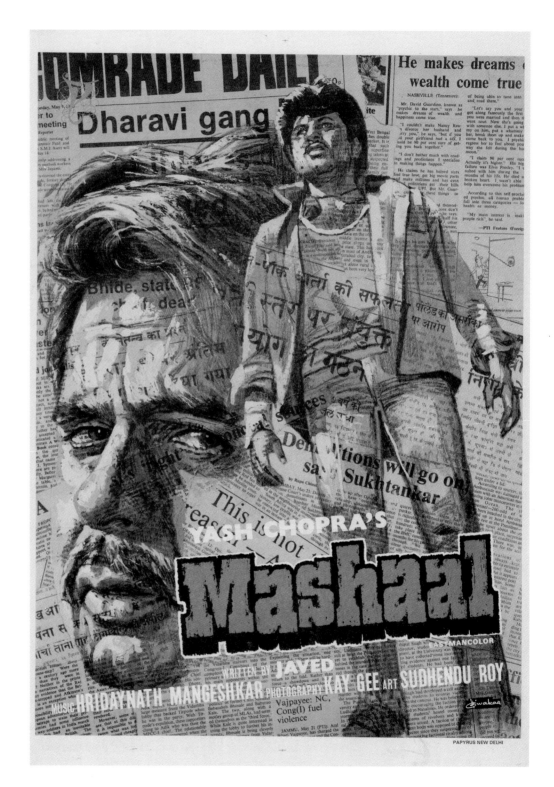

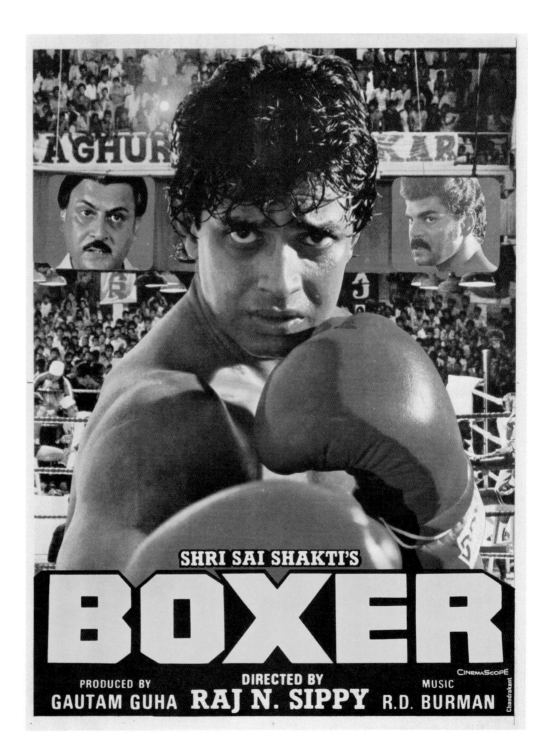

BOXER
1984
HINDI – COLOUR
FILM GENRE **ACTION DRAMA**
DIRECTOR **RAJ N. SIPPY**
PRODUCER **GAUTAM GUHA**
PRODUCTION **SHRI SAI SHAKTI**
CAST **TANUJA,**
MITHUN CHAKRABORTY,
RATI AGNIHOTRI
MUSIC **R.D. BURMAN**
POSTER ARTIST **CHANDRAKANT**
POSTER SIZE **100.6** X **74.8 CM**

SOHNI MAHIWAL
1984
HINDI – COLOUR
FILM GENRE **DRAMA**
DIRECTOR **UMESH MEHRA**
PRODUCER **F.C. MEHRA**
PRODUCTION **EAGLE FILMS**
CAST **SUNNY DEOL, TANUJA, POONAM DHILLON,**
MUSIC **ANNU MALIK**
LYRICS **ANAND BAKSHI**
POSTER ARTIST **PRABHAKAR, J.P. SINGAL**
POSTER PRINTER **J.P. MEHTA & SONS, BOMBAY**
POSTER SIZE **100.5 X 74.1 CM**

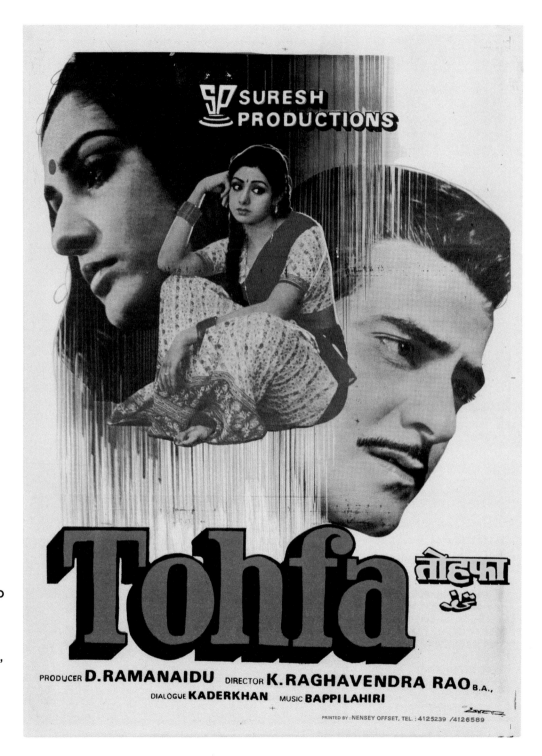

TOHFA
1984
HINDI – COLOUR
FILM GENRE **SOCIAL**
DIRECTOR **K. RAGHAVENDRA RAO**
PRODUCER **D. RAMA NAIDU**
PRODUCTION **SURESH PRODUCTIONS**
CAST **JEETENDRA, SRIDEVI, JAYAPRADA, KADER KHAN, SHAKTI KAPOOR**
MUSIC **BHAPPI LAHIRI**
LYRICS **INDEEVAR**
POSTER PRINTER **NENSEY OFFSET PVT. LTD., BOMBAY**
POSTER SIZE **101.2 X 73.4 CM**

**MAIN KHILONA
NAHIN**
1985
HINDI – COLOUR
FILM GENRE **SOCIAL**
DIRECTOR **QAMAR NARVI**
PRODUCER **MOHAN T. GEHANI**
PRODUCTION **DEVI FILMS**
CAST **KAJAL KIRAN,
PUNEET ISSAR,
RAZA MURAD**
MUSIC **ANWAR USMAN**
LYRICS **KHALID-JALAL JHANSVI**
POSTER ARTIST **SELBEST VIKAR**
POSTER PRINTER **NEW APSARA
ARTS, BOMBAY**
POSTER SIZE **99** X **71.4 CM**

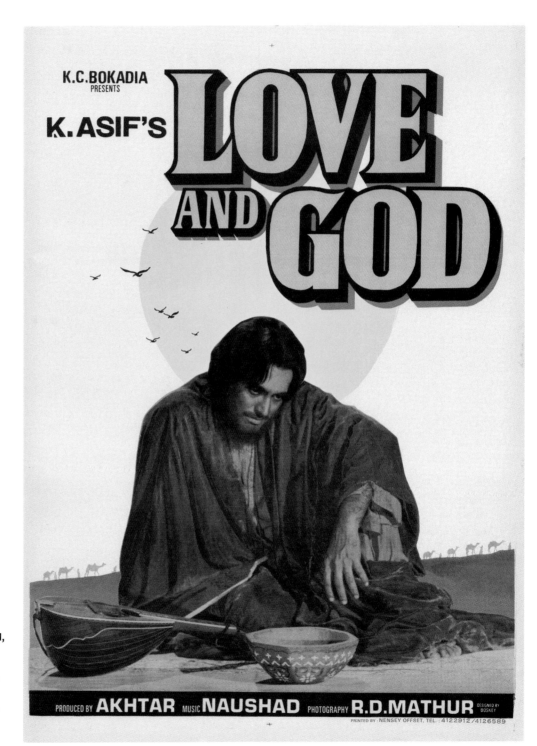

LOVE AND GOD
1986
URDU – COLOUR
FILM GENRE **COSTUME DRAMA**
DIRECTOR **K. ASIF**
PRODUCER **K.C. BOKADIA,**
AKHTAR ASIF
PRODUCTION **K.C. BOKADIA**
CAST **SANJEEV KUMAR, PRAN,**
NIMMI, SIMI GAREWAL,
MUSIC **NAUSHAD**
LYRICS **KUMAR BARABANKVI,**
ASAD BHOPALI
POSTER ARTIST **BOSKEY**
POSTER PRINTER **NENSEY OFFSET**
PVT. LTD., BOMBAY
POSTER SIZE **101.5 X 73.3 CM**

UTTAR DAKSHIN

1987
HINDI – COLOUR
FILM GENRE **SOCIAL**
DIRECTOR **PRABHAT KHANNA**
PRODUCER **ASHOK KHANNA**
PRODUCTION **DEEPALI ARTS**
CAST **JACKIE SHROFF,**
RAJNIKANT,
MADHURI DIXIT,
ANUPAM KHER
MUSIC **LAXMIKANT PYARELAL**
LYRICS **ANAND BAKSHI**
POSTER ARTIST **SINGHAL**
POSTER PRINTER **DYANSAGAR**
LITHO PRESS, BOMBAY
POSTER SIZE **100.5 × 74.7 CM**

MR INDIA
1987
HINDI – COLOUR
FILM GENRE **COMEDY**
DIRECTOR **SHEKHAR KAPOOR**
PRODUCER **BONEY KAPOOR**
PRODUCTION **NARSIMHA**
ENTERTAINMENTS
CAST **ANIL KAPOOR, SRIDEVI,**
AMRISH PURI,
ASHOK KUMAR
MUSIC **LAXMIKANT PYARELAL**
LYRICS **JAVED AKHTAR**
POSTER ARTIST **SINGHAL**
POSTER PRINTER **DNYANSAGAR**
LITHO PRESS, BOMBAY
POSTER SIZE **100.8** X **74.5 CM**

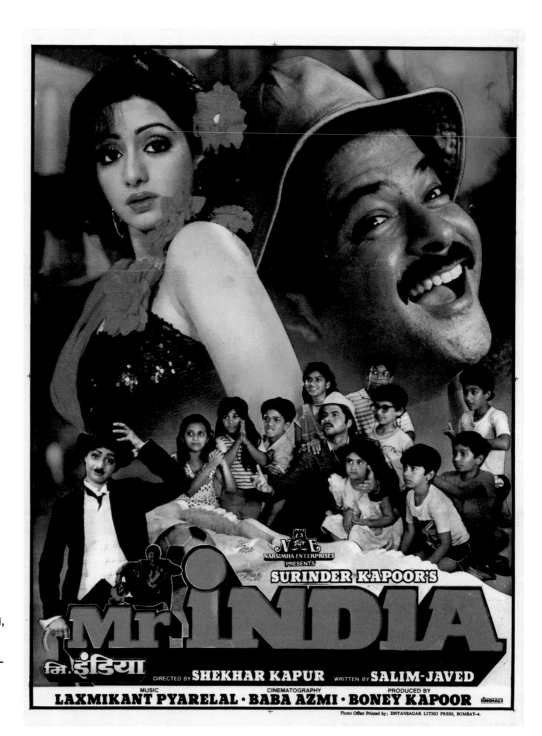

MR INDIA
1987
HINDI – COLOUR
FILM GENRE **COMEDY**
DIRECTOR **SHEKHAR KAPOOR**
PRODUCER **BONEY KAPOOR**
PRODUCTION **NARSIMHA ENTERTAINMENTS**
CAST **ANIL KAPOOR, SRIDEVI, AMRISH PURI, ASHOK KUMAR**
MUSIC **LAXMIKANT PYARELAL**
LYRICS **JAVED AKHTAR**
POSTER ARTIST **SINGHAL**
POSTER PRINTER **NENSEY OFFSET PVT. LTD., BOMBAY**
POSTER SIZE **101.2 X 73.6 CM**

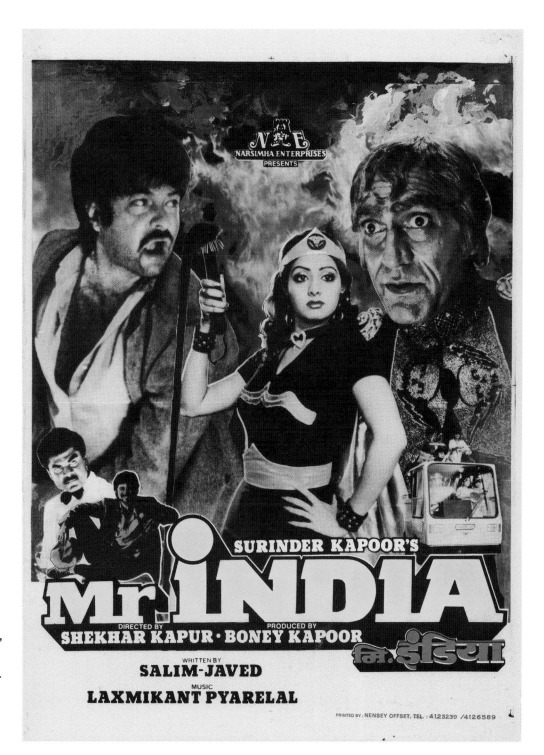

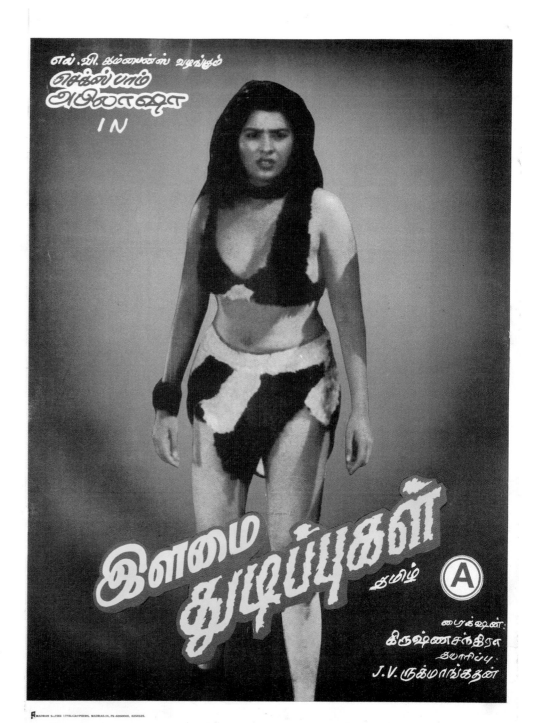

ILAMAI THUDIPPUGAL

1988
TELUGU (DUBBED IN TAMIL) – COLOUR
FILM GENRE **ADULT SEX**
DIRECTOR **J.V. RUKMANGADAN**
PRODUCER **KRISHNA CHANDRA**
PRODUCTION **L.V. RAMANAN FILMS**
CAST **ABHILASHA, KAPIL DEV**
MUSIC **RAJ KOTTI**
POSTER ARTIST **S. DAVOOD**
POSTER PRINTER **MADRAS SAFIRE LITHOGRAPHERS, MADRAS**
POSTER SIZE **98.6 X 70.5 CM**

JAWANI KI PYAAS
1988
MALAYALAM (DUBBED IN HINDI) – COLOUR
FILM GENRE **ADULT SEX**
DIRECTOR **N. SHANKARAN NAIR**
PRODUCER **BABUBHAI H. SHAH**
PRODUCTION **HANSA PICTURES**
CAST **ANURADHA, SOMAN**
MUSIC **JOI KISHEN**
LYRICS **MADHUKAR**
POSTER ARTIST **KETHA ARTS**
POSTER PRINTER **ADVANCE LITHOGRAPHERS, BOMBAY**
POSTER SIZE **102 X 76 CM**

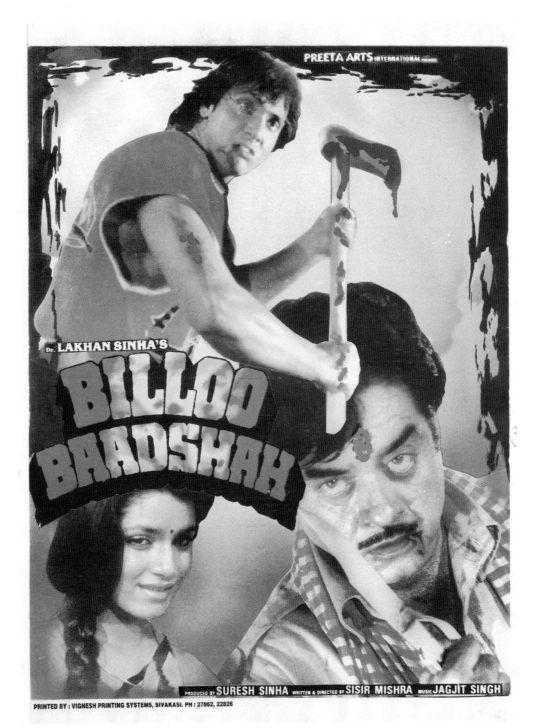

**BILLOO
BAADSHAH**
1989
HINDI – COLOUR
FILM GENRE **ACTION**
DIRECTOR **SISIR MISHRA**
PRODUCER **SURESH SINHA**
PRODUCTION **PREETA ARTS
INTERNATIONAL**
CAST **SHATRUGHAN SINHA,
ANITA RAJ, GOVINDA,
NEELAM, KADER KHAN**
MUSIC **JAGJIT SINGH**
POSTER ARTIST **LOOMBA ARTS**
POSTER PRINTER **VIGNESH
PRINTING SYSTEMS,
SIVAKASI**
POSTER SIZE **95.6** X **70.4 CM**

221

CHANDNI

1989
HINDI – COLOUR
FILM GENRE **ROMANCE**
DIRECTOR **YASH CHOPRA**
PRODUCER **YASH CHOPRA**
PRODUCTION **YASH RAJ FILMS**
CAST **VINOD KHANNA,
RISHI KAPOOR, SRIDEVI,
WAHEEDA REHMAN**
MUSIC **SHIV HARI**
LYRICS **ANAND BAKSHI**
POSTER ARTIST **YASHAWANT**
POSTER PRINTER **SUPER ART
PRINTERS**
POSTER SIZE **101.7 X 75.8 CM**

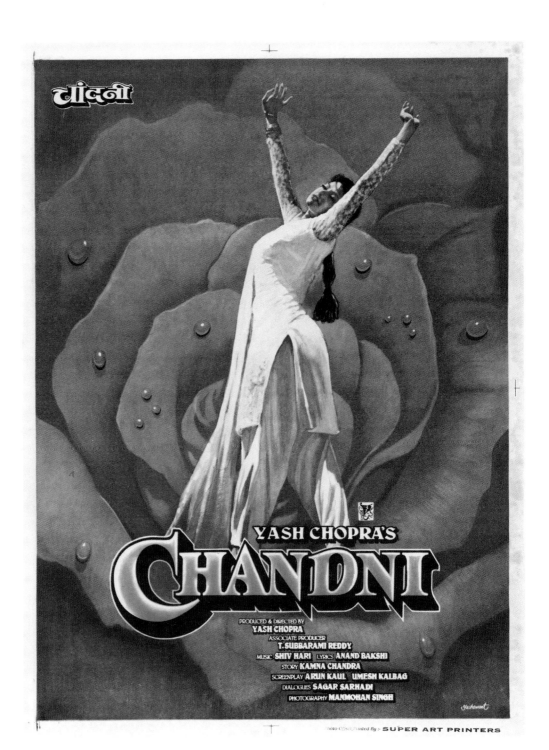

KACHCHI UMAR MEIN
1998
MALAYALAM (DUBBED IN HINDI) – COLOUR
FILM GENRE **ADULT SEX**
DIRECTOR **PREM SAGAR**
PRODUCER **DINESH SALGIA**
PRODUCTION **SALGIA & CO.**
CAST **SHARDA, HEMA, USMAN, PADMA MANMOHAN,**
MUSIC **RAJ BHASKAR**
POSTER SIZE **96.5** X **70.6 CM**

LOVE
MALAYALAM (DUBBED IN HINDI) – COLOUR
FILM GENRE **ADULT SEX**
DIRECTOR **SA. J. JAN**
CAST **PRADEEPA**
POSTER PRINTER **EMPIRE CINE PROCESS**
POSTER SIZE **96.4 X 70.7 CM**

**SHAADI SE PEHLE
AUR SHAADI KE
BAAD**
1989
**TAMIL (DUBBED IN
HINDI) – COLOUR**
FILM GENRE **ADULT SEX**
DIRECTOR **KOMMINENI**
PRODUCER **J.V. RUKMANGADAN**
PRODUCTION **LEO INTERNATIONAL**
MUSIC **JOY JAIKISHAN**
POSTER ARTIST **S. DAVOOD**
POSTER PRINTER **JOTHI FINE ARTS,
SIVAKASI**
POSTER SIZE **102.6 X 75.6 CM**

225

PUNNAMI RATRI
MALAYALUM (DUBBED IN
TELUGU) – COLOUR
FILM GENRE **ADULT HORROR**
DIRECTOR **S.R. RAJAN**
PRODUCER **M. SIVAPRASAD,**
P. SAI JITESH
PRODUCTION **SRI VENKAT SAI**
DURGA ARTS
CAST **CHARANRAJ, MOHINI**
POSTER PRINTER **MADRAS SAFIRE**
LITHOGRAPHERS, MADRAS
POSTER SIZE **98.5 X 70.6 CM**

PUNNAMI RATRI
MALAYALUM (DUBBED IN TELUGU) – COLOUR
FILM GENRE **ADULT HORROR**
DIRECTOR **S.R. RAJAN**
PRODUCER **M. SIVAPRASAD,
P. SAI JITESH**
PRODUCTION **SRI VENKAT SAI
DURGA ARTS**
CAST **CHARANRAJ, MOHINI**
POSTER PRINTER **MADRAS SAFIRE
LITHOGRAPHERS, MADRAS**
POSTER ARTIST **NEETHI**
POSTER SIZE **98.5** X **70.5 CM**

S. S. PRINTERS

SALEM VISHNU
1990
TAMIL – COLOUR
FILM GENRE **DRAMA**
DIRECTOR **THYAGARAJAN**
PRODUCER **THYAGARAJAN**
PRODUCTION **LAKSHMI SHANTHI MOVIES**
CAST **THYAGARAJAN, RUPINI, SARATKUMAR, RATHISH, VAISHAVI**
MUSIC **SANGEETHARAJAN**
LYRICS **VAIRAMUTHU VALI, KENNADAI, THYAGARAJAN,**
POSTER ARTIST **N.B. GURUSWAMY**
POSTER PRINTER **S.S. PRINTERS**
POSTER SIZE **97.4** X **71 CM**

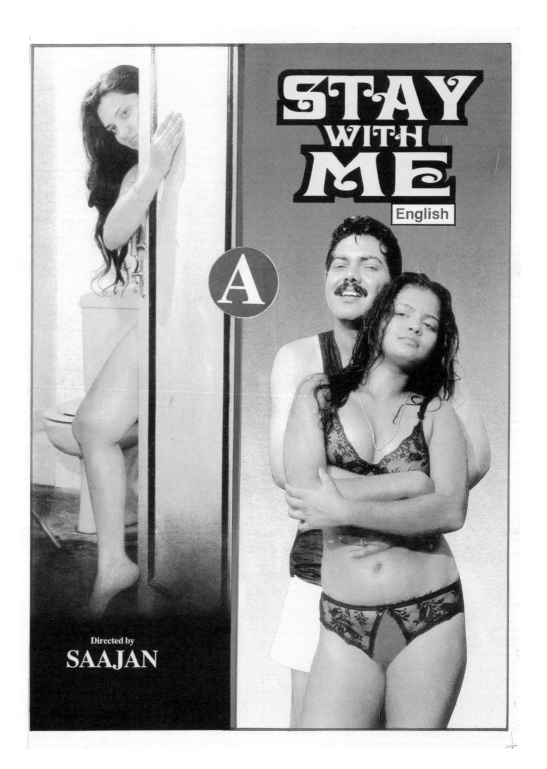

STAY WITH ME
MALAYALAM (DUBBED IN
HINDI) – COLOUR
FILM GENRE **ADULT SEX**
DIRECTOR **SAAJAN**
POSTER SIZE **98.5** X **70.5 CM**

AAJ KA ARJUN
1990
HINDI – COLOUR
FILM GENRE **ACTION**
DIRECTOR **K.C. BOKADIA**
PRODUCER **K.C. BOKADIA**
PRODUCTION **B.M.B. FILMS**
CAST **AMITABH BACHCHAN,
JAYAPRADA, KIRAN KUMAR,
AMRISH PURI,
SURESH OBEROI**
MUSIC **BAPPI LAHIRI**
LYRICS **ANJAAN**
POSTER PRINTER **RELIANCE
PROCESSORS, SIVAKASI**
POSTER SIZE **97.3 X 70.2 CM**

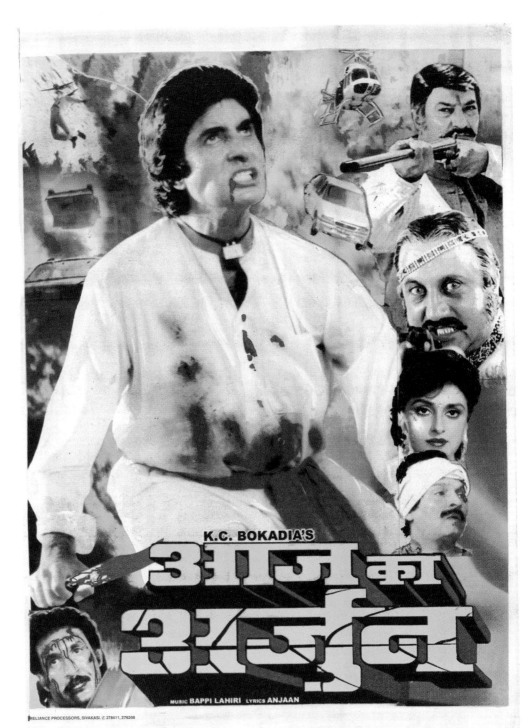

230

AGNI POOKKAL
1990
KANADA (DUBBED IN
TAMIL) – COLOUR
FILM GENRE **ADULT SEX**
DIRECTOR **SUNIL KUMAR DESAI**
PRODUCER **SUNIL KUMAR DESAI**
PRODUCTION **RACHANNA
MOTION PICTURES
PRODUCERS**
CAST **ABHILASHA, ANJALI,
AMBRISH, VANITA BASU**
MUSIC **GUNASINGH**
POSTER ARTIST **H.C. VENU**
POSTER PRINTER **MADRAS SAFIRE
LITHOGRAPHERS, MADRAS**
POSTER SIZE **98.8** X **70.5 CM**

AJOOBA

1991
HINDI – COLOUR
FILM GENRE FANTASY
DIRECTOR SHASHI KAPOOR
PRODUCER SHASHI KAPOOR
CAST AMITABH BACHCHAN,
DIMPLE KAPADIA,
SHASHI KAPOOR,
SHAMMI KAPOOR,
AMRISH PURI,
RISHI KAPOOR, SONAM,
MUSIC LAXMIKANT PYARELAL
LYRICS ANAND BAKSHI
POSTER ARTIST RAVI
POSTER PRINTER DNYANSAGAR
LITHO PRESS, BOMBAY
POSTER SIZE 99.5 X 74.8 CM

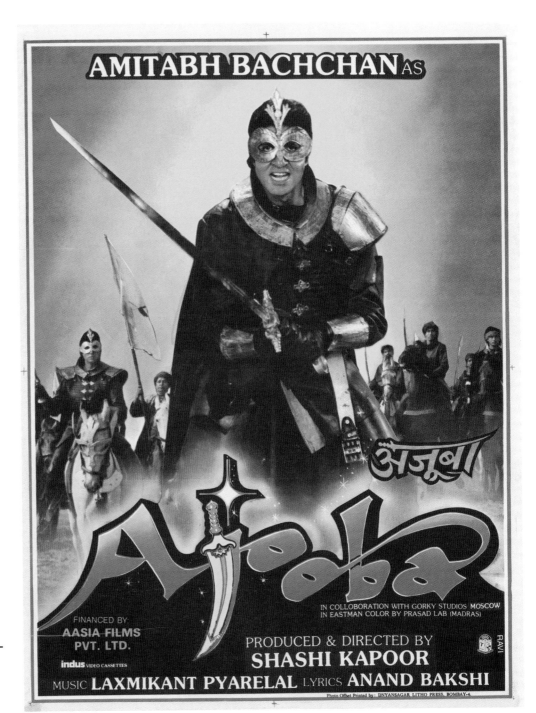

AKAYLA
1991
HINDI – COLOUR
FILM GENRE **ACTION**
DIRECTOR **RAMESH SIPPY**
PRODUCER **MUSHIR RIAZ**
PRODUCTION **M.R. PRODUCTIONS PVT. LTD.**
CAST **AMITABH BACHCHAN, JACKIE SHROFF, MEENAKSHI SHESHADRI, AMRITA SINGH, SHASHI KAPOOR**
MUSIC **LAXMIKANT PYARELAL**
LYRICS **ANAND BAKSHI**
POSTER ARTIST **YASHAWANT**
POSTER PRINTER **GLAMOUR PHOTO LAB PVT. LTD., BOMBAY**
POSTER SIZE **100** X **75 CM**

233

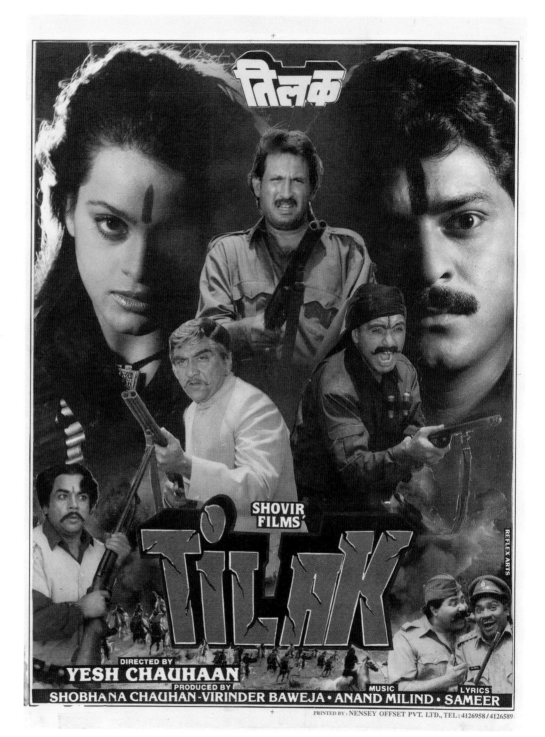

TILAK
1992
HINDI – COLOUR
FILM GENRE **SOCIAL**
DIRECTOR **YASH CHAUHAN**
PRODUCER **SHOBHANA**
CHAUHAN,
VIRINDER BAWEJA
PRODUCTION **SHOVIR FILMS**
CAST **SIDDHARTH,**
SHILPA SHIRODKAR,
PARESH RAWAL,
GOGA KAPOOR
MUSIC **ANAND MILIND**
LYRICS **SAMEER**
POSTER ARTIST **REFLEX ARTS**
POSTER PRINTER **NENSEY OFFSET**
PVT. LTD., BOMBAY
POSTER SIZE **101 X 73.4 CM**

POLICEWALA
1993
HINDI – COLOUR
FILM GENRE **ACTION**
DIRECTOR **SIKANDAR BHARTI**
PRODUCER **SANDEEP KUMAR**
PRODUCTION **SUNDEEP FILMS**
CAST **CHUNKEY PANDEY,
KIRAN KUMAR,
SHAKTI KAPOOR, SONAM**
MUSIC **BAPPI LAHIRI**
LYRICS **ANJAAN,
SIKANDAR BHARTI**
POSTER ARTIST **AMARNATH
STUDIO K.B.**
POSTER PRINTER **NENSEY OFFSET
PVT. LTD., BOMBAY**
POSTER SIZE **100.9 X 73 CM**

RANG

1993
HINDI – COLOUR
FILM GENRE **SOCIAL**
DIRECTOR **TALAT JANI**
PRODUCER **MANSOOR AHMED SIDDIQUI**
PRODUCTION **ANAS FILMS**
CAST **JEETENDRA, AMRITA SINGH, KAMAL SADANAH, BINDU, AYESHA JHULKA, KADER KHAN**
MUSIC **NADEEM-SHRAVAN**
LYRICS **SAMEER, SURINDER SAATHI**
POSTER ARTIST **CREATIVE HYD.**
POSTER PRINTER **SURESH OFFSET PRINTERS, HYDERABAD**
POSTER SIZE **96.4 X 69.9 CM**

BANDIT QUEEN
1994
HINDI – COLOUR
FILM GENRE **SOCIAL**
DIRECTOR **SHEKAR KAPUR**
PRODUCER **S.S. BEDI**
PRODUCTION **KALEIDOSCOPE (INDIA) – CHANNEL FOUR FILMS (LONDON)**
CAST **SEEMA BISWAS, NIRMAL PANDEY, MANOJ BAJPAI,**
MUSIC **NUSRAT FATEH ALI KHAN, M. ARSHAD**
POSTER ARTIST **MANJEET BAWA**
POSTER PRINTER **AJANTA OFFSET, DELHI**
POSTER SIZE **94.9 X 70 CM**

MADAM X

1994
HINDI – COLOUR
FILM GENRE **CRIME**
DIRECTOR **DEEPAK SHIVDASANI**
PRODUCER **R.S. THAKUR**
PRODUCTION **NISHITA PRODUCTIONS**
CAST **REKHA, MOHSIN KHAN, PARIKSHIT SAHNI**
MUSIC **ANU MALIK**
LYRICS **HASRAT JAIPURI, SAMEER**
POSTER ARTIST **BOSKEY & PRABHU**
POSTER PRINTER **GLAMOUR PHOTOLAB PVT. LTD., BOMBAY**
POSTER SIZE **99 X 73.6 CM**

AUZAAR

1997
HINDI – COLOUR
FILM GENRE **ACTION**
DIRECTOR **SOHAIL KHAN**
PRODUCER **RAMESH TAURANI,**
KUMAR TAURANI
PRODUCTION **TIPS FILMS PVT. LTD.**
CAST **SALMAN KHAN,**
SANJAY KAPOOR,
SHILPA SHETTY
MUSIC **ANU MALIK**
LYRICS **RAHAT INDORI,**
QATEEL SHIFAI, ILA ARUN,
ANU MALIK
POSTER ARTIST **RAHUL AND**
HIMANSHU NANDA –
H.R. ENTERPRISES
POSTER PRINTER **VIGNESH PRINTING**
SYSTEMS, SIVAKASI
POSTER SIZE **96.4** X **138.6 CM** 2 SHEET

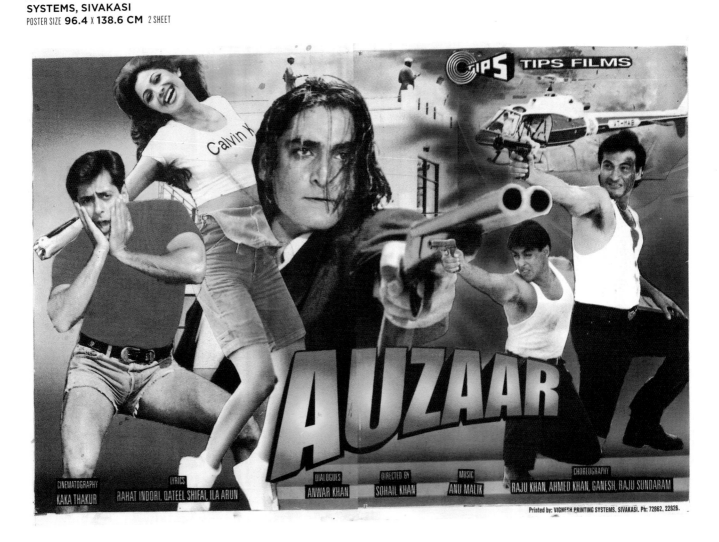

DADA
1999
HINDI – COLOUR
FILM GENRE **ACTION**
DIRECTOR **T.L.V. PRASAD**
PRODUCER **MAHENDRA DHARIWAL**
PRODUCTION **MAKE WELL FILMS**
CAST **MITHUN CHAKRABORTY,
DILIP TAHIL, RAZA MURAD**
MUSIC **GHULAM ALI**
LYRICS **NAWAB ARZOO AND
NAVDEEP BIKANERI**
POSTER ARTIST **AYOUB'S**
POSTER PRINTER **NENSEY OFFSET
PVT. LTD., BOMBAY**
POSTER SIZE **95.7 × 70.4 CM**

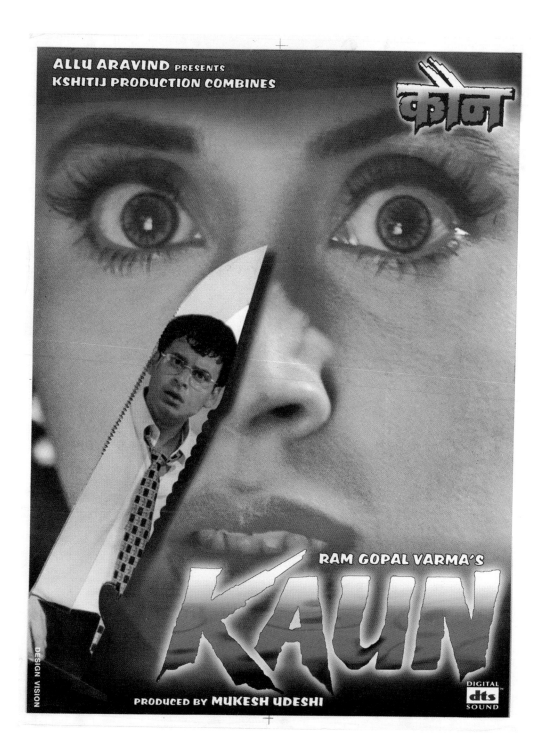

KAUN
1999
HINDI – COLOUR
FILM GENRE **CRIME DRAMA**
DIRECTOR **RAM GOPAL VARMA**
PRODUCER **MUKESH UDESHI**
PRODUCTION **KSHITIJ**
PRODUCTION COMBINES
CAST **URMILA MATONDKAR,
MANOJ BAJPAI,
SUSHANT KUMAR**
MUSIC **SANDEEP CHOWTHA**
LYRICS **NITIN RAIKWAR**
POSTER ARTIST **DESIGN VISION**
POSTER PRINTER **GLAMOUR,
BOMBAY**
POSTER SIZE **96.4** X **71.8 CM**

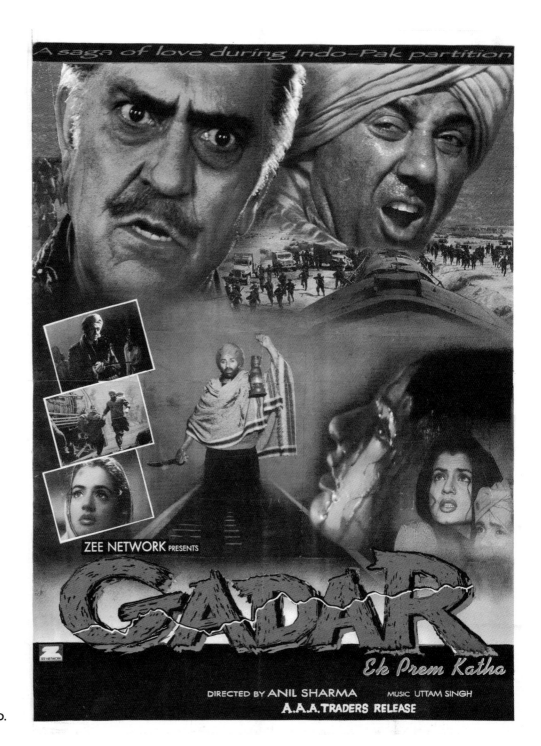

GADAR
2001
HINDI – COLOUR
FILM GENRE **SOCIAL**
DIRECTOR **ANIL SHARMA**
PRODUCER **NITIN KENI**
PRODUCTION **ZEE TELEFILMS**
CAST **SUNNY DEOL,**
AMISHA PATEL,
AMRISH PURI
MUSIC **UTTAM SINGH**
LYRICS **ANAND BAKSHI**
POSTER ARTIST **J.P. SINGHAL**
POSTER PRINTER **FUNTECH PVT. LTD.**
POSTER SIZE **96.5** X **70.6 CM**

KAAMA
2001
HINDI (DUBBED IN TELUGU)
– COLOUR
FILM GENRE **ADULT SEX**
DIRECTOR **K. JAGDISHWAR REDDY**
PRODUCER **K. JAGDISHWAR**
REDDY
PRODUCTION **S & S PRODUCTION**
CAST **KAMLESH, SUSHMITA RAI,**
KASHMIRA SHAH,
MUSIC **RAM**
LYRICS **MOHAMMED**
POSTER ARTIST **BHASKAR,**
SPECTRUM GRAPHICS
POSTER PRINTER **MADRAS SAFIRE,**
MADRAS
POSTER SIZE **98.7 X 78.6 CM**

243

KAANTE
2002
HINDI – COLOUR
FILM GENRE **CRIME**
DIRECTOR **SANJAY GUPTA**
PRODUCER **PRITISH NANDY
COMMUNICATION LTD.**
PRODUCTION **WHITE FEATHER
FILMS – FILM CLUB LTD.**
CAST **AMITABH BACHCHAN,
SANJAY DUTT,
KUMAR GAURAV,
SUNIL SHETTY, LUCKY ALI**
MUSIC **ANAND RAJ ANAND,
VISHAL, SHEKHAR,
LUCKY ALI**
POSTER ARTIST **IN HOUSE (P.N.C)**
POSTER PRINTER **GLAMOUR,
BOMBAY**
POSTER SIZE **96 X 67 CM**

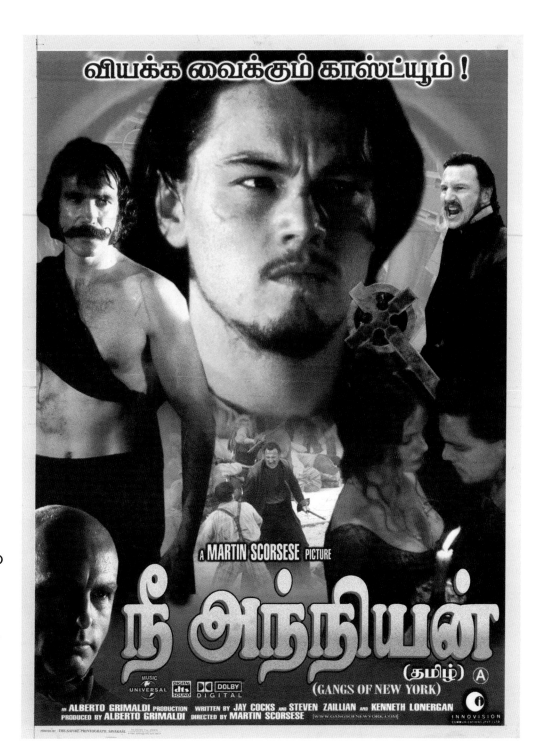

NEE ANNIYAN
2002
ENGLISH (DUBBED IN TAMIL)
– COLOUR
FILM GENRE **DRAMA**
DIRECTOR **MARTIN SCORSESE**
PRODUCER **ALBERTO GRIMALDI**
PRODUCTION **INNOVISION
COMMUNICATIONS PVT. LTD.
ALBERTO GRIMALDI**
CAST **LIAM NEESON,
LEONARDO DI CAPRIO,
DANIEL DAY-LEWIS,
CAMERON DIAZ**
POSTER PRINTER **THE SAFIRE
PRINTOGRAPH, SIVAKASI**
POSTER SIZE **96.9** X **70.9 CM**

245

CHEHRAA
2004
HINDI – COLOUR
FILM GENRE **DRAMA**
DIRECTOR **SAURABH SHUKLA**
PRODUCER **DILKHUSH DOSHI**
PRODUCTION **KHAWAISH MOVIES**
CAST **BIPASHA BASU,**
DINO MOREA,
PREETI JHANGIANI,
IRRFAN KHAN
MUSIC **ANU MALIK**
POSTER ARTIST **STUDIO LINK**
POSTER PRINTER **BHARAT LITHO**
PRESS, MUMBAI
POSTER SIZE **99 X 70.3 CM**

CHEHRAA
2004
HINDI – COLOUR
FILM GENRE **DRAMA**
DIRECTOR **SAURABH SHUKLA**
PRODUCER **DILKHUSH DOSHI**
PRODUCTION **KHAWAISH MOVIES**
CAST **BIPASHA BASU,
DINO MOREA,
PREETI JHANGIANI,
IRRFAN KHAN**
MUSIC **ANU MALIK**
POSTER ARTIST **MOIE**
POSTER PRINTER **BHARAT LITHO
PRESS, MUMBAI**
POSTER SIZE **76.7 X 51.2 CM**

247

gift
vouchers

unattended
bags

GLOSSARY

ZIMBO AND SON MEET THE GIRL WITH A GUN

BOMBAIWALI – Woman from Bombay
DESHI – Indian, home-grown, local
HANUMAN – Monkey God of Hindu religion
HUNTERWALI – Hunter woman – the Islamic wali
meaning friend or protector
JUNGLEE – Pl. Junglo, originally uncivilized jungle or
wilderness dweller, later meaning metamorphosed
into an individual of dangerous sexual energy
and ultra-modernity
KALIYUG – Age in Hindu astrology
QAWWALI – Devotional music of the Sufis originating
from 8th Century Persia and performed throughout what
is now India and Pakistan.
TOPIS – A hard white hat worn as protection against
the sun
VIRANGANA – Warrior woman

NOTES ON THE EPIDEMIOLOGY OF ALLURE

FILMI – Indian popular music as written and performed
for Indian cinema and sold commercially
JHANKI – Display stand
MOFUSSIL – Provincial areas and outlying rural districts
PANCHAYAT – Indian political system that grouped five
villages. Each had appointed tasks and responsibilities
TANUKA – Administrative division in India below
a district

PICTURE LIVES

ACHARIS – An artisanal Tamil caste
BEEDI – Tobacco rolled in tobacco leaf to make a
rudimentary cigarette
BHARATHANATYAM DRESS – Traditional costume worn
to perform Southern Indian classical dance form
Bharathanatyam
MUDRA – Ritual hand gesture

THE POSTER ON THE BEDROOM WALL

HALVA – Sweet dish made from ground sesame seeds,
fruit or vegetables

THE PAIN OF LOVE AND THE LOVE OF PAIN

BELLIES/BELLEYS – Etymology unknown, but perhaps
denoting "ballet" shoes
BRAHMO – Member of the Brahmo Samaj, an Indian
theistic organisation
GHULAM – Servant
GHULAMI – Female servant
LEHNGA – Bridal or dance attire
MUJRA – Performance by a tawaif
NAWABI – Relating to Muslim equivalent of a
Maharajah, a senior official
SINDUR – Vermilion powder credited with love
inducing powers
TAWAIF – Professional dancing girl

BIOGRAPHIES

SARA DICKEY

Sara Dickey is Professor of Anthropology at Bowdoin College in the U.S. Her research has examined film-watching, fan clubs and politics, domestic service, and class identities and relations in southern India, as well as poverty in the U.S. Her publications include: *Cinema and the Urban Poor in South India* (Cambridge, 1993) and the co-edited volume, *Home and Hegemony: Domestic Service and Identity Politics in South and Southeast Asia* (Michigan, 2000). She has written articles on cinema and politics in the *Journal of Asian Studies,* on the anthropological study of media in *International Social Science Journal,* and on domestic service relationships in *American Ethnologist,* as well as essays on fan clubs and on class mobility in edited volumes, such as Christopher Pinney and Rachel Dwyer's *Pleasure and the Nation: The History, Politics and Consumption of Popular Culture in India* (Oxford, 2001) and Diane P. Mines and Sarah Lamb's *Everyday Life in South Asia* (Indiana, 2002).

EMILY KING

Emily King is a writer and curator specialising in graphic design. She is the design editor of *Frieze* magazine and editor-at-large of the Berlin-based publication *032C.* Her books include *Movie Poster* (Mitchell Beazley, 2003) and the edited monograph, *Designed by Peter Saville* (Frieze, 2003). She has curated a number of graphic design exhibitions including, *The Book Corner* (British Council, 2002) and the graphic design section of the Design Museum's *2003 European Design Show.* She is currently working on a biography of the seminal designer Robert Brownjohn.

M.S.S. PANDIAN

M.S.S. Pandian is currently a Visiting Fellow of the Sarai Programme at the Centre for the Study of Developing Societies, Delhi. Prior to that he was on the faculty of the Centre for Studies in Social Sciences, Kolkatta, and the Madras Institute of Development Studies, Chennai, and has taught at the University of Wisconsin, Madison, and George Washington University, Washington DC. He is also on the Subaltern Studies Editorial Collective and the South Asia Regional Advisory Panel of the Social Science Research Council, New York. His publications include, *The Image Trap: M.G. Ramachandran in Film and Politics* (New Delhi: Sage Publications, 1992).

CHRISTOPHER PINNEY

After completing his doctoral studies on Indian industrial labour at the London School of Economics, Christopher Pinney taught at the School of Oriental and African Studies and has held visiting positions at the Australian National University and the University of Chicago and University of Cape Town. He is currently Professor of Anthropology and Visual Culture at University College London. His recent publications include the monographs, *Camera Indica: The Social Life of Indian Photographs* (Reaktion, 1997); *Photos of the Gods: The Printed Image and Political Struggle in India* (Reaktion, 2004) and the co-edited volumes, *Beyond Aesthetics: Art and the Technologies of Enchantment* (Berg, 2001); *Pleasure and The Nation: The History, Politics and Consumption of Public Culture in India* (Oxford, 2001) and *Photography's Other Histories* (Duke, 2003).

ROSIE THOMAS

Rosie Thomas is Reader in Art and Media Practice at the University of Westminster where she is Director of the Centre for Research and Education in Art and Media (CREAM). Trained as a social anthropologist, she did fieldwork in the Bombay film industry in the early 1980s and published pioneering articles on Indian cinema in *Screen, Quarterly Review of Film and Video* in the late 1980s, as well as contributing essays to various edited collections, including Carol Breckenridge's *Consuming Modernity* (University of Minnesota Press, 1995). Throughout the 1990s she also built a track record as an independent television producer, making more than thirty programmes for Channel Four Television, ranging from two series of, *On the Other Hand,* an innovative multi-cultural discussion program hosted by Shekhar Kapur, to arts programmes, documentaries and current affairs investigations for C4's prestigious *Dispatches* strand. Her current research interests lie in documentary theory and practice, and Indian cinema history.

PATRICIA UBEROI

Patricia Uberoi was born in Canberra, Australia, but has lived and worked in India for over 30 years. She is presently Professor, Social Change and Development, at the Institute of Economic Growth, Delhi, and concurrently Honorary Director, Institute of Chinese Studies (Centre for the Study of Developing Societies), Delhi. She has published widely on aspects of family, kinship, sexuality, popular culture and anthropological history in reference to both India and China. Her publications include the popular and well-regarded text, *Family, Kinship and Marriage in India* (Oxford University Press, 1993) and *Social Reform, Sexuality and The State* (Sage Publications, 1996). She has recently completed a book entitled *Dharma and Desire: Gender and Family in Indian Popular Culture*, which draws on several different genres of Indian popular culture – calendar art, popular films, and women's magazines – for sociological insights into contemporary questions of family and gender. Along with her husband, J.P.S. Uberoi, she has been collecting Indian calendar art for the past three decades, and has curated several exhibitions of Indian calendar art in India and abroad.

OPEN EDITIONS

Founded in London in 1992, Open Editions operates as an independent agency for the dissemination and promotion of innovative critical and artistic dialogue. Projects are realised by engaging a network of creative partnerships, between artists, writers, designers and industrialists. An ethos of exploration and collaboration underpins this publishing: theory and practice are combined and artists and writers exchange ideas on a common platform. Titles include, *Here, There, Elsewhere: Dialogues on Location and Mobility*, edited by David Blamey (2002). A new guest edited critical series titled *Occasional Table* is launched in 2006.

DAVID BLAMEY

David Blamey is an artist. He teaches at the Royal College of Art, where he is currently Director of the Buryport Critical Forum and is also a Senior Lecturer in Fine Art at The Surrey Institute of Art & Design. His first edited book, *Here, There, Elsewhere: Dialogues on Location and Mobility* was published by Open Editions in 2002 and his other critical work has been published in Circa (2001–2003) and The George Hanson Critical Forum (RCA, 2004). His recent and forthcoming exhibitions include: *David Blamey*, Glassbox, Paris (2006), *La-La-Land*, Project Gallery, Dublin (2005); *Open (The Big Nothing)*, Arcadia University Gallery, Philladelphia (2004); *Tonight*, Studio Voltaire, London (2004); *Ways of Saying*, Loman Street Studio, London (2003); *Happy Outsiders*, Zachéta Museum, Warsaw (2002) and *Are We There Yet?*, Glassbox, Paris (2001).

ROBERT D'SOUZA

Robert D'Souza is an artist and designer. He teaches in the School of Media, Art & Design at the University of Luton, where he is currently the Director of the Centre For Diversity in Cultural Production in the Research Institute for Media Art & Design. His research interests and practice lie in cross-cultural interactions and the overlapping areas of visual art, cultural study and social science.

GRAPHIC THOUGHT FACILITY

Graphic Thought Facility is a graphic design consultancy, working for public and private clients on a variety of national and international projects. The studio produces both print and three-dimensional graphics for publishing, marketing, press, exhibition, events, product development and brand applications. Clients include: The Design Museum, Science Museum, Habitat, Shakespeare's Globe, Carnegie Museum of Art and the Frieze Art Fair.

BIBLIOGRAPHY

ROSIE THOMAS

Chakravarty, Sumita, *National Identity in Indian Popular Cinema: 1947–1987*, Austin: University of Texas Press, 1993

Creed, Barbara *Me Tarzan: You Jane! – A Case of Mistaken Identity in Paradise*, Continuum Vol 1, No 1, 1987

Essoe, Gabe *Tarzan of the Movies*, New York: Citadel Press, 1968

Gandhy, Behroze and Thomas, Rosie, *Three Indian Film Stars* in Christine Gledhill (Ed.), Stardom: Industry of Desire, London: Routledge, 1991

Hansen, Kathryn, *Grounds for Play: The Nautanki Theatre of North India*, Berkeley: University of California Press, 1992

Nandy, Ashis, *At the Edge of Psychology*, New Delhi: Oxford University Press, 1980

Pinney, Christopher, *Moral Topophilia: The Significations of Landscape in Indian Oleographs* in Hirsch, E and O'Hanlon, M (Eds.), The Anthrolopology of Landscape, Clarendon Press, 1985

Thomas, Rosie, *Indian Cinema: Pleasures and Popularity*, Screen, Vol 26, nos 3–4, 1985

Thomas, Rosie, *Not Quite (Pearl) White* (in press) in Raminder Kaur and Ajay Sinha (Eds.), Bollyworld: Indian Cinema Through a Transnational Lens, New Delhi: Sage, 2005

Torgovnick, Marianne, *Gone Primitive: Savage Intellects, Modern Lives*, Chicago and London: University of Chicago, 1991

Wadia, J.B.H., *Those Were the Days* in Cinema Vision India: The Indian Journal of Cinematic Art, Vol 1, No.1, 1980

Wadia, J.B.H., *The Making of Toofani Tarzan*, unpublished manuscript in Wadia Movietone archives

Yule, Sir Henry, A.C. Burnell, William Crooke (Eds.) *Hobson-Jobson: A Glossary of Colloquial Anglo-Indian Words and Phrases*, London: Routledge, 1985

PICTURE USAGE

Every reasonable attempt has been made to identify and contact owners of copyright. The editors would like to extend their gratitude to the following rights holders for supporting this project:

AG Films (AA Nadiadwala), *Mela, Rampur Ka Lakshman*

Amudham Pictures, *Punnagai*

Arun Prasad Movies, *Pattikada Pattanana*

Basant Pictures, *Khilari, Madhosh, Maya Bazaar, Reporter Raju, Toofani Teerandaz, Zimbo Finds A Son*

Baweja Movies Pvt. Ltd. (Harry Baweja), *Tilak*

BM Art Productions (Ishwar Ratan Agarwal), *Pran Jaaye Per Vachan Na Jaaye*

BMB Productions (Sudhakar Bokadia), *Love and God, Aaj Ka Arjun*

BR Films (BR Chopra), *Waqt*

CS Ratna Prasad, *Yashoda Krishna*

Devar Films (C Balasundaram), *Nalla Neram, Vettaikaran*

Devi Films, *Main Khilona Nahin*

Dhandayadhapani Films, *Deivam*

Dhariwal Films, *Dada*

Eagle Films (Umesh Mehra), *Sohni Mahiwal*

Emgeeyar Pictures, *Ulagam Sutrum Valiban*

Film Dhaara, *Insaan Aur Shaitan*

Film Wallas (Shashi Kapoor), *Ajooba*
FK Films International (Feroz Khan), *Dharmatma*
Gemini Films, *Thangapatumai*
Geethanjali Minidue Pvt. Ltd. (Jayanth Mukharjee), *Bees Saal Pahele*
Grihalakshmi Productions (PV Gangadharan), *Ahimsa*
Guru Dutt Films Pvt. Ltd. (Arun Dutt), *Sahib Bibi Aur Gulam, C.I.D., Mr & Mrs 55*
Hansa Pictures (Babubhai H Shah), *Jawani Ki Pyaas*
Integrated Films (Muzaffar Ali), *Umrao Jaan*
Iris Movies, *Neeyum Naanum*
Jayanthi Films Pvt. Ltd. (Madurai), *Raman Thediya Seethai*
JB Productions (VB Bhatas), *Do Badan*
Jubilee Films, *Kaveri*
Kaleidoscope (Rohit Ved Prakash), *Bandit Queen*
KC Films, *Uzhaikum Karangal*
Ketnav Dubbing Theatre (Vijaya Anand), *Ghungroo Ki Awaaz*
Kishendas Chhabra & Co. (Chitra Chhabra), *Sone Ki Chidiya, Sarhad, Bheegi Raat*
Lakhan Sinha, *Billoo Baadshah*
Lakshimikanti Movies, *Salem Vishnu*
Leo Films International, *Ilamai Thudippugal, Shaadi Se Pehle Aur Shaadi Ke Baad*
Mahal Pictures Pvt. Ltd., *Pakeezah*
Maya Movietone, *Daadi Maa*
Mehboob Productions (Mrs Saukat Khan), *Mother India*
MKD Films & Aasia Management & Consultancy Pvt. Ltd., *Coolie, Chehraa*
Movie Tee Vee Enterprises (Kewal Suri), *Dilruba, Uttar Dakshin*
Mukesh Movies, *Insaan*
Mukta Arts Ltd., (Subash Ghai), *Karz*
Muktha Films, *Then Mahzi*
Nariman Films (Mrs Nariman Irani), *Don*
Nasir Husain Films Pvt. Ltd. (Mrs Nuzhat Khan), *Jab Pyar Kisise Hota Hai*
Nishita Productions (Deepak Shivdasani), *Madam X*
NN Sippy Productions, *Shatranj*
O.K. Films (RV Mani), *Kuddi Irrinda Koil*
Prakash Mehra Productions (Prakash Mehra), *Laawaris, Zanjeer*
Pramod Chakravorty, *Jagir*
Pramod Films, *Love In Tokyo*
Prasad Productions (Ramesh Prasad), *Jeene Ki Raah*
Pritish Nandy Communications, *Kaante*
Rajshree Films Pvt. Ltd., *Deedar*
Ramakrishna Horticultural Cine Studios (Nandamuri Ramakrishna), *Shri Krishna Pandaviyam*
Reel Poster Gallery, London, *Jaws, The Outlaw*
Rehmat Enterprise, (Liaquat Gola), *Chehraa, Sholay*
Rena Films Pvt. Ltd. (Romu N Sippy), *Diwana, Satte Pe Satta*
RK Films (Randhir Kapoor), *Shri 420, Sangam, Barsaat*
Rono Mukerjee, *Haiwan*
Roop Enterprises (Kailash Chopra), *Shakka*

Sagar Entertainment Ltd. (Prem Sagar), *Ankhen, Ramayan*
Sargam Chitra, *Sampoorna Devi Darshan*
Sarvana Films, *Rajkumar*
Shakti Films (Shakti Samanta), *Kati Patang*
Sippy Films (GP Sippy), *Shaan, Sholay*
Shankar Movies, *Jaani Dushman*
Sharda Finance & Trading Co. (Chitra Chhabra), *Manzil, Half Ticket*
Shivaji Films, *Pudhiya Paravai*
Shree Sai Shanthi Enerprises, *Janma Rahasya*
Sri Sai Shakthi, *Boxer*
Sri Venkata Sai Durga Arts, *Punnami Ratri*
Sreekala Arts, *Bulundi*
Sudharshan Chitra, *Kaanch Aur Heera, Ganga Maang Rahi Balidaan*
Sultan Productions (Sultan Ahmed), *Heera*
Sunil Kumar Desai Productions, *Agni Pookkal*
Super Film Makers, *Mehboob Ki Mehndi*
Suresh Productions (Dr D Rama Naidu), *Tohfa*
The Factory Productions, *Kaun*
Swarnambika Productions, *Pakadai Panirendhu, En Kadamai*
Talpade Films, *Sant Namdev, Tarana*
The Roop Enterprise (Kailash Chopra), *Shakka*
Tips Films Pvt. Ltd., *Auzaar*
Trimurti Films (Ravi Rai), *Deewar*
Ultra Distributors (Sushilkumar Agarwal), *Namak Haraam*
Venus Pictures (AV Srinivasan), *Apna Desh*
Vijayalakshmi Pictures (Trivikrama Rao), *Farz*
Vijaya Productions (B Nagi Reddy), *Swarag Narak*
Vikas Productions, *Talwar Ka Dhani*
VR Pictures (Vinod Doshi), *Faulad*
Yashraj Films (Yash Chopra), *Sawaal, Silsila, Mashaal, Nakhuda, Kala Patthar, Chandni*
Zee Telefilms (Nitin Keni), *Gadar*

ACKNOWLEDGEMENTS

The Editors would like to extend their special thanks to:
Sara Dickey, Emily King, M.S.S. Pandian,
Christopher Pinney, Rosie Thomas and Patricia Uberoi
(*Living Pictures* writers)

And in approximate chronological order:
Wahid, Sajid and Zahid Mansoori (Mini Market,
Mumbai)
Divia Patel (Indian and South-East Asian Department
of the V&A)
Arif Nensey (Nensey Offset Pvt. Ltd., Mumbai)
J Rustom (Madras Safire Lithographers, Chennai)
K Loganathan (Film and TV Institute of Tamil Nadu)
KS Sasidharan, Arti V Karkhanis and Subbalakshmi Iyer
(National Film Archive of India, Pune)
Rachel Dwyer (SOAS)
Kapil Jariwala (Curator)
Ashish Rajadhyaksha (Co-author with Paul Willemen
Encyclopedia of Indian Cinema)
Grant Watson (Project Gallery, Dublin)
Suman Gopinath (Curator, COLAB Bangalore)
Maithili Rao (Film Critic, Bombay)
Shez Dawood and Runa Islam (Artists, London)
Jyotindra Jain (School of Arts and Aesthetics at
Jawaharlal Nehru University, Delhi)
Kajri Jain (Writer and much valued critical friend to
Living Pictures)
Steve Kirk (Partner at Loman Street Studio and much
valued critical friend to *Living Pictures*)
Abid Hussain Vora (Farida Traders, Mumbai)
Vinod "Raju" Rajani and Gulab Kanal (The Garden
Hotel, Mumbai)
Henry and Philo Lobo (Preema Packaging, Mumbai)
Adam Proctor, Gordon Hon, Chryssa Toka (University
of Luton)
Professor Bashir Makhoul (University of Luton)
K Moti Gokulsing (University of East London)
Tim Metcalf (Designer)
Tony Nourmand and Kim Goddard (Reel Poster Gallery,
London)
Alnoor Mitha (SHISHA)
Mike Willis (Data Image Ltd.)
Radhika Subramaniam (Arts International, New York)
P Venkatesh (National Film Archive of India, Pune)
Aissa Deebi (Art East, New York)

Filmnews Anandan (Film Information Centre,
Chennai and author of *The Encyclopedia of South
Indian Cinema*)
S Raju (Central Board of Film Certification, Chennai)
PS Kamble (Advocates Supreme Court of India, Pune)
Sanjit Narwekar (Rajkamal Academy of Cinematic
Excellence)
Alex Coles (Art Critic and valued critical friend to *Living
Pictures*)
Dan Fern and Virginia Ferreira (RCA)
Feroz Sheik and Liaquat Gola (Rehmat Enterprise)
Ranjani Mazumdar (Writer)
Ramesh Roy (Film Director)
Hema (Cherry Square, Mangalore)
Martyn Shouler (Designer)
James & Monica D'Souza (Mumbai)
Neville Tuli and Angira Arya (Osians, Mumbai)
Jude Greenaway (The Light Surgeons and purveyor of
Indian movie posters)
Andy Stevens and Paul Neale (Graphic Thought
Facility)
Omkar Potdar (Glamour Design Studio, Mumbai)
Stephen Hooley (Kemistry)
Safina Uberoi (*My Other Mother India*)
Tosh Lakhani and Surojit Walawaker (Far East Beer
Company)
Deena Ingham (Ingham Ink)
Patrick Thomas (laVista Design, Barcelona)
Leonard Doyle (The Independent Newspaper)
Rosa and Kai (David's people)
Caroline and Benedicta (Ed's people)

Christopher Pinney would like to thank Balkrishna
Vaidya, Omkar Potdar and everyone at Glamour
Studios, Chandrakant Potdar, Arif Nensey at Nensey
Offset, J. P. Singhal, Ashish Rajadhyaksha, Ravi
Aggrawal and Mrs Lobo.

David Blamey would like to thank Ed D'Souza
Ed D'Souza would like to thank David Blamey

INDEX

COLOPHON

Designed by Graphic Thought Facility
Text set in Berthold Concorde
with Hoefler Knockout and Hoefler Gotham headlines
Printed on Arctic Extreme 115gsm
and Munken Print Extra 115gsm

Scanning by Data Image Limited
Production by Robert D'Souza at Loman Street Studio
and Regal Litho
Printed by Grup 3, Barcelona

PHOTOGRAPHY

Film stills:
Front cover – *Raman Thediya Seethai*
Back cover – *Love And God*
Inside front cover – *Love And God*
Inside back cover – *Swarag Narak*

Poster section contextual photography:
Page 89 – Madonna's *Body of Evidence*, Mumbai 2004
Page 90 – Street scene, Madurai c1990
Page 110 – Rickshaw ride, Delhi c1992
Page 118 – Beach boys, Chennai 2004
Page 136 – Rooftops, Delhi c1989
Page 168 – Krishna's Butterball, Mahabalipuram 2004
Page 174– Flute Vendors, New Delhi c1990
Page 190 – Alley, Delhi c1989
Page 220 – Couple, Chennai 2004
Page 248 – Re-cyled hoarding art, Habitat, London 2004

All contextual photography by David Blamey
except page 3 by Robert D'Souza

SUPPORT

The Arts & Humanities Research Board
The Royal College of Art
The University of Luton

DISTRIBUTION

Distributed by Art Data
Telephone 00 44 (0)20 8747 1061

E-orders:
orders@openeditions.com
orders@artdata.co.uk